Francine Hébert, M.Ed.

Construction of a
GARMENT

DARNLEY
PUBLICATIONS
INC.

Legal deposit – Bibliothèque et Archives nationales du Québec, 2007
Legal deposit – Library and Archives Canada, 2007

ISBN 978-2-923623-09-2

Copyright © 2008 Darnley Publications Inc.

Printed in Canada

Catalog No.: TBYD2

Author:
Francine Hébert, M.Ed.

Editor-in-Chief:
Dr. Claude Major, Ph.D.

Copy Editors:
John Alarie
Matthew Testa

Project Manager:
Francine Hébert, M.Ed.

Design and Layout:
Saskia Nieuwendijk
Michael Gonzalez

TABLE OF CONTENTS

TABLE OF CONTENTS

TABLE OF CONTENTS

TABLE OF CONTENTS

TABLE OF CONTENTS

PART ONE

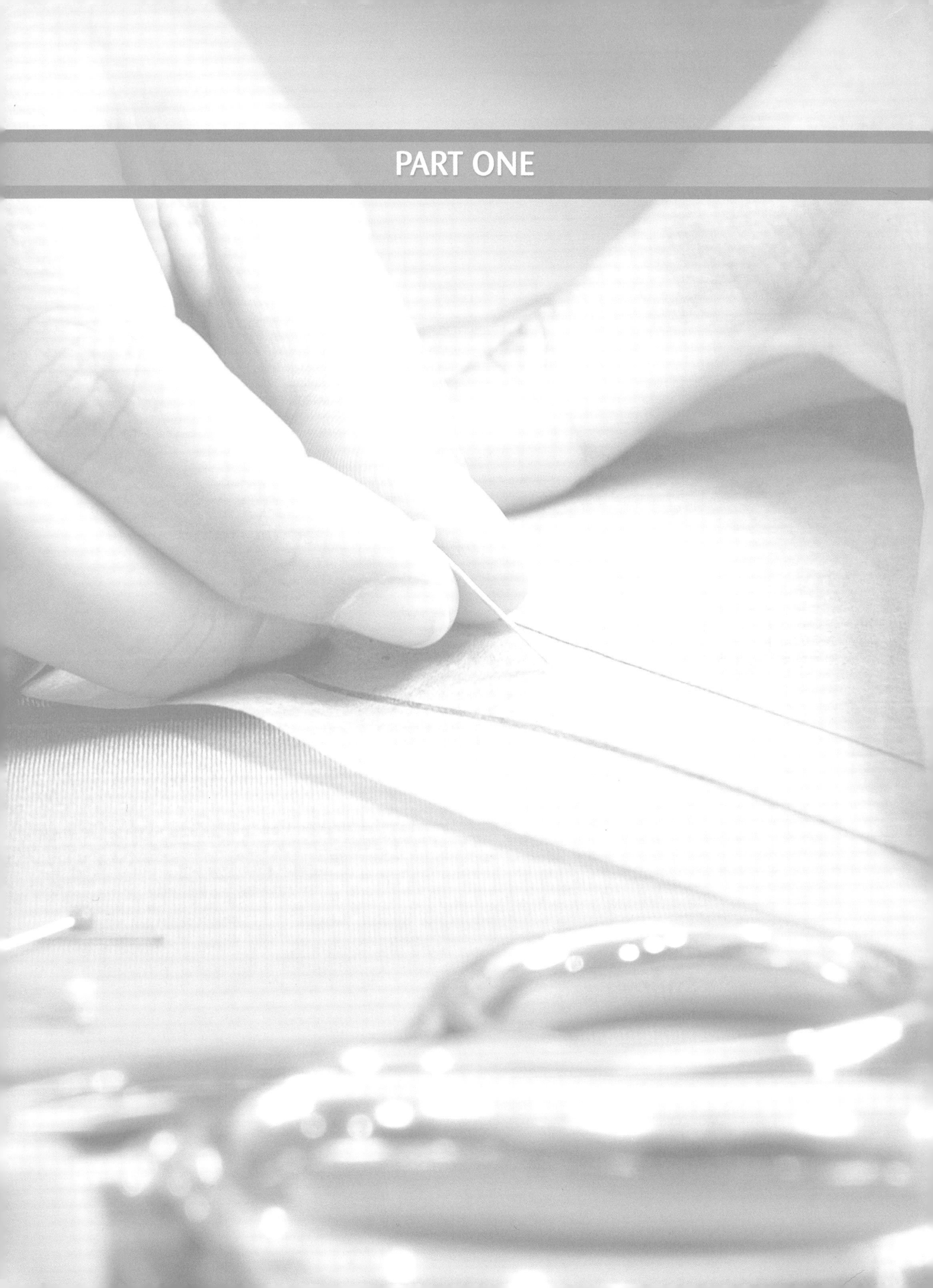

PATTERN USE

Overview

In this first part, we will cover adjusting the pattern, layout, cutting, and marking. Upon completion of this part, you will be able to

- Describe how to adjust a pattern to your measurements if they vary from those of the pattern. These include adjustments in length, bust size, waist, hip, abdomen, shoulder, chest, and back.

- Identify and list terms connected with layout, cutting, and marking

- Describe the layout and cutting procedures

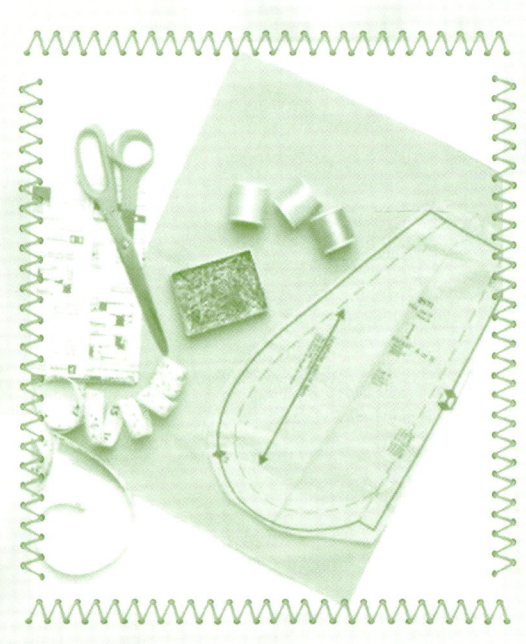

ADJUSTING THE PATTERN

Introduction

Once you have chosen your pattern and fabric, you should study the instruction sheet that comes in the pattern envelope. There may be more than one; read them all. There's a wealth of information on them that will help you to do a good job of cutting and sewing. Look at the fabric layout charts and pick the one you need to follow. They're arranged according to pattern view, size, and width of fabric. If your material has nap or a one-way design, be sure to follow the layout that says "with nap." Circle the one you're going to use. This will prevent any mix-up as you lay out your pattern. Go through all

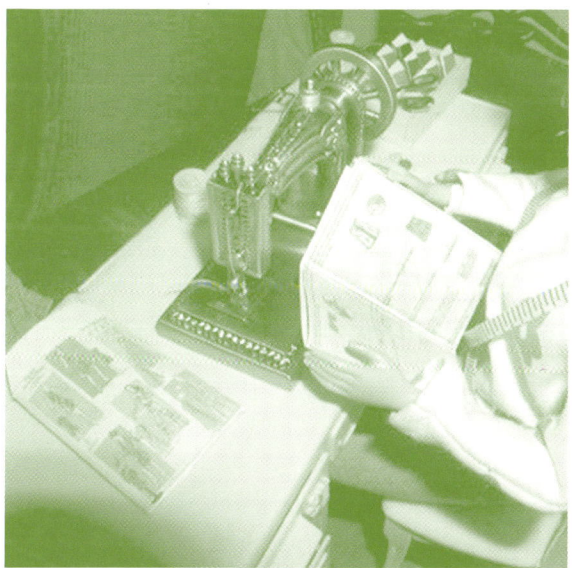

the pattern pieces and pick out the ones you need for the view you are making. The pattern sheet will tell you which ones they are. Put the rest of the pieces away. Don't lose any of them; you may want to make a different pattern view the next time around.

Adjusting the Pattern

Look back at your body measurements to determine what adjustments, if any, are necessary. Make them on your pattern according to the instructions on the following pages. Although some of these adjustments may sound complicated to you at first, you will soon learn to do the ones that are required for your particular figure. Once you are able to make your own special corrections, you will find it quite simple to apply them to all future patterns. A good fit is worth the effort.

Each stitching line provides one opportunity for a pattern adjustment. These lines include seams, darts, tucks, gathers, and any other area of fullness control. Making a dart smaller adds width to a garment; making it larger makes the garment narrower.

Large adjustments should be evenly distributed at each of the stitching lines across a pattern section. The number of pieces determines the fraction of adjustment to be made at each one. For instance, a 2" hip adjustment in a 4-gore skirt would require a 1/2" adjustment on each quarter of the skirt. Each pattern piece would be adjusted 1/2" (there would be only 2 pattern pieces for the 4 gores). To do this, adjust both side seams of each pattern piece by 1/4" each.

Here are a few things to remember as you make your pattern adjustments:

· Make your adjustments in this order: length (critical to a good fit); bust darts; width at bust, waist, hip; width at shoulder, chest, back; special problems.

· Use adjustment lines printed on the pattern to aid you in making changes in length.

· Keep all grainlines and foldlines straight.

· Redraw and straighten all cutting lines after making folds in the pattern. Redraw stitching lines 5/8" (or the width of the seam allowance) inside cutting lines.

· In most cases, an adjustment on one pattern piece will mean that an adjustment must be made on the corresponding pieces that will be used with it. This includes linings, facings, and any pieces to be seamed to it, such as backs, fronts, and sleeves. In length adjustments, buttonholes and pockets may need to be repositioned.

· Remember that you are working with a pattern piece that represents one fourth of your body. Keep this in mind when making width adjustments.

· Any adjustment made in the width of one pattern piece will be doubled when you cut two layers of fabric.

· Any fold in the pattern will give you an adjustment twice the size of the fold. For example, a 1/2" fold *across* a skirt pattern will *shorten* the pattern 1".

How to Adjust

Have on hand some mending tape, tissue paper, a pencil, and a ruler. To make a pattern piece smaller, take a tuck in it. To make a pattern piece larger, slash it and insert a piece of tissue paper. For basic adjustments, follow these simple rules:

Length—Make bodice adjustments between bust and waistline. If bustline needs to be raised or lowered as well, make adjustment above bustline dart

extra tissue where needed (don't rely on yourself to remember to cut the seams larger—you won't). Add or subtract one fourth the total amount from side seams of both back and front. For example, 1/4" off the side seam of each front and back skirt piece would result in a skirt 1" smaller.

Basic adjustments mainly concern changes in length and width. Use only adjustments that apply to your particular needs. Remember to straighten all cutting and stitching lines after making your adjustments.

instead of below it. Remember to make adjustments in both back and front pieces. Make sleeve adjustments equally divided above and below the elbow. Small adjustments in a sleeve or garment length can be made at the bottom edge of the pattern.

Width—Adjustments of 2" or less can usually be made at the side seams. There is often enough tissue around the edge of the pattern to allow for adjustments in the seams. If not, use

Length Adjustments

To shorten bodice, skirt, sleeve, or pants, mark the amount to be shortened above the adjustment line. Fold pattern on the adjustment line, as shown in Figure 1.1, and bring fold up to the mark. Tape in place.

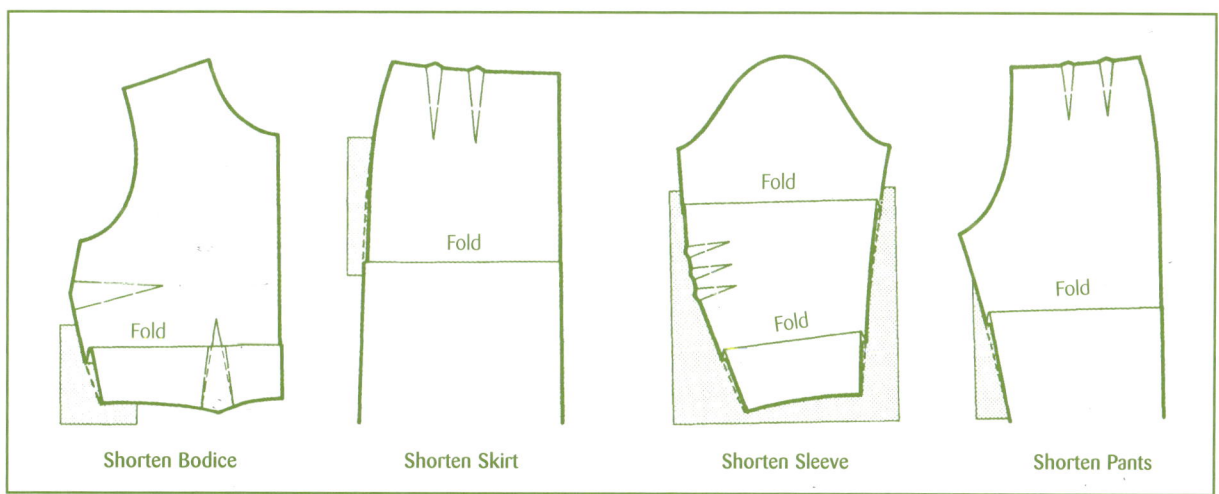

| Shorten Bodice | Shorten Skirt | Shorten Sleeve | Shorten Pants |

Figure 1.1—Shortening

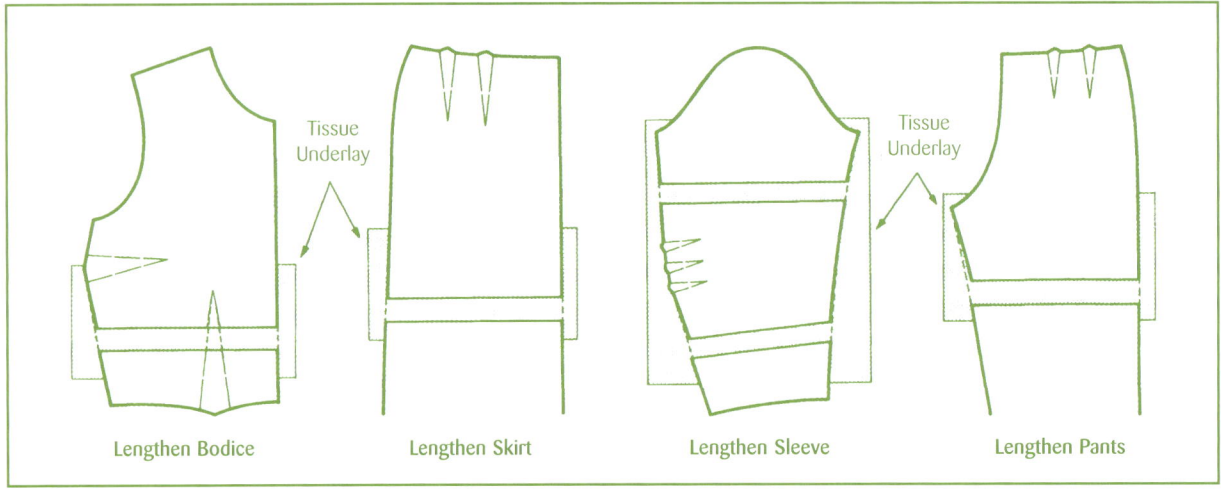

Figure 1.2–Lengthening

To lengthen bodice, skirt, sleeve, or pants, slash pattern across adjustment line. Place tissue paper underneath and separate pattern the amount to be lengthened, as shown in Figure 1.2. Tape to tissue.

To lengthen armhole, draw a line across the bodice front and bodice back between shoulder and bottom of armhole. Make a corresponding line across the sleeve between shoulder and bottom of armhole. Slash along this line, spread pattern the desired amount, and insert tissue paper. Tape in place. To restore bodice to its original length, shorten on adjustment line. Shorten the bodice the same amount that the armhole was lengthened. Do the same with the sleeve if it is a long sleeve. If it is a short sleeve, simply take this amount from the bottom. See Figure 1.3.

To shorten the armhole, reverse the above procedure, taking a tuck in the

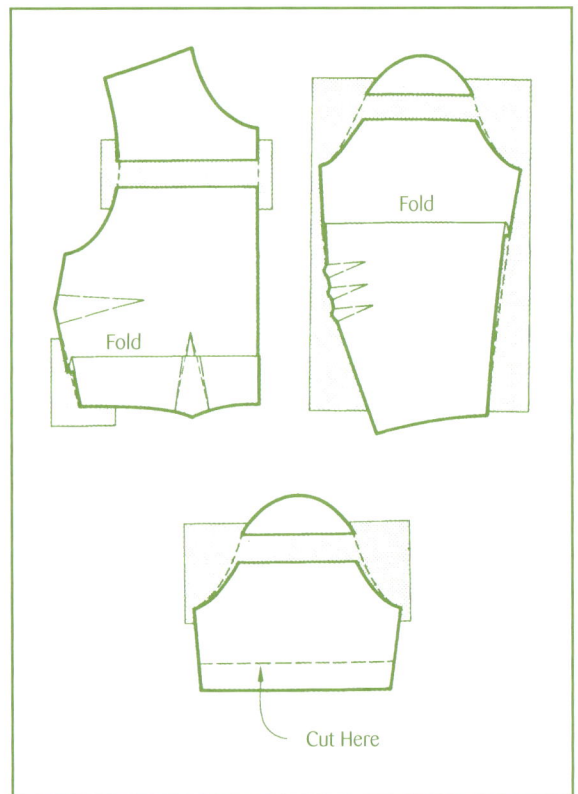

Figure 1.3–Lengthening Armhole

armhole area and lengthening the bodice and sleeve area. Add the required amount to the bottom of a short sleeve. See Figure 1.4.

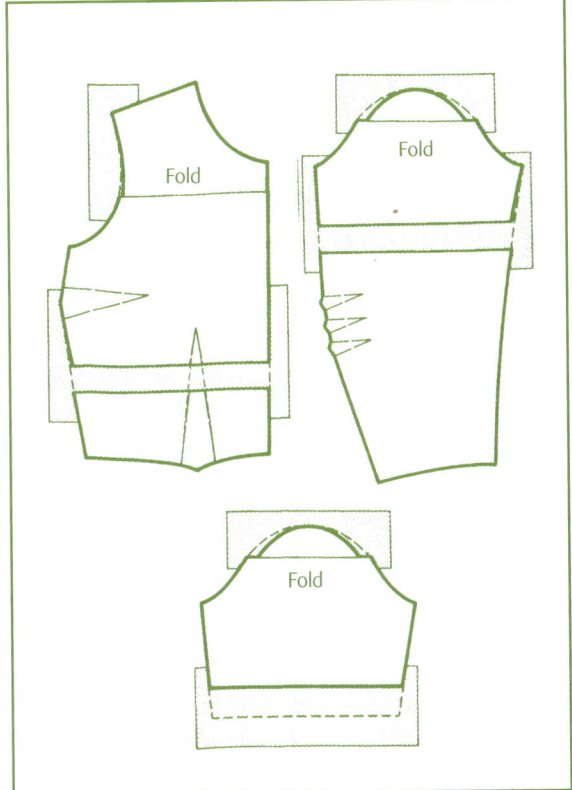

Figure 1.4—Shortening Armhole

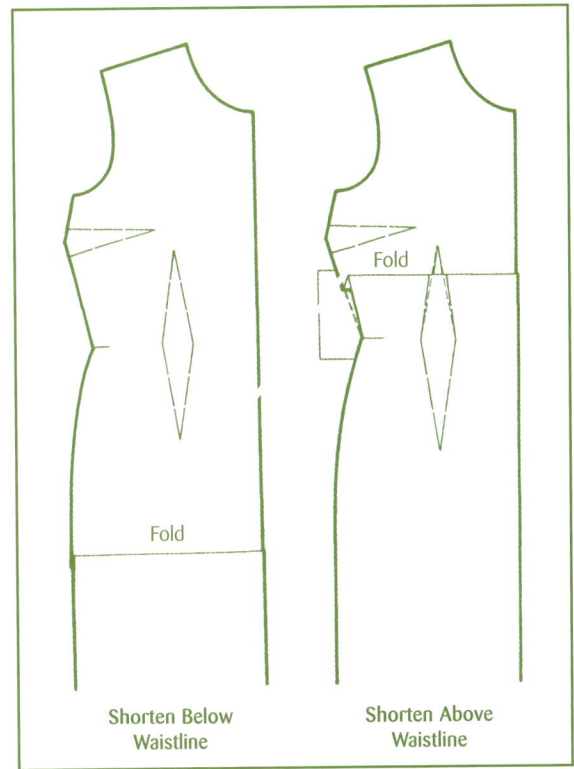

Figure 1.5—Shortening One-Piece Dress

To shorten a one-piece dress, use adjustment lines on pattern. Check waistline placement. If it is correct, shorten below waistline. If waistline is too low, shorten above waistline. Be sure to adjust all back and front pattern pieces. See Figure 1.5.

To lengthen a one-piece dress, follow the above procedure, slashing and spreading pattern instead of taking a tuck. If waistline is correct, adjust below waistline. If waistline is too high, adjust above waistline. See Figure 1.6.

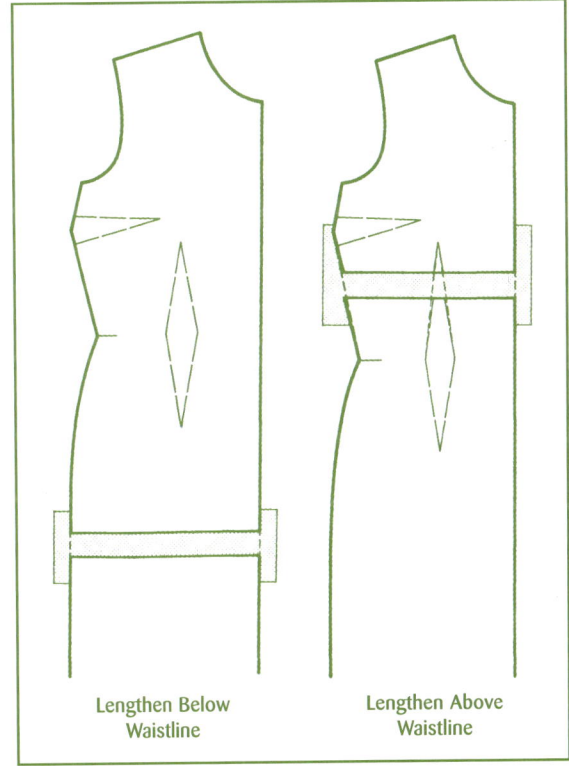

Figure 1.6—Lengthening One-Piece Dress

Width Adjustments

To increase waistline by 2" or less, add one fourth the required amount to the side seams of back and front pattern pieces. Taper to cutting lines. Remember to increase both bodice and skirt waistlines in garments with waistline seams. If more than 2" is needed, take remaining fullness from waistline darts. For large adjustments in princess style dresses or gored skirts, spread the adjustment equally among all seams. See Figure 1.7.

To decrease waistline by 2" or less, follow the same procedure, taking in the side seams the required amount. For more than 2", take larger waistline darts. For larger adjustments on princess dresses or gored skirts, distribute adjustment evenly. See Figure 1.8.

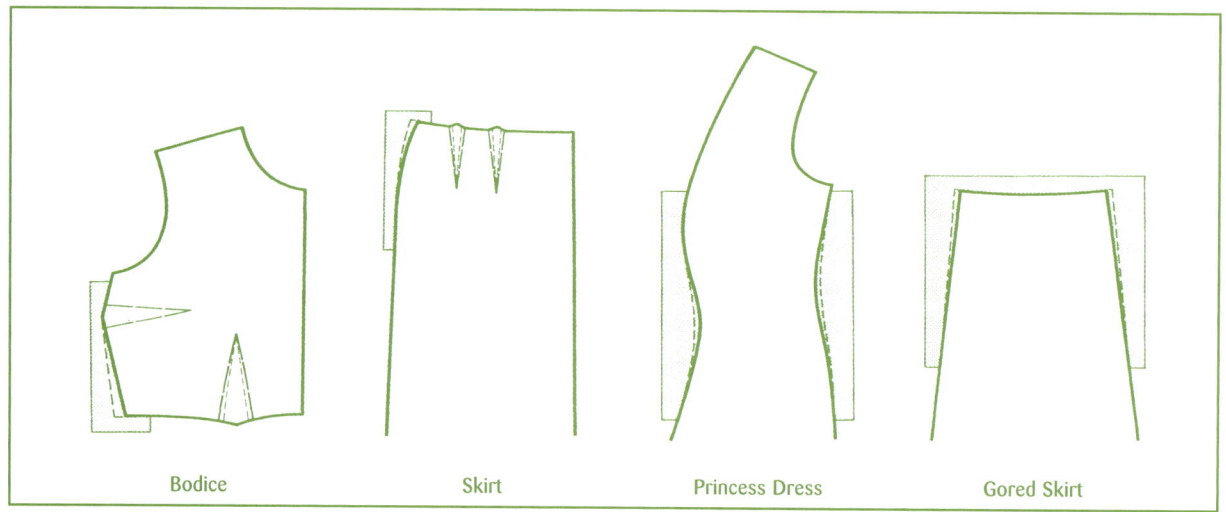

| Bodice | Skirt | Princess Dress | Gored Skirt |

Figure 1.7–Increasing Waistline

| Bodice | Skirt | Princess Dress | Gored Skirt |

Figure 1.8–Decreasing Waistline

Remember to increase or decrease skirt or pants waistbands by the same amount and in the same places, usually at the side seam markings on the waistband. See Figure 1.9.

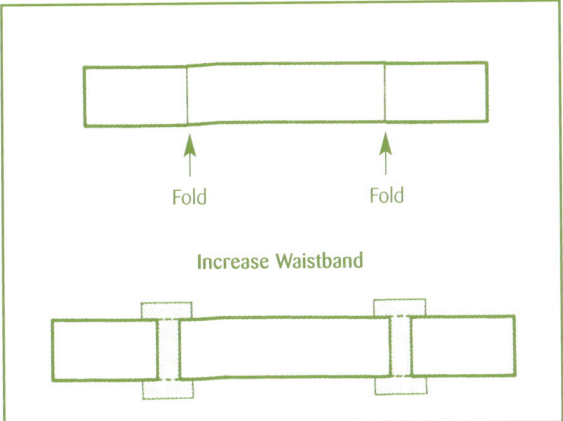

Figure 1.9—Altering Length of Waistband

To increase hip measurement by 2" or less, measure from waist to point on pattern where hip measurement was taken (usually 7"-9" below waistline). At this point, add one fourth the required amount to side seams of front and back pattern pieces. Taper to waistline. Carry the hipline increase all the way to the bottom of the pattern to preserve the shape of the skirt, as shown in Figure 1.10.

To increase hipline more than 2", use either of the following methods, as shown in Figure 1.11:

Method 1: Draw a straight line near side seam from waist to bottom of skirt. Slash and spread pattern desired amount. Take tuck where pattern folds.

Insert tissue and tape in place. Redraw hemline to match pattern piece.

Method 2: Draw a straight line near side seam from waist to bottom of skirt. Slash open completely and spread pattern desired amount. Insert tissue and tape in place. Make new dart to take up added fullness in waist.

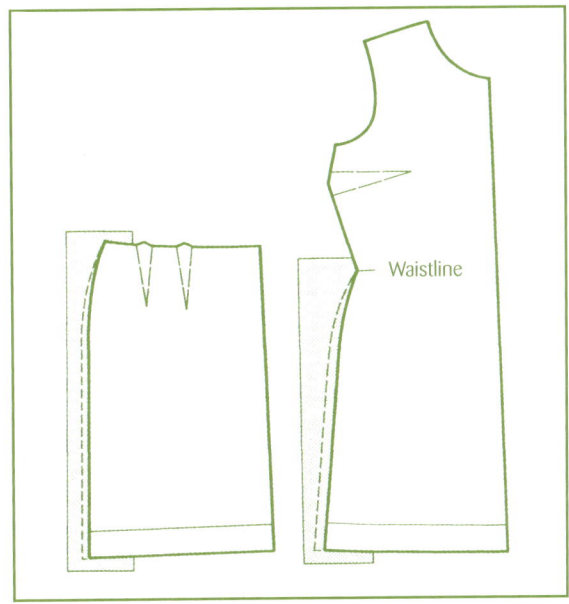

Figure 1.10—Increasing Hipline 2" or Less

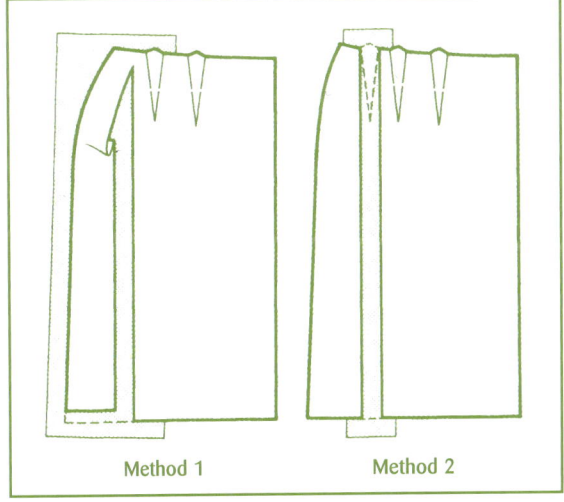

Figure 1.11—Increasing Hipline More than 2"

To decrease hipline less than 2", follow above method for increase, taking in side seams instead of adding on. To decrease hipline more than 2", slash as in Method #1 of Figure 1.11. Overlap slash required amount and tape in place. Make tuck where pattern

folds. Redraw side cutting line. See Figure 1.12.

To increase bustline 2" or less, add one-fourth the required amount of adjustment to side seams of bodice front and back. Taper to waistline. Add the same amount to both seams of sleeve pattern. Taper to cutting line. See Figure 1.13 on the following page.

To decrease bustline 2" or less, subtract one fourth the required amount of adjustment from side seams of bodice front and back. Taper to waistline. Subtract the same amount from both seams of sleeve pattern. Taper to cutting line. See Figure 1.14 on the following page.

To increase or decrease bustline more than 2", refer to the following section on special problems.

Waistline

Figure 1.12–Decreasing Hipline 2" or Less

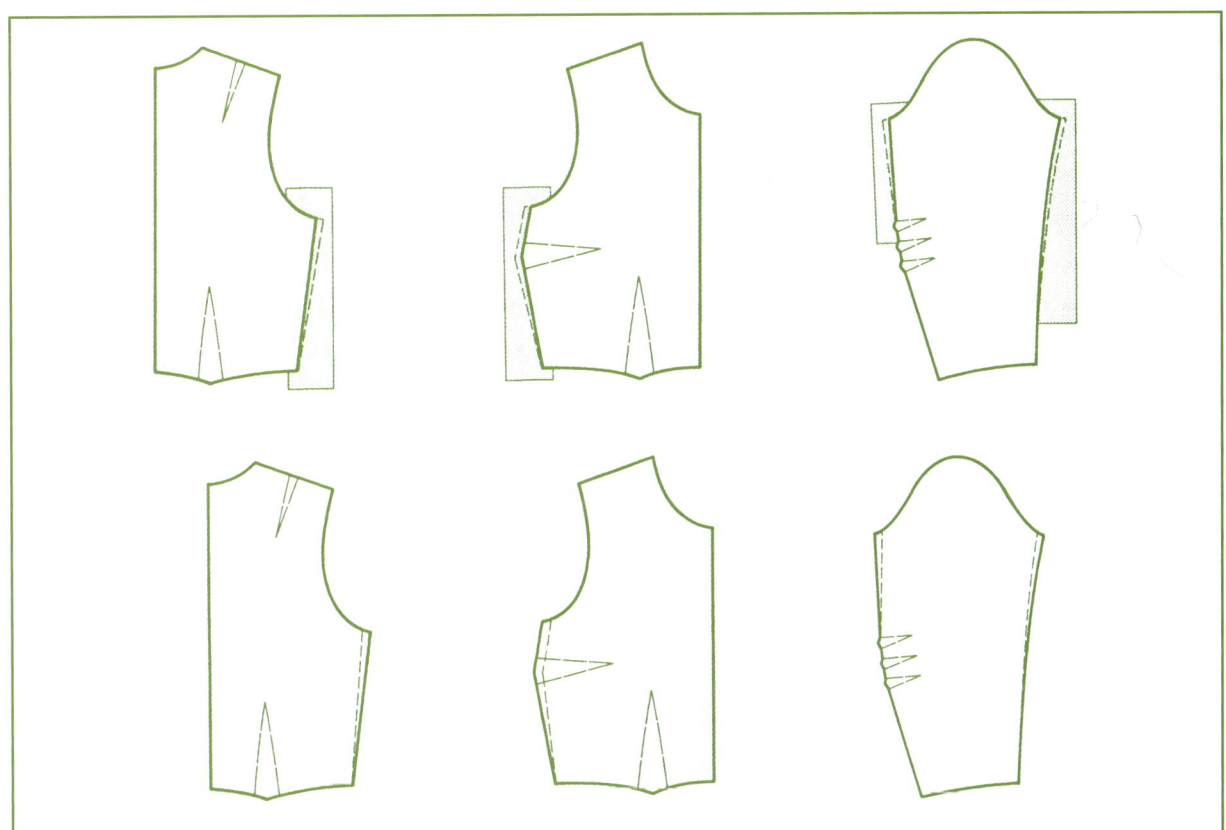

Figure 1.13–(Top) Increasing Bustline 2" or Less
Figure 1.14–(Bottom) Decreasing Bustline 2" or Less

Special Problems

Large Bust

Draw a straight line through center of waist dart and center of bust dart. Draw another straight line from center of shoulder to point where first two lines meet. Slash along vertical line from waist to shoulder seamline; slash underarm dart to within 1/8" of first slash. Tape bottom edges of pattern together. Spread vertical slash desired amount; bust dart will spread open. Insert tissue underneath and tape in place. Redraw side seamlines. Redraw waistline dart to original point, as in Figure 1.15.

For princess style, slash side front pattern piece from front edge to side seamline, as in Figure 1.16. Spread pattern desired amount. Insert tissue and tape in place. Cut front pattern section straight across bust area. Spread pattern same amount as side front. Insert tissue and tape in place.

Small Bust

Follow directions under "Large Bust" for slashing. Overlap center of

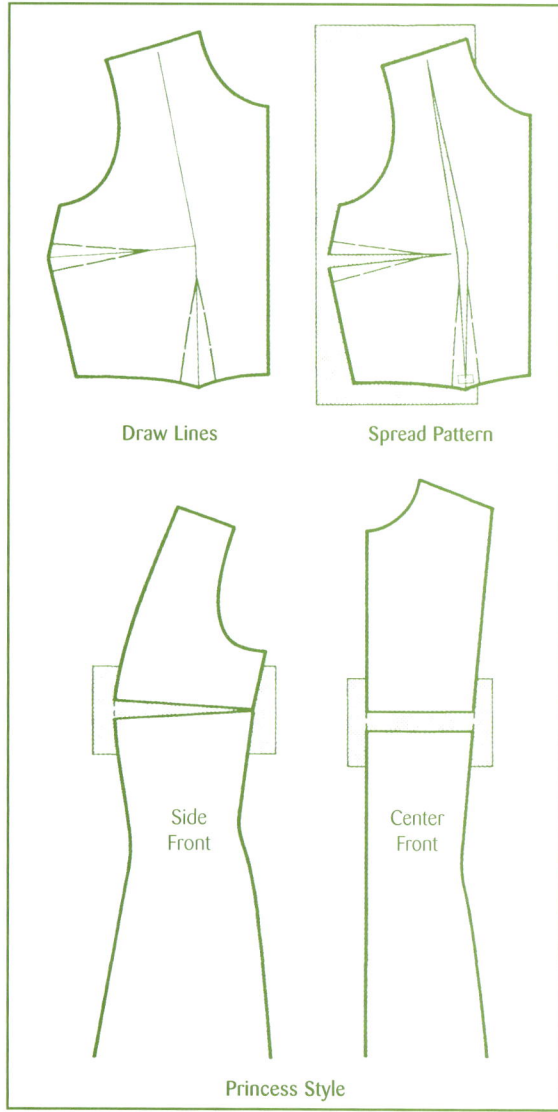

Draw Lines   Spread Pattern

Side
Front

Center
Front

Princess Style

Figure 1.15—(Top) Altering for a Large Bust
Figure 1.16—(Bottom) Altering for a Large Bust
on Princess Style

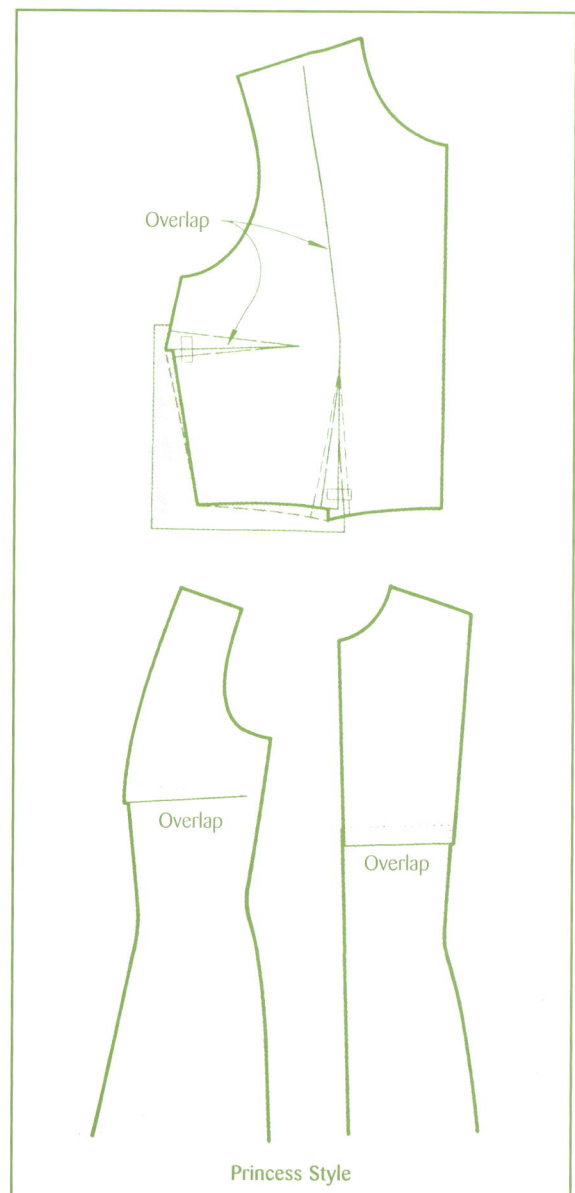

Overlap

Overlap

Overlap

Princess Style

Figure 1.17—(Top) Altering for Small Bust
Figure 1.18—(Bottom) Altering for Small Bust on
Princess Style

vertical slash desired amount; bust dart
will overlap. Tape in place. Straighten
side and bottom seamlines. Redraw
waistline dart to original point. Refer to
Figure 1.17.

For princess style, overlap dart
slash and center front slash, as shown
in Figure 1.18. Tape in place.

Raising or Lowering Bust Darts

For French darts or minor bustline
adjustments, mark the desired bust
point position on pattern. Redraw
lines for bust dart. See Figure 1.19.
Remember that the side and lower bust

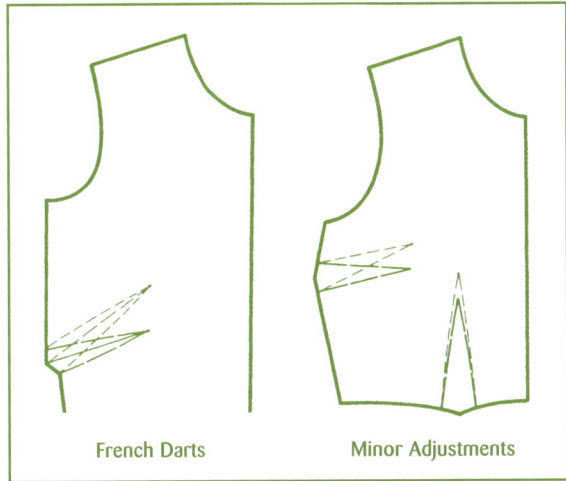

French Darts   Minor Adjustments

Figure 1.19—Adjusting Bust Darts

darts should end 1/2" - 1" from the most prominent part of the bust.

For larger adjustments, move the entire bust dart. Draw a rectangle around bustline dart. Cut on these lines, removing entire bust dart. Place tissue under opening. Move dart up or down desired amount. Tape in place. Taper end of waistline dart up or down the same amount as bustline dart, as shown in Figure 1.20.

To correct side seam cutting lines after bust dart adjustment, bring dart together on sewing lines and fold dart down. Redraw cutting line and cut across folded dart on cutting line, as shown in Figure 1.21 on the following page. Unfold dart.

Broad Shoulders

Slash pattern from center of shoulder to center of armhole seamline, as shown in Figure 1.22 on the following page. Spread desired amount. Insert tissue and tape in place. Redraw shoulder cutting line. Adjust both front and back bodice pieces.

For pattern with yoke, slash through entire yoke and spread desired amount. Slash and increase bodice front and bodice back the same amount.

Narrow Shoulders

Slash pattern pieces the same as for broad shoulders. Overlap pattern

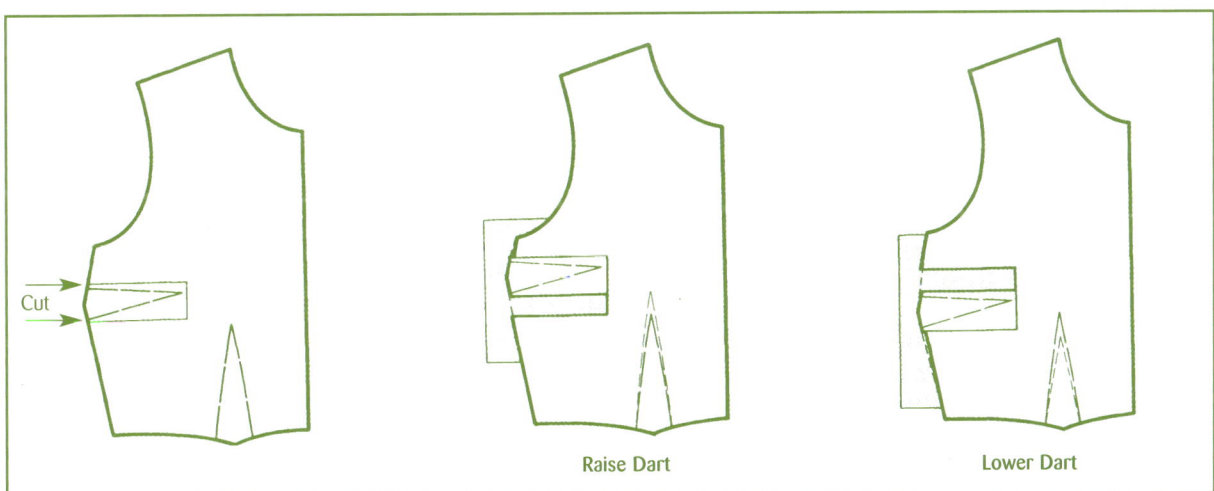

Cut   Raise Dart   Lower Dart

Figure 1.20—Moving the Bust Dart

Figure 1.21—(Top left) Correcting Side Seam after Bust Dart Adjustment
Figure 1.22—(Top right) Adjusting for Broad Shoulders
Figure 1.23—(Bottom) Narrow Shoulders

desired amount, as in Figure 1.23, and tape in place. Redraw cutting lines.

Square Shoulders

Use either one of the following two methods, shown in Figure 1.24, adjusting both front and back bodice pieces:

Method 1: Draw a horizontal line 1" below armhole. Draw a vertical line 1" from armhole, from shoulder to the horizontal line. Cut on this L-shaped line and raise armhole desired amount. Place tissue under opening and tape in place. Redraw shoulder and side seam cutting lines.

Method 2: Slash pattern just below shoulder from armhole to neck seamline. Place tissue under slash and spread pattern desired amount. Tape in place. Redraw armhole, restoring original cutting line.

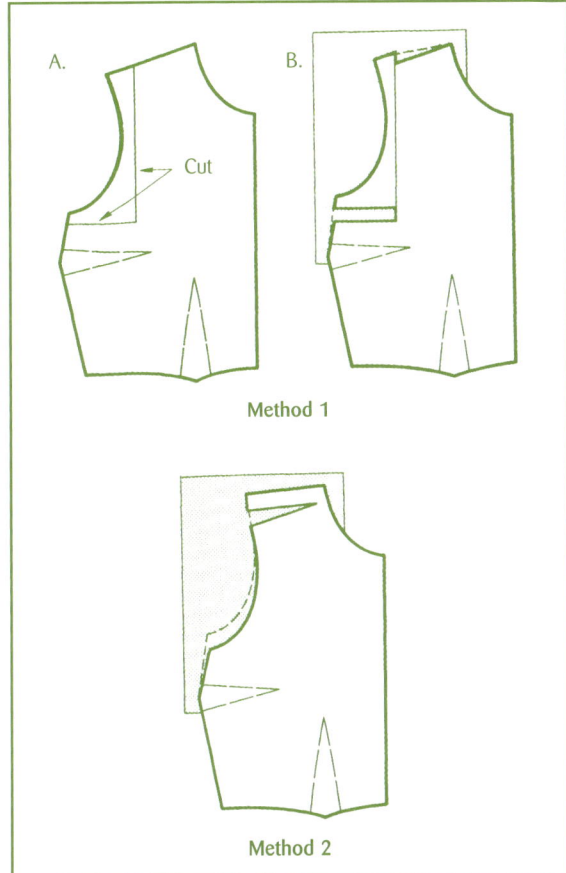

Figure 1.24–Adjusting for Square Shoulders

Sloping Shoulders

Either of the following two methods, shown in Figure 1.25, will give the desired results:

Method 1: On both front and back bodice pieces, redraw shoulder cutting line, lowering shoulder desired amount at armhole edge. Lower armhole edge at side seam by equal amount to restore original cutting line.

Method 2: On both front and back bodice pieces, redraw shoulder cutting lines, raising shoulder desired amount at neckline edge. Raise front neckline edge by equal amount to restore original cutting lines.

Large Upper Arm

Following grainline, as in Figure 1.26, draw a straight line down center of sleeve, from shoulder seamline to

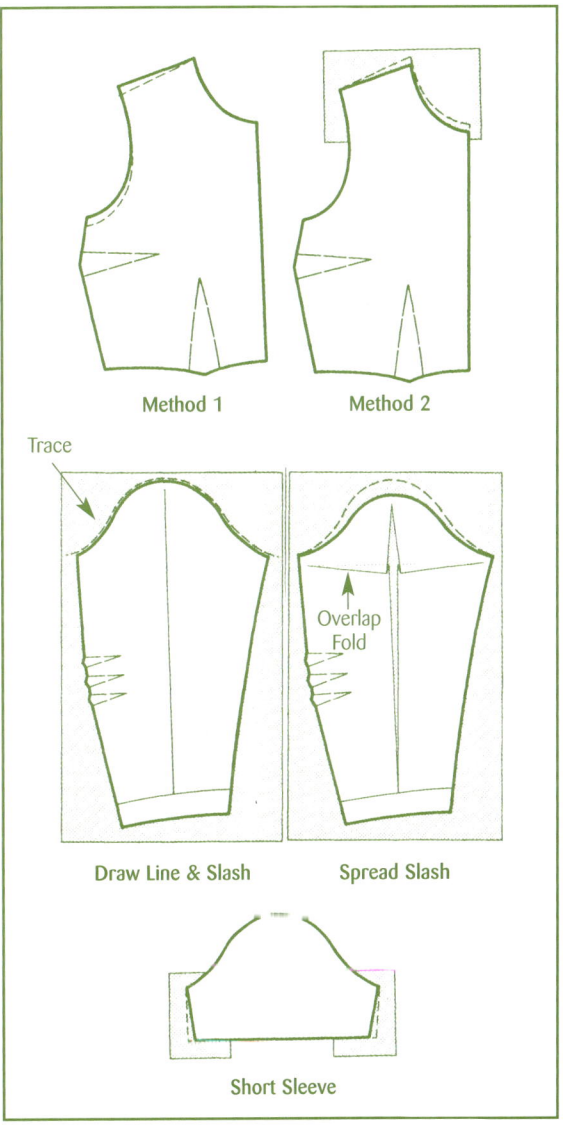

Figure 1.25–(Top) Adjusting for Sloping Shoulders

Figure 1.26–(Bottom) Large Upper Arm

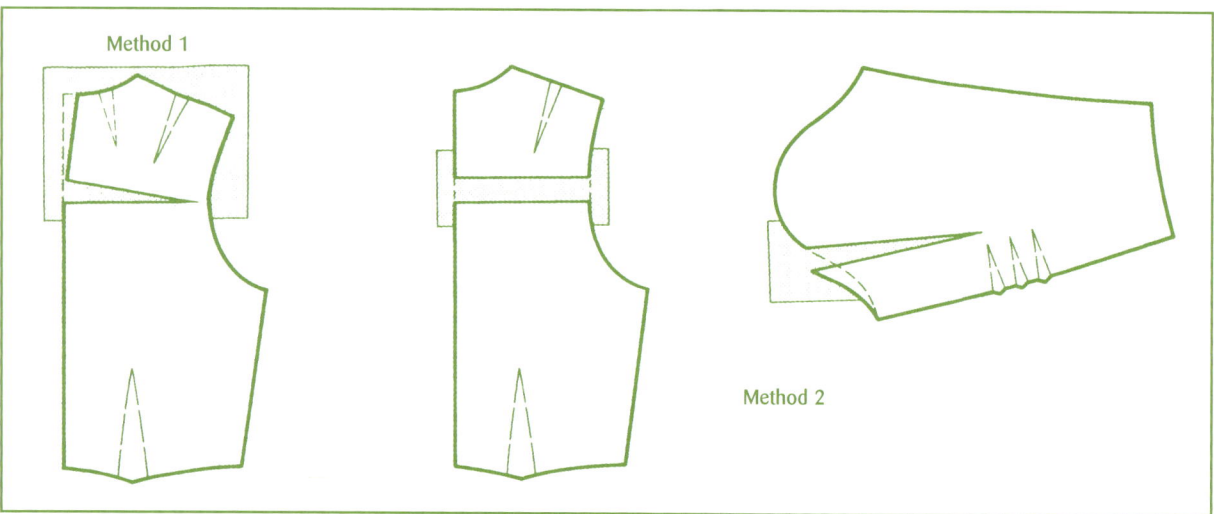

Figure 1.27—Adjusting for Round Shoulders

hemline. Slash along line. Place tissue under sleeve pattern and trace around sleeve cap. Spread slash desired amount, allowing folds to form each side of slash. Tape in place. Redraw top of sleeve following tracing line. Bodice front and back side seams may need increased width to allow for additional ease in sleeve cap. For short sleeves, add width at the underarm seam.

Round Shoulders

Either of the following two methods, shown in Figure 1.27, will give the desired result:

Method 1: Slash pattern from center back to armhole seam midway between shoulder and bottom of armhole. Spread pattern desired amount and place tissue underneath. Straighten center back line. If needed, add small neckline dart or increase existing neckline dart to restore original neckline size. Make dart the width of the distance between the old and new center back lines.

Method 2: Slash back bodice pattern from center back to armhole edge midway between shoulder and bottom of armhole. Separate pattern desired amount and insert tissue. Tape in place. Slash back of sleeve from sleeve edge almost to elbow, parallel to underarm seamline. Spread pattern same amount as bodice back. Insert tissue and tape in place. Redraw sleeve cutting line.

Very Straight Back

Slash across bodice back from center back to armhole seamline, midway between shoulder and bottom of armhole, as shown in Figure 1.28. Overlap slash desired amount and tape

Figure 1.28–Very Straight Back

in place. Straighten and redraw center back line.

Broad Back

Draw a vertical line on bodice back from center of shoulder to just below armhole. Spread pattern desired amount and insert tissue, as shown in Figure 1.29. Bring shoulder edges of pattern together, allowing small tuck to form in outer pattern piece. Tape in place and redraw shoulder cutting line. If small tuck forms in side seam, add

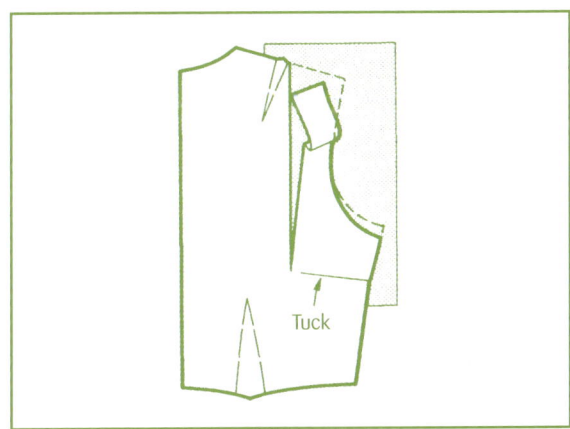

Figure 1.29–Broad Back

this amount to underarm seam at armhole.

Narrow Back

If bodice has waist and shoulder darts, join lines of dart, stitching from top to bottom, as in Figure 1.30. This will create a continuous seamline down back of bodice.

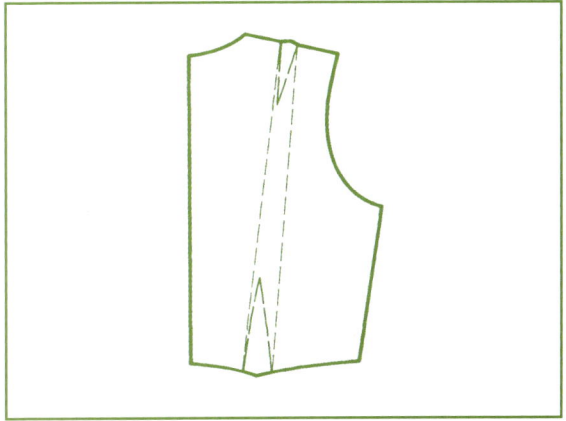

Figure 1.30–Narrow Back Adjustment

Alternate method: Take tuck the entire length of back, following center lines of darts, as shown in Figure 1.31.

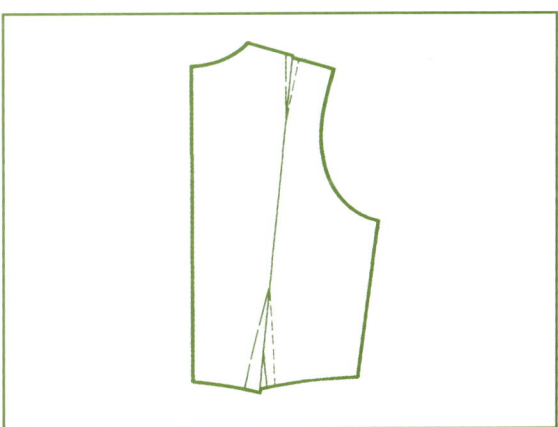

Figure 1.31–Alternate Method for Narrower Back Adjustment

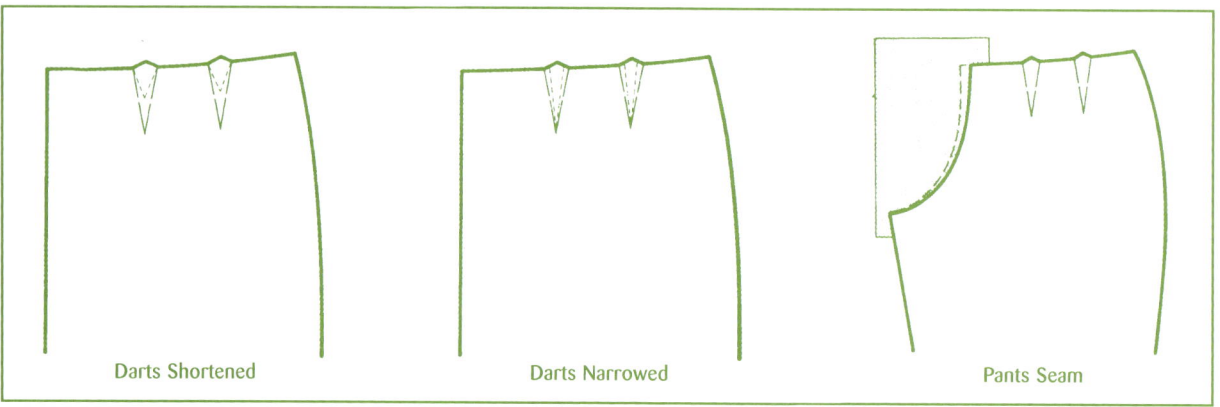

Figure 1.32–Increasing Width for Large Abdomen

Tuck should be one-fourth the desired amount to be taken in. Leave dart markings in position. Darts will be smaller. Waistline dart may need to be extended to original point. Shoulder dart may disappear entirely.

Large Abdomen

To increase width across abdomen, waistline darts in skirt front may be shortened or reduced in width. Any adjustment in waist measurement of skirt or pants will require an adjustment in adjoining bodice or waistband. Darts in skirt front can be eliminated altogether if necessary. For additional width in pants, or skirt with center front seam, add to center front seam. See Figure 1.32.

For larger increase in abdomen, slash pattern straight down from front darts to bottom of pattern. Slash across abdomen from center front to side seamline. Spread pattern one half the desired width and all the desired

length. Keep side of pattern straight, allowing a crosswise fold to form. Insert tissue and tape in place. Redraw waistline dart or add new waistline dart if needed. Straighten cutting lines. See Figure 1.33.

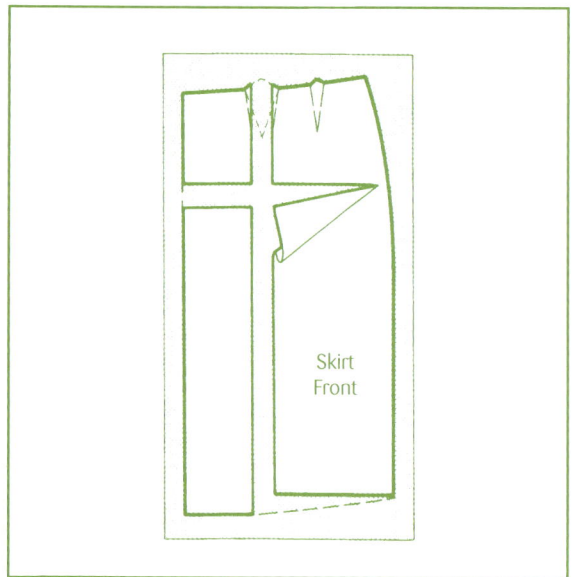

Skirt Front

Figure 1.33–For larger increase in abdomen, slash the pattern, as shown.

For A-line style, slash up front of skirt into bust area of bodice. Insert tissue and spread pattern one-half desired amount of increase, as in Figure 1.34. Tape in place.

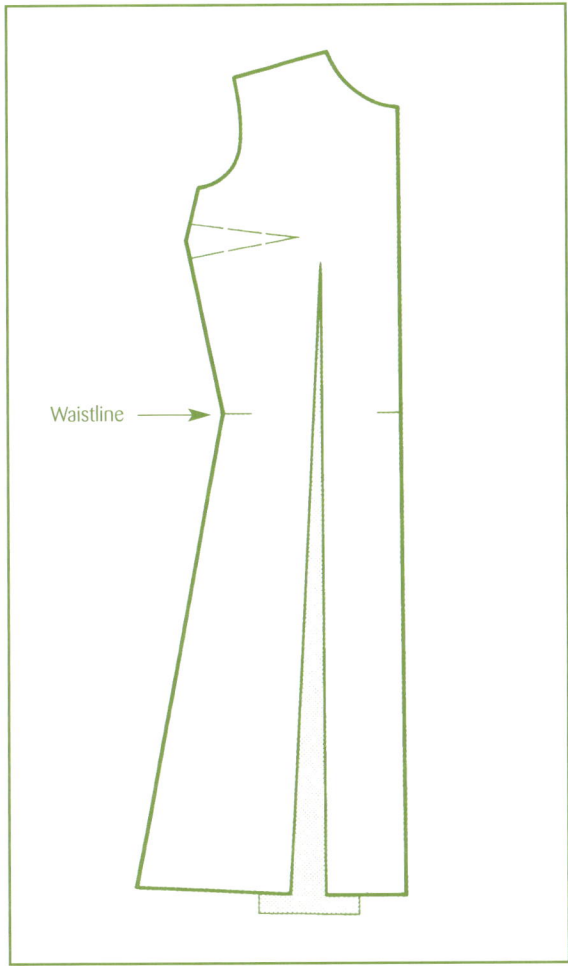

Figure 1.34–Large Abdomen Adjustment in A-line Style

Large Buttocks

Draw a horizontal line across skirt back at hipline from center back to side seamline. Draw a vertical line from dart to bottom of skirt. Slash on both lines. Spread pattern one-half the desired width and all of the desired length. Keep side seam straight, allowing pattern to form a crosswise fold.

Redraw dart to form new point. Redraw bottom edge of skirt, as shown in Figure 1.35.

Figure 1.35–Large Buttocks Adjustment

Flat Buttocks

Draw lines and slash as above for large buttocks. Overlap pattern one half the desired amount of width and all of desired length. Redraw dart to form new point. Dart will be narrower. Redraw center back seam. See Figure 1.36.

Sway Back

Slash across skirt back above hipline from center back to side seamline, as in Figure 1.37. Overlap desired amount and tape in place (usually about 1/2"). Redraw dart lines and center back cutting line.

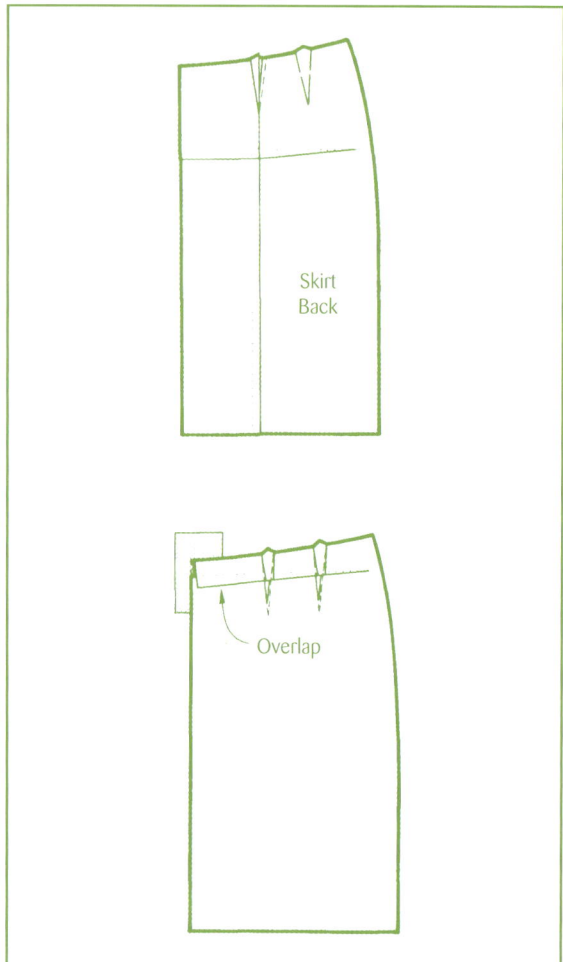

Figure 1.36 – (Top) Flat Buttocks Adjustment
Figure 1.37 – (Bottom) Sway Back Adjustment

For Pants Only

When both crotch depth and crotch length need adjusting, change crotch depth first, since this will affect crotch length.

Altering Crotch Depth

Make adjustments on pattern adjustment line between waist and bottom of crotch. To lengthen, slash, spread desired amount, add tissue and

tape in place. To shorten, take a tuck one half the total amount desired. Alter both front and back pieces. Redraw cutting lines. See Figure 1.38.

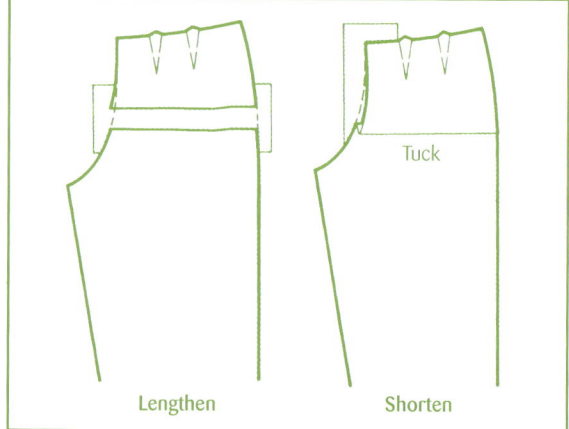

Figure 1.38 – Altering Crotch Depth

Altering Crotch Length

This can be done at the crotch point or in the crotch seam. Alter either in front or back, wherever length is needed.

Crotch point: If pattern does not have a crotch line, draw a straight line from crotch point to side seam, at right angles to grainline. To increase crotch length, continue the line past crotch point for amount needed. Draw new cutting lines in both directions. To decrease crotch length, shorten line at crotch point. Draw new leg cutting lines. See Figure 1.39.

Crotch seam: Cut and spread pattern on adjustment line from center cutting line to side seamline. To

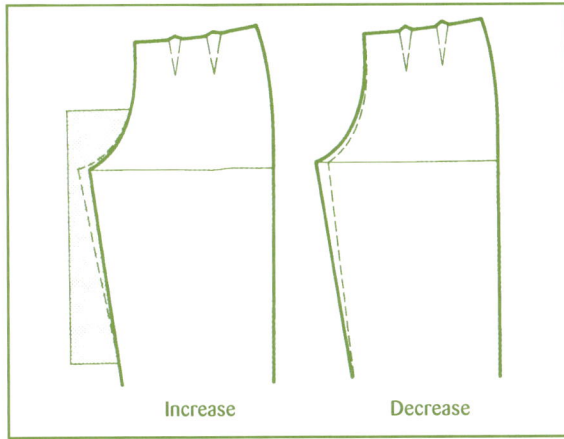

Figure 1.39–Altering Crotch at Point

increase crotch length, spread desired amount, insert tissue and tape in place. Redraw cutting lines on center seam. See Figure 1.40.

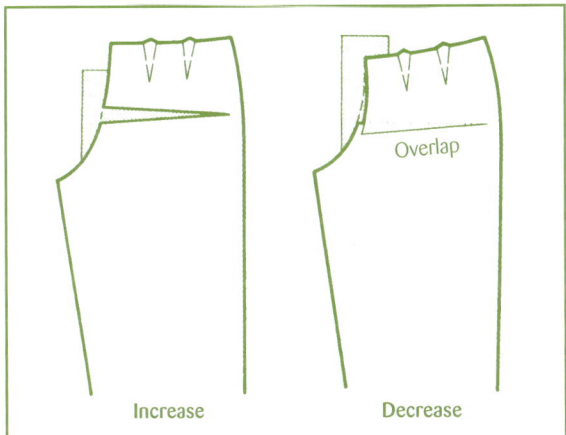

Figure 1.40–Altering Crotch at Seam

These are some of the most common fitting problems that will require adjustment. Of course, they will not apply to one person. Many may not apply to you at all. Once you've made all the corrections that are needed for your particular garment, it's a good idea to try on your adjusted paper pattern.

Try It On

Pin all darts and tucks together on the right side of the pattern, along the stitching line. Fold the horizontal darts down, the vertical darts toward the center line. Pin the pattern pieces together right side out along the seamlines. Place the pins close together in a straight, even line. Turn the waistline seam up after pinning. Carefully try the pattern on the right side of your body with the seams outside, as shown in Figure 1.41. Do not pin in the sleeves or put on the collar. Slip the sleeve over your arm and pin it to the shoulder seam with one pin. Pin the center front line to the center of your undergarments. Have someone do

Figure 1.41–Checking Basic Fit

the same in the center back, or hold center back in place with your left hand.

Now stand in front of a mirror. Don't expect this creation to look or fit like a finished product, since it will not drape the way your fabric will. *What you're concerned about here is the basic fit.* If there is a high round neckline, it will fit snugly due to the seam allowance. Clip this if you like, to make it lie flatter. Check to see if the seamline falls in the right place on your neck. The same will be true of the armhole edge: it will feel snug due to the seam allowance. Check to see if the seamline falls properly on the shoulder and under the arm. Make sure the center front line falls straight down the center of your body. Check the back center line, also. Look to see if the bust darts fall in the proper place. If they are too high or too low, they will need adjusting. Side and lower bodice darts should end 1/2"-1" from the most prominent part of the bust. See if the waistline falls in the proper place. If there are any adjustments to be made, make a mark on the pattern where they should be. Remember that a paper pattern will not conform to the body the way cloth does. All you're looking for is the basic fit. The correct drape will come with the finished product.

Unpin the pattern, smooth out the pieces, and make any necessary corrections according to the markings you made on the pattern.

Making a Trial Muslin

If you find there are a number of corrections involved, or if you want to be absolutely sure of a perfect fit, you might want to make a "trial muslin" before cutting into your precious material. A trial muslin is a garment made from your pattern in a fabric that will fit and drape the same way your finished garment will. It is used especially in the following instances:

• If you are using a very expensive fabric for your finished garment.

• If the style of the garment is especially complicated or difficult.

• If there is a part of the garment you are unsure of, such as the fit of an armhole or neckline. A too-low neckline cannot be raised once it's been cut.

• If the fabric you are using would show pin and needle marks, such as vinyl or leather.

① Use a plain material for your trial muslin, so that markings may be easily seen. ② Use a good quality material with a high thread count. A poor quality fabric will tend to stretch and will give you an inaccurate fit. Cut out the basic pattern pieces, using a 1" seam allowance to allow for alterations. You do not need to use facings, collars, or

pockets. Transfer the pattern markings, including the seamlines. Sew the pieces together with a large machine basting stitch (remember to take that 1" seam allowance).

Leave all edges unfinished—neck, hem, zipper opening, etc. For neck and armhole edges, sew a line of stitching around the opening, directly on the seamline, and slash to the stitching.

This will make the neck and armhole edges fit more accurately. Make a line of machine basting down the center front and center back. Try the garment on and check for fit. Pin zipper or button openings closed. Make sure center front and center back basting lines hang straight. Pin, mark, and adjust wherever necessary. If garment is too tight, slash it open and insert a piece of material. Start making your adjustments at the shoulders; work from the top down. Adjustments made at the top sometimes solve problems farther down.

When the fit of your trial muslin is correct, take the muslin apart and transfer all markings and corrections to the paper pattern. Now you can cut into your fabric with confidence. You are assured a perfect fit.

True or False?

1. Include seam allowances when measuring pattern pieces.

2. Making a dart smaller adds width to a garment.

3. Each pattern piece represents one half of your body.

4. If the bustline needs to be lowered, make the adjustment at the bustline darts.

5. Adjustments of 2" or less can usually be made at the side seams.

6. To shorten a one-piece dress, always shorten below the waistline.

7. You do not need to correct side seam cutting lines after bodice adjustments are made.

8. To alter the crotch length, always alter at the crotch point.

9. Side and lower bodice darts should end 1/2"-1" from the most prominent part of the bust.

10. A trial muslin is a garment made from your pattern in a fabric that will fit and drape the same way your finished garment will.

Check your answers with those provided on page 199.

LAYOUT, CUTTING, AND MARKING

Introduction

The pattern has been adjusted, the fabric has been prepared, and now you're ready for cutting. Cutting into your fabric is a big step—one that must be taken cautiously. A mistake in cutting cannot be undone. Check your pattern instruction sheet. It will tell you what layout to use according to your pattern size and the width of your material. Circle it—your eye will go directly to it.

Since you've chosen the correct layout for your particular garment, follow it as closely as possible. Pattern layouts are pretested for the most satisfactory use of material. Sometimes you will come out with a little fabric left over. Remember that adjustments must be made on the pattern *before* cutting—pattern companies allow for these alterations when they estimate yardage. If you find that your cutting layouts *consistently* require less yardage, you will learn how much less fabric to purchase in the future. If you make any changes in your pattern layout, be sure to do a trial layout *before* you cut—lay all the pattern pieces on the

fabric to make sure you have enough. Don't attempt to economize on fabric by laying pieces slightly off grain. It won't work! You'll end up with a poorly hanging garment. See Figure 2.1.

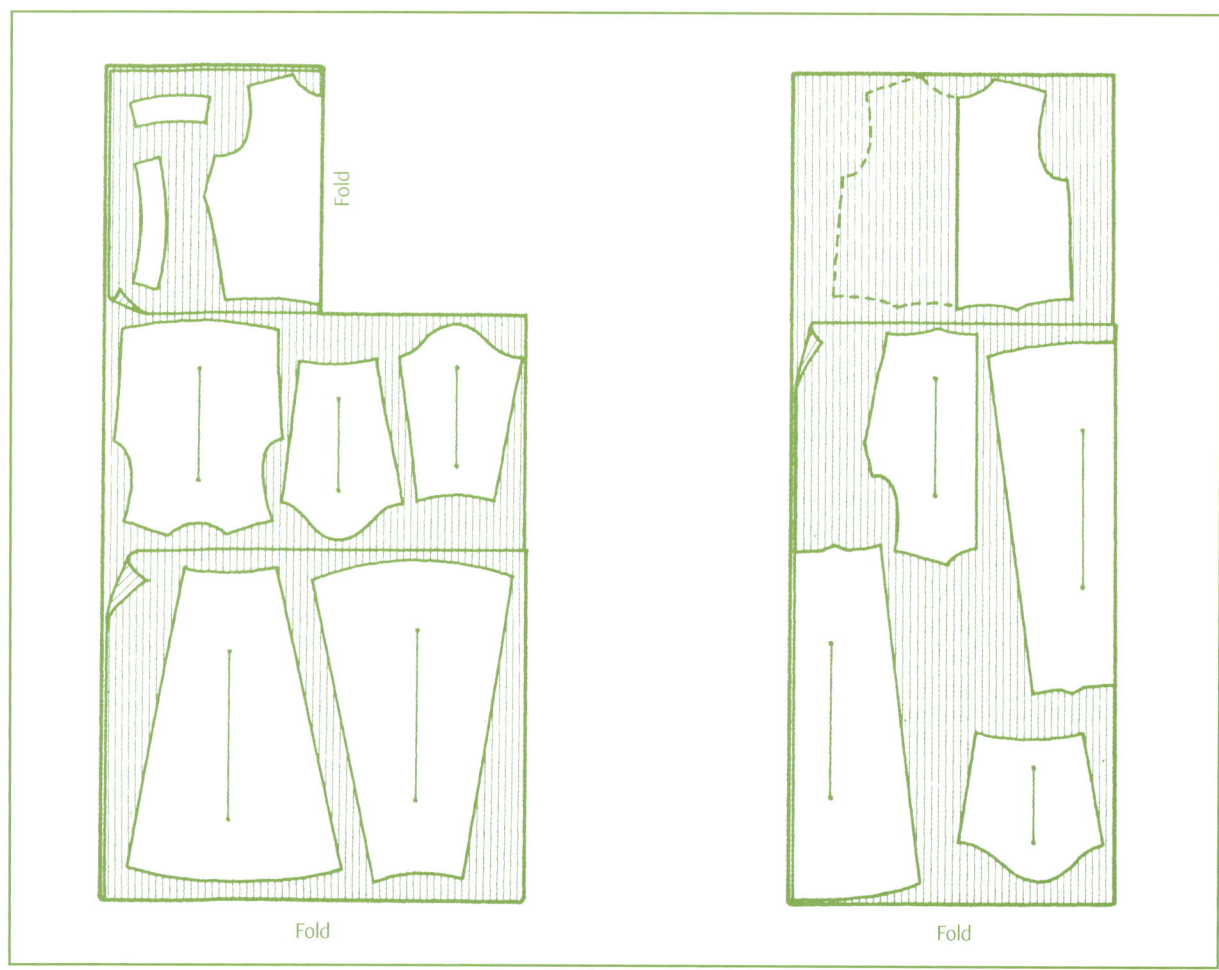

Figure 2.1—Be sure all pieces fit and are on the grain.

Remove the Crease

Before you spread out your fabric, press it lightly to remove all wrinkles and creases. Most fabrics come from the bolt folded in half. Check that fold to see if it will press out. You don't want to use it in your layout if you're going to end up with a permanent crease down the front of your dress. On most permanent press fabrics, this crease is exactly that—permanent. Test to see if it's removable. Sponge it with a mixture of 1 tablespoon white

vinegar and 1 cup water (test this on a scrap first for spotting or colorfastness). If that doesn't work, sponge or spray it with plain vinegar, then press. If this won't remove it, nothing will—you'll have to avoid it when cutting. You can usually refold the fabric satisfactorily by opening it out flat and bringing the outside edges to the center (Figure 2.2), or measure the widest part of the pattern piece to be laid on a fold, measure that distance from the selvage, and fold the fabric on that line. (Figure 2.3).

Figure 2.2 – (Left) Refolding Fabric to Avoid Crease
Figure 2.3 – (Right) Folding Fabric to Fit the Pattern Piece

Right or Wrong?

Sometimes it is difficult to tell the right side of a fabric from the wrong side. Here are a few clues to help you in determining which side to use:

- Cottons and linens are usually folded right side out (this also aids in showing the patterns on printed fabrics).

- Wools, delicate fabrics, and imported fabrics are usually placed on the bolt right side in, to protect them from damage.

- Napped fabrics, vinyls, and velvets are rolled, usually right side out, to avoid creasing.

- Prints are always sharper and more defined on the right side.

- The selvage is usually more smoothly woven on the right side.

- Textured fabrics, such as shantung or tweed, have more textured surface on the right side than on the wrong side. Small irregularities sometimes appear on the wrong side.

- When knits are stretched crosswise, they usually roll to the right side of the material.

- Smooth fabrics are usually smoother and softer to the touch on the right side.

- Some fabrics, such as checked gingham or woven wool plaids, do not have a right or wrong side. Use either one.

- When all else fails, pick the side you like best and stick with it. When cutting, be sure to make all fabric folds to the same side. Make a mark on the wrong side of the fabric on each piece to avoid confusion when sewing.

Grain

Most garments are cut on the lengthwise grain of a woven fabric for greater wear and durability. The lengthwise grain of a fabric has more strength and stability than the crosswise grain. The crosswise grain has a slight amount of give and works best going around the contours of the body. True bias is the 45° angle to any straight edge and has the most elasticity. It is used where a great amount of stretch and drape is desired.

Knits have varying degrees of stretch. Unlike woven fabrics, they do *not* have the most stretch on the bias. Knits usually have the most stretch on the crosswise grain. Knits have an up and down because they are constructed of loops—they should be cut in one direction. Use the "with nap" layout when cutting knits.

With Nap

Fabrics that have an up and down must always be cut with all pattern pieces running in the same direction, as shown in Figure 2.4.

Prints sometimes have an up and down design; these should be cut in one direction. Fabrics with nap or pile must also be laid out in one direction. A *nap* is created when surface fibers on a fabric are brushed after weaving; a *pile* is created when surface fibers are cut after weaving.

Run your fingers lightly over the surface of a napped or piled fabric along the lengthwise grain. It will feel smooth in the direction of the nap (down) and rough against the nap (up). Velvet, velveteen, and corduroy are all fabrics with a short pile. They look best when cut with the nap running up—the colors

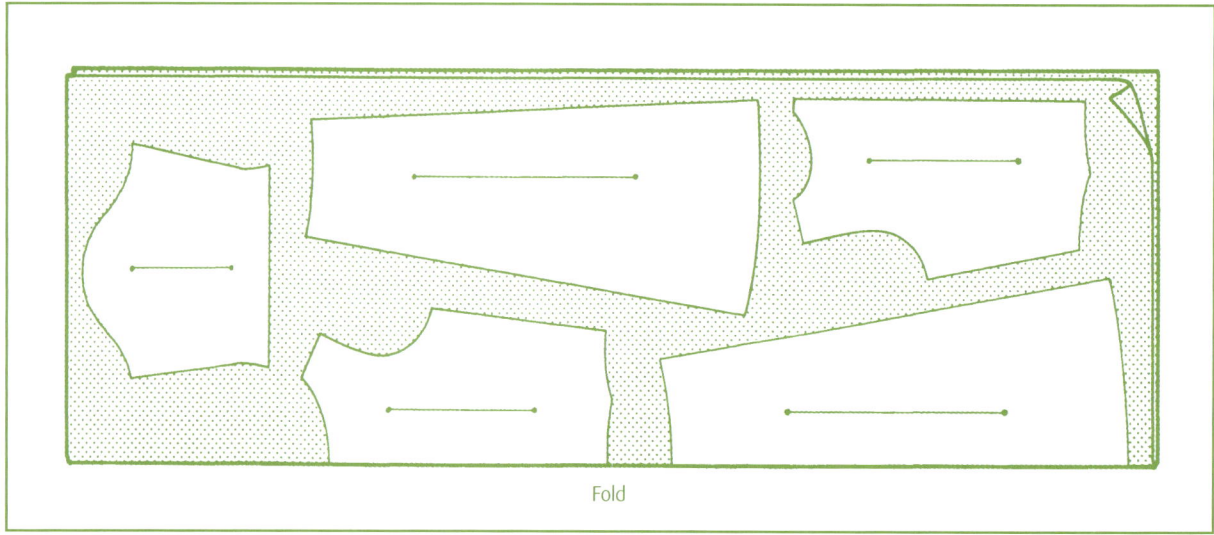

Figure 2.4—On a napped fabric, all pieces must run in the same direction.

will be darker and richer. Suede cloth is a short-napped fabric that wears best when cut with the nap running down. Fabrics with a long nap or pile, such as fleece, velour, or camel hair, look and wear better with the nap running down.

Check your fabric for variations in color and shading. Drape one end of the fabric over your right shoulder and the other end over your left shoulder, letting the fabric in between hang down in front of you. Stand in front of a mirror. If the fabric on one side looks slightly darker or different in color from the other side, use the "with nap" layout. Satins, knits, or iridescent taffetas often reflect light differently in opposite directions and should be cut using "with nap" layouts.

Pattern Layout

Lay your fabric on a large, flat surface (a cutting board is ideal). Do not let the end of the fabric hang over the edge—it will stretch the fabric and you will not get an accurate cutting. Fold the ends over on the table if necessary. Circle your cutting layout if you haven't already done so. Smooth out the pattern pieces or press them with a warm, dry iron if they are very wrinkled. Cut apart small pieces that are printed on the same piece of tissue.

Do a rough layout: spread out all the pattern pieces on the material before

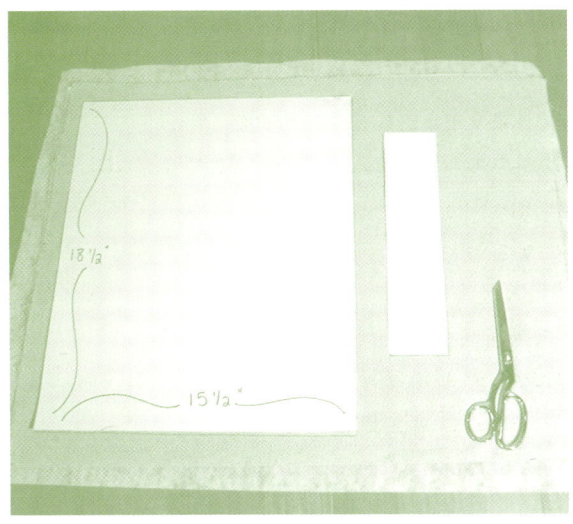

cutting to make sure they will fit. Lay out as many pieces as you can; then, if necessary, fold over or roll up this section, moving it down to the end of the table.

Spread out the next section of fabric. If a crisis develops and you discover you don't have enough material, here are a few suggestions to save the day:

- Facings can sometimes be cut on the crosswise grain (not the front facings of a jacket with lapels, however, because they will show).

- Cuffs, pockets, tabs, and other small decorative pieces can sometimes be cut on the crosswise grain or the bias for an interesting effect.

- Sleeve length can be changed from long to short.

- Hems can be eliminated; use hem facing instead.

• Collars, cuffs, yokes, pockets, and other decorative trims can be cut from a contrasting fabric.

Once you've determined that everything will fit, follow your layout and start pinning. First lay out the pattern pieces that go on a fold. Then do the lengthwise pieces, then the crosswise pieces, if any. Cut single thicknesses last. Start with the large pieces and work your way down to the smallest ones.

Be sure to use each pattern piece the correct number of times (each piece will tell you how many are needed). Selvages can be used as cutting edges for straight seams but should be clipped every few inches to prevent puckering. They are especially good to use for seams where zippers will be inserted, since they require no seam finishing.

Overlap excess tissue paper outside the cutting lines unless it was used to enlarge the pattern (do *not* overlap the cutting lines). Rearrange the layout if necessary where pattern pieces have been enlarged, staying as close as possible to the original layout. Watch out for placement of motifs on large prints. You don't want to put large flowers right across the bust or buttocks. Small prints are no problem.

Keep all grainlines straight, following the printed arrow on the pattern. It's easier to keep grainlines straight if you extend them to both ends of each pattern piece (be sure to use a ruler). Measure the distance from each end of the grainline to the edge of the fabric, as shown in Figure 2.5—both ends should be the same. Put a pin at each end of the grainline. Pin outer edges of pattern.

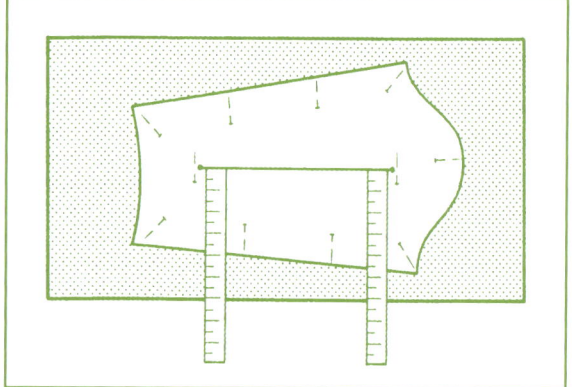

Figure 2.5–Keeping the Grainline Straight

Use pins sparingly (about every 6" - 8")—just enough to hold pattern in place. Pick up only a few threads of fabric with each pin. Too much pinning will make the material buckle—you want it to lie nice and flat for cutting. Use very sharp dressmaker pins to avoid damaging the fabric (bent or dull pins will make snags). Ball-point pins are good on knit fabrics. If you have a cutting board, you can try using push pins to hold the pattern and fabric to the board. Be sure your pins do not cross the cutting line.

You might try using upholstery weights as a substitute for pins (they can be purchased at a yardage store) or try masking tape or spray pattern holder, also obtainable at fabric stores. These are especially good on fabrics that will be damaged by pins.

Cutting

Keep the fabric flat while cutting. Bent-handled shears, shown in Figure 2.6, work the best because they do not raise the fabric as you cut. Use one hand to hold the pattern and material flat while you cut with the other hand. If you're left-handed, use left-handed shears.

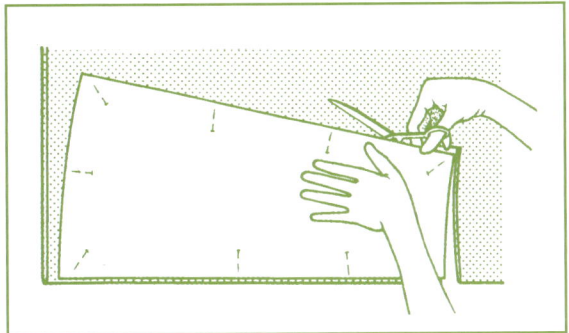

Figure 2.6—Use bent-handled shears to keep the fabric flat.

Take long, even strokes, not quite closing the blades of the shears, since closing completely causes chopping. Cut directly on the outer edge of a single cutting line or directly between a double cutting line, whichever is marked on your pattern. Don't try to cut *around* corners—cut *into* corners from each side. Wipe lint off the shears as you go, especially if you're cutting synthetics.

Shears *must* be sharp. Dull shears will chew the fabric and you will not get a clean cutting line. Slightly dull shears can be sharpened by cutting through fine sandpaper; very dull ones should be sharpened by a professional.

Serrated shears are an aid in cutting thin, slippery fabrics such as chiffon or tricot. Never use pinking or scalloping shears for cutting out a garment. You will not get a true cutting edge and it will be difficult to determine your seam allowance when sewing. You will also have difficulty locating the notches.

Cut all notches outward rather than inward to preserve the seam allowance (Figure 2.7). If you're sure you will not need to alter the seam allowance, you can make short clip marks into the seam allowance instead. Clip no further than the point of the printed notch (Figure 2.8).

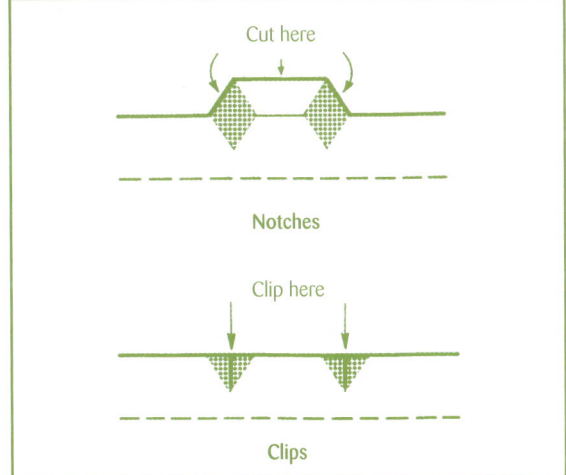

Figure 2.7—(Top) Cut notches outward.
Figure 2.8—(Bottom) If no altering is needed, clip notches.

Clips are also handy at center front and center back lines, foldlines, and shoulder markings on sleeves. Clip dart lines at seam allowances and mark each end of gathering lines with a small clip (Figure 2.9).

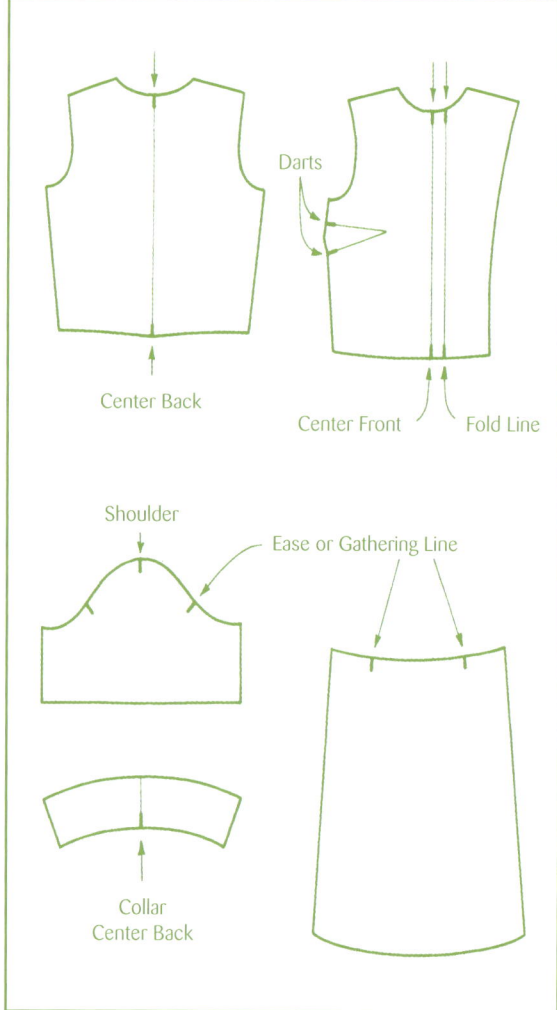

Figure 2.9–Use clip marks to indicate important points.

Save all your cutting scraps. They'll come in handy for making trial buttonholes, for testing stitch and tension control, and for checking pressing temperatures.

Knits

Don't try to cut knit fabrics on grain. Many knit fabrics are made on circular knitting machines; this causes them to be slightly off grain. Follow the straight line of the weave, print, or stripe. The finished look is more important than the grainline.

If your knit fabric has a lengthwise rib that is easily recognizable, open the fabric, press out the fold, and re-press it along one of the ribs closest to the foldline. The edges will not match exactly, but you will be able to cut your fabric double.

If the fabric is too far off grain, it should be cut in a single layer, rather than double. If the fabric is tubular, cut one edge and lay the fabric out flat. *Be sure to reverse your pattern when cutting the second piece.* Cut one piece with the pattern right side up and one piece with the pattern face down. You don't want to end up with two right sleeves and no left sleeve.

For pattern pieces that need to be placed on a fold, you might want to make an extended piece for cutting on a single layer of fabric. Lay the pattern piece on a folded piece of tissue paper, placing the fold edge of the pattern along the fold of the paper (Figure 2.10). Cut around the remaining edges of the pattern. Open the tissue paper and you

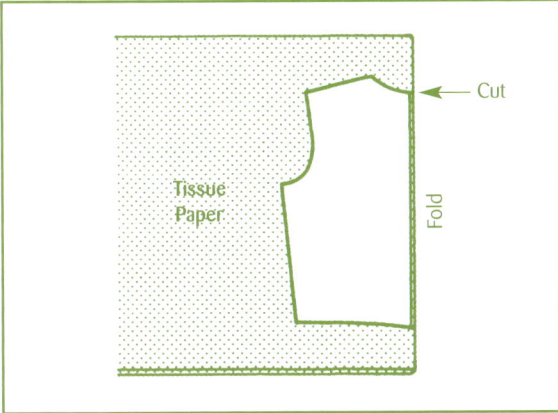

Figure 2.10—Making an Extended Pattern Piece

have a whole pattern piece that can be cut on a single layer (Figure 2.11).

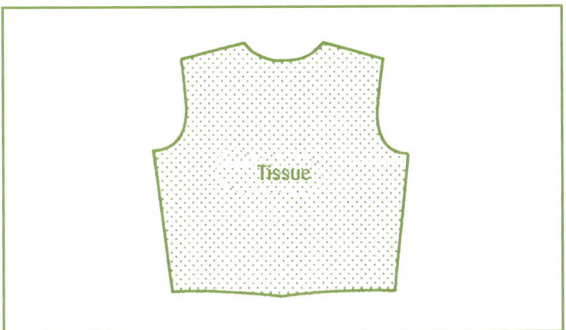

Figure 2.11—Extended Pattern Piece

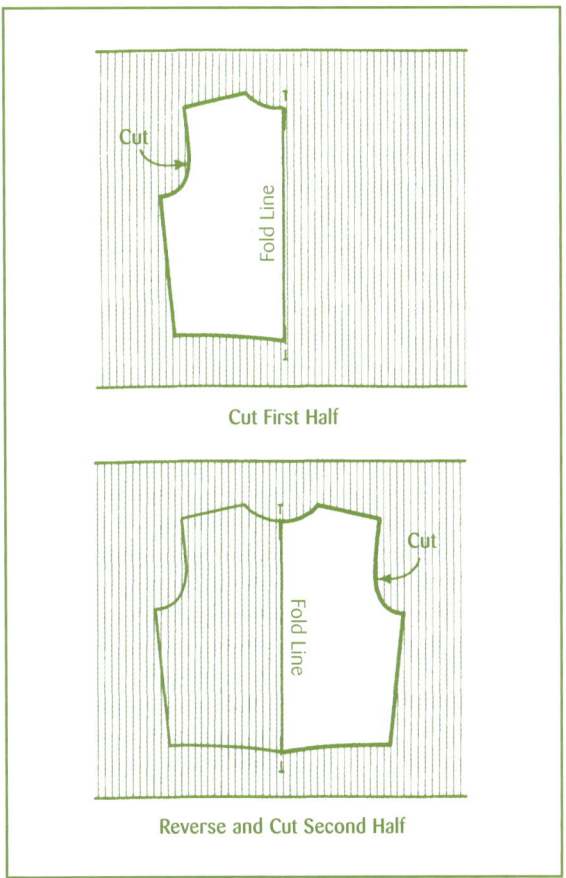

Cut First Half

Reverse and Cut Second Half

Figure 2.12—(Top) Cutting First Half of Pattern with Fold Line.
Figure 2.13—(Bottom) Reversing and Cutting Second Half of Pattern

If you don't want to bother making an extended pattern piece, lay the pattern on the fabric, mark the foldline with pins, and cut around the pattern to the foldline (Figure 2.12). Reverse pattern to the other side, finish cutting (Figure 2.13), and put pins *across the cutting line on the fold*. You don't want to accidentally cut down that foldline. It's been known to happen.

Test your knit fabrics for stretch. Most knits have the greatest stretch in the crosswise grain. Cut your knit fabric with the greatest stretch going around the body for ease and comfort. Remember to lay all pattern pieces in the same direction when cutting knits. Use ball-point pins; fine, sharp silk pins; or needles for pinning the pattern to a knit fabric. Use very sharp shears or serrated shears for cutting.

Accuracy in cutting any fabric is absolutely essential. Patterns are designed precisely, to accurate measurements. In order for your garment pieces to fit together properly, all pieces must be cut exactly on the cutting lines. These lines must be straight and clean. Your stitching will be simplified if you have nice, straight lines to follow, and all your pieces will match each other perfectly.

Marking

After your garment is cut, you will need to transfer a number of markings to your fabric before you remove the pattern pieces. There are several methods that can be used. Choose the one that will work the best on the fabric you are using and will be the most convenient for you.

Tracing Wheel and Dressmaker's Carbon Paper

A tracing wheel is used with dressmaker's carbon paper—both can be purchased in the notions department of a fabric store. Carbon paper comes in assorted colors. Choose the one that is the closest in color to the fabric you are using. Use light colors on light fabrics and dark colors on dark fabrics. There should be just enough difference between the carbon and the fabric to make the markings visible. *Carbon markings do not wash out.* On sheers and laces they will show through—you will have to use a different marking method on these fabrics. Always try

your carbon on a test scrap first. Tweeds and other soft fabrics do not always show carbon markings; leather and vinyl may be permanently marked by the tracing wheel. Test first to be sure this method is usable on your fabric.

There are three kinds of tracing wheels. The most commonly used wheel has a serrated edge—it will work well on most fabrics (Figure 2.14). A plain, unserrated wheel should be used on delicate fabrics or fabrics with a smooth finish. This wheel is sometimes used without tracing paper because it leaves an impression on the material (Figure 2.15). A needlepoint wheel can be used on heavier, hard-finish fabrics: it gives a more definite mark (Figure 2.16).

To mark fabric, unpin the pattern enough to insert the carbon paper. If fabric is folded *right* sides together, put one piece of carbon between the pattern

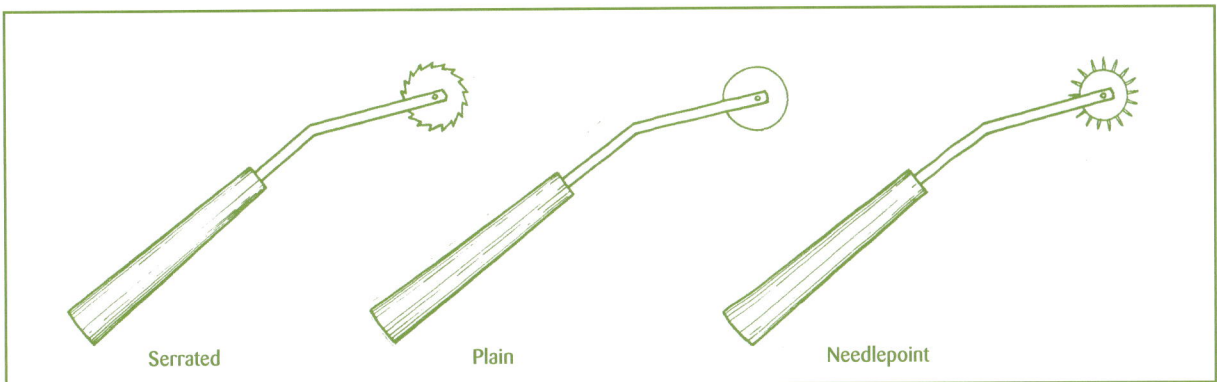

Figure 2.14 – (Left) Serrated Tracing Wheel
Figure 2.15 – (Center) Plain Tracing Wheel
Figure 2.16 – (Right) Needlepoint Tracing Wheel

and the top layer of material; put another piece of carbon underneath the bottom layer of material.

If fabric is folded *wrong* sides together, put two pieces of carbon between the two layers of fabric. Be sure the carbon side of the paper is toward the wrong side of the fabric. Use the tracing wheel to follow the printed lines and markings on the pattern (a ruler will help you to draw straight lines). See Figure 2.17. Sometimes you can fold back the pattern on the marking line and use the folded edge as a guide (Figure 2.18).

Mark all darts, tucks, buttonholes, pocket placements, etc. Dots and other symbols can be marked with an X. You don't need to mark the stitching line unless it is other than the standard 5/8". You can use a seam guide or marking line on your sewing machine to make an accurate stitching line. Do *not* transfer the grainline marking. Be sure

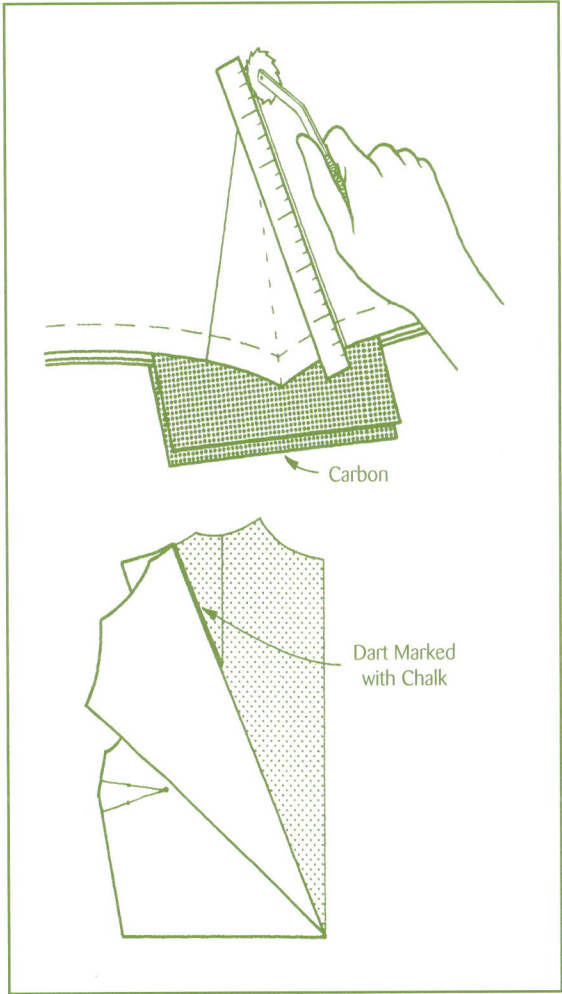

Figure 2.17 – (Top) Marking with Carbon Paper
Figure 2.18 – (Bottom) Marking with Chalk on a Folded Edge

to protect the surface under your fabric. Tracing wheels can make damaging marks on your furniture.

When marking is finished, remove the pattern. To transfer markings that are needed on the right side of the fabric—buttonholes, for instance—use thread tracing. Thread tracing is a line of hand basting made directly on top of the marking line on the fabric (Figure 2.19). Use a contrasting color thread—it will show easily on the right side. No need to fasten the thread ends. Leave them loose for easy removal.

Figure 2.19–Transferring marking with thread tracing.

Machine basting can be used on fabrics that do not show needle marks. For a quick method of transferring markings to the right side, pin-marking can be used. Push a pin through the markings and place another pin in that same spot on the right side. This is good for marking placement of pocket corners (Figure 2.20).

If your garment is to be underlined, you will need to place your pattern

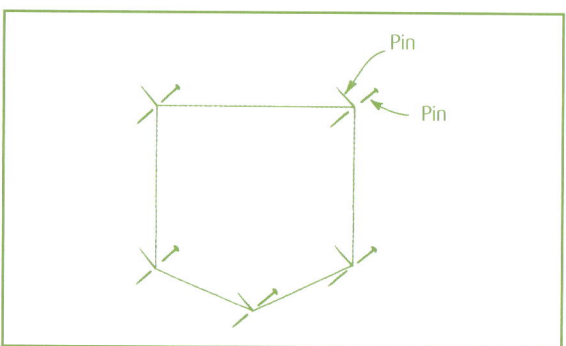

Figure 2.20–Transferring markings with pin-marking.

markings on the underlining fabric rather than the outer fabric. If your garment is to be lined, transfer all necessary markings to the lining pieces.

Pins and Chalk

For a quick and easy method of marking your fabric, use pins and chalk. A chalk pencil is handy for this.

Step 1. Poke pins through pattern and material where dots and other markings occur. Turn pattern and material over so that pins are sticking straight up (Figure 2.21).

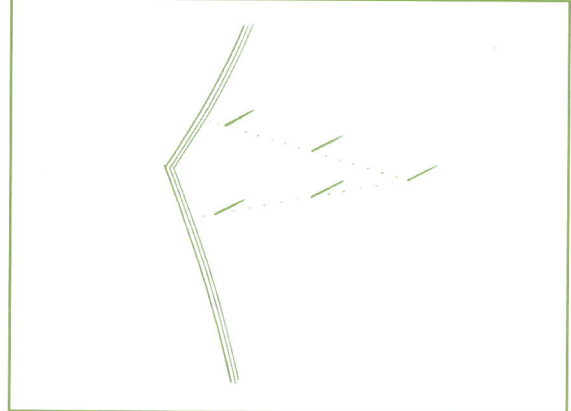

Figure 2.21–Step 1. Pin-and-Chalk Method

Step 2. If fabric has been folded *right* sides together, make a chalk mark where each pin sticks out through the fabric. Gradually lift both layers of fabric off the pattern piece, making a chalk mark where pins enter the fabric (Figure 2.22).

Step 3. If fabric has been folded *wrong* sides together, gradually lift top layer of fabric and mark *both* pieces with chalk where pins pass through fabric (Figure 2.23).

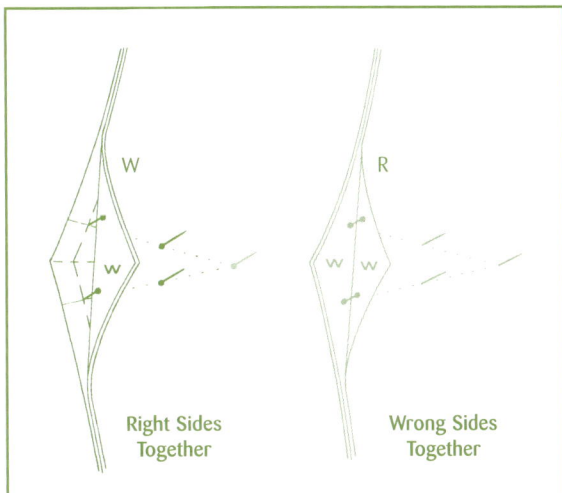

Figure 2.22–(Left) Step 2. Pin-and-Chalk Method
Figure 2.23–(Right) Step 3. Pin-and-Chalk Method

Chalk marks do not stay forever; it's a good idea to do your marking just before you sew. Otherwise, put a few pins into your chalk marks so you can find them later. You might want to connect the chalk marks on darts and other lines by drawing a chalk line from one to another (use your ruler).

Clips

Clip marks are a quick and useful method of marking many construction points. We've mentioned them before. A 1/8" clip into the seam allowance is all that is needed and will not interfere with seam construction. Use clips whenever dots or other symbols appear on a seamline. Simply clip 1/8" into the seam allowance at that point. They are especially useful for marking center front and center back lines, foldings, dart placement lines, shoulder markings on sleeves, and ends of zipper openings. Use them also to mark waistlines, seamlines, and hemlines. The more you use them, the more you'll like them. Be accurate with your clipping and you'll find that your sewing will be simplified.

Tailor's Tacks

This is the most time-consuming method of marking fabrics, but it is the one that should be used on delicate fabrics and those that would be permanently damaged by any other method. Use soft threads that are not slippery—they will stay in the fabric better. Cotton thread, darning cotton, and embroidery thread are good choices.

Tailor's tacks are made by hand with a long double strand of thread. Do not make a knot in the end of the thread. Take a small stitch through pattern and material, leaving about 1" of thread at the end. Take another stitch in the same place, forming a loop. Cut the thread, leaving another 1" end. Do this at every construction symbol. For longer lines, make several tailor's tacks in a row, cutting them apart when you finish. Raise the top layer of fabric and clip the threads between the layers (Figure 2.24). Carefully remove pattern, clipping loops if necessary. If threads are clipped short, they will be less apt to pull out of the fabric.

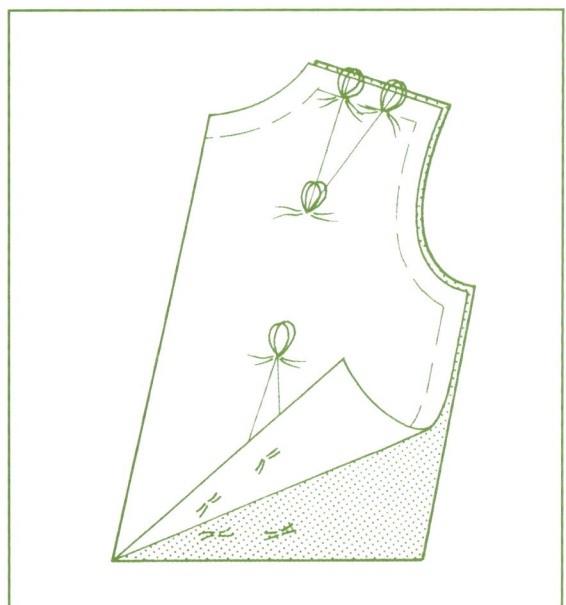

Figure 2.24–Tailor's Tacks

Some machines are equipped to make tailor's tacks but require a special foot. Consult your manual. Some machines make a chain stitch that can be used for marking, since it is easily removed. However, both of these methods require sewing directly through the pattern. If you plan to use your pattern again, you'd better not use these methods, since the tissue will be torn when it is removed from the fabric.

Simplified tailor's tacks are generally used when marking a single layer of fabric. This is basically a line of uneven basting stitches. Take a tiny stitch through pattern and material with a double, unknotted strand of thread. Leave a long, loose stitch on top and take another tiny stitch through pattern and material. Continue along marking line, then clip threads apart between stitches (Figure 2.25). Remove pattern, being careful not to pull out marking threads. This is a good method to use when marking center front and center back lines, foldlines, or hemlines. When marking pleat lines, use one color thread for the foldlines, and another color thread for the placement lines.

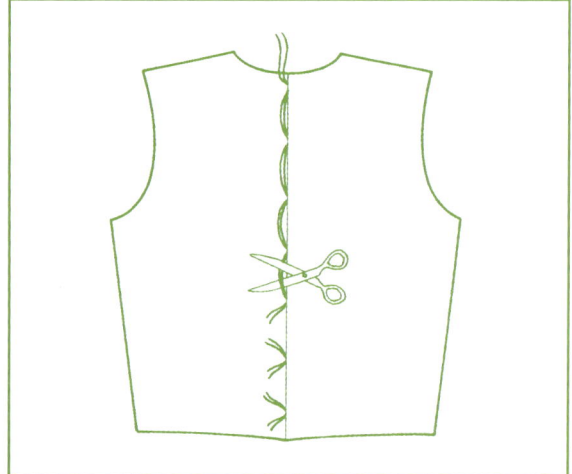

Figure 2.25–Simplified Tailor's Tacks

What Pattern Markings Mean

Every pattern consists of markings that are necessary to ensure accuracy when laying out the pattern, pinning the pieces to the fabric, fitting to your figure, and cutting out. The following are symbols and their meanings.

Notches: Diamond-shaped symbols used for accurate joining.

Added aides for matching or end of stitch line.

Place-on-fold bracket: Grainline marking with directional arrows that indicates to place thin outer line on fold.

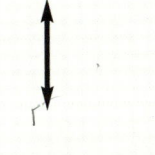

Grainline: Means to place on straight of grain, done by measuring distance at both ends of arrow to selvage or fold.

Cutting line: Heavy outer line on patterns (on patterns of more than one size there will be lines within lines).

Seamline: Indicated by broken line. 5/8" unless otherwise stated.

Scissors: Directional symbol: indicates which direction to cut.

Small arrows: On seamline: indicates which direction to sew in.

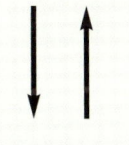

Lengthen or shorten symbols: Double lines specify the place to make these adjustments.

Darts: Broken stitching lines.

Answer the following multiple-choice questions.

1. Cottons and linens are usually folded _____.

     a. right side out
     b. right side in
     c. woven side out

2. Most garments are cut with the grainlines laid parallel to the _____.

     a. crosswise grain
     b. the bias
     c. lengthwise grain

3. Fabrics that have an up and down are _____.

     a. knits
     b. with nap
     c. woven

4. Facings can sometimes be cut on the _____.

     a. crosswise grain
     b. lengthwise grain
     c. bias

5. When cutting the fabric, cut all notches _____.

     a. outward
     b. inward
     c. off

6. Carbon markings _____.

   a. are best
   b. do not wash out
   c. show up on all fabrics

7. Tailor's tacks are made _____.

   a. with chalk
   b. by hand with thread
   c. with scissors

8. The pattern symbol ⌐⌐⌐ signifies _____.

   a. a notch
   b. the grainline
   c. that the pattern should be placed on a fold

9. The seam allowance is _____.

   a. indicated by a solid line
   b. 5/8" unless otherwise stated
   c. indicated by a diamond-shaped symbol

10. Scissors appearing on pattern pieces are _____.

   a. directional symbols
   b. used for end of stitch line
   c. used for matching

Check your answers with those provided on page 199.

PART TWO

BASIC CONSTRUCTION METHODS

Overview

At this point, all your careful measuring, pattern adjusting, layout, and cutting are ready to pay off. You can finally begin to put your garment together. You can start that construction as soon as you have read this second part. In this part, you will read about the various types of seams and seam finishes and learn the processes for your final fitting of a garment. You will also read about some time-saving methods, such as unit construction.

Upon completion of this part, you will be able to

- Identify and list terms used in construction of a garment

- Name and define stitches and seams used in clothing construction

- Explain steps in garment fitting

- List notions and time-saving steps connected with shortcut construction

STITCHING AND SEAM

Stitching and Seam Construction

Stitching is the mainstay of your garment. Straight, strong seams hold it together. Stitching done with correct tension, pressure, and stitch length will keep your garment from coming apart at the seams. Correct stitching procedures done in the proper sequence will give you a neat, professional-looking result.

Needle and Thread Selection

The selection of your needle and thread is determined by the fabric you are using. Fine fabrics require fine needles; heavy fabrics require heavier needles. Special fabrics should have special needles, shown in Figure 3.1. For best results, use ball-point needles on knits and wedge-shaped needles on leathers and vinyls. Twin and triple needles are joined together and are used on some machines for decorative stitching.

Imported needles are sized differently from domestic needles. Here are the corresponding sizes:

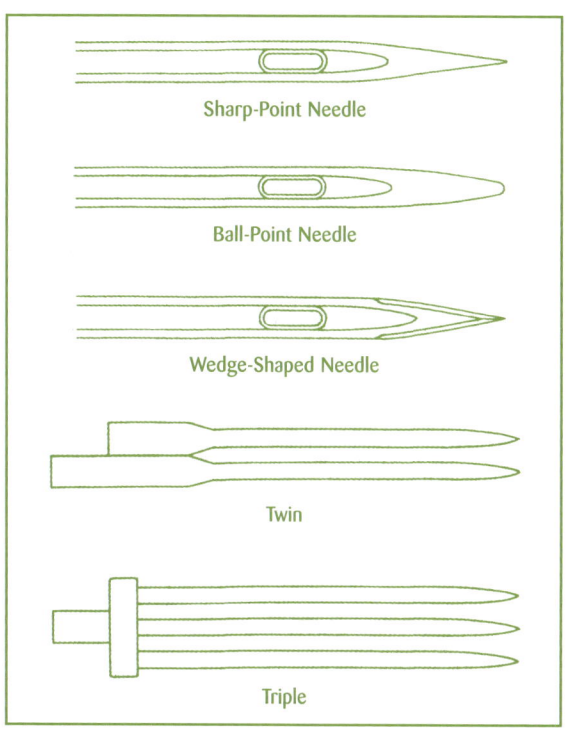

Figure 3.1—Types of Needles

Imported	Domestic
65	9
70	10
75	11
80	12
90	14
100	16

Thread is sized by numbers or letters. Size 50 is the most commonly used. Higher numbers denote finer thread, lower numbers heavier thread. Letters range from A to D—A is fine, D is heavy. Silk and nylon threads are usually labeled by letter; cotton and polyester threads by number. Choose a color that is one shade darker than your fabric—it will look lighter when sewn.

Straight Stitching Practice

There's no better way to become an expert at sewing than to practice. Your goal is to turn out professional-looking garments with a minimum of time, effort, and fuss. Learn to use the sewing techniques that will give you these professional results. Practice sewing on two layers of fabric. That's what sewing is all about—joining two layers of fabric together. Learn to handle your fabric carefully, without stretching, pulling, or tugging. Train your eye to recognize the basic 5/8" seam allowance—this will prove to be an invaluable time-saver. Sew at a steady pace—don't try to rush.

You don't want to spend all your time ripping.

Staystitching

Staystitching is used for reinforcement, particularly on curved or bias seamlines. It is done on a single layer of fabric before the seams are sewn, as shown in Figure 3.2. It should be done as soon as the pattern is removed from the fabric, to prevent stretching. Stitch within the seam allowance, 1/8" from the seamline. Follow the grain of the fabric. To find the grain on a cut edge, run your finger along the edge. The edge will fray and feel rough *against* the grain. Threads will lie smoothly *with* the grain. See Figure 3.3. If in doubt, stitch from the widest part to the narrowest part on each garment piece: this will usually be with the grain. If interfacing or interlining will be sewn

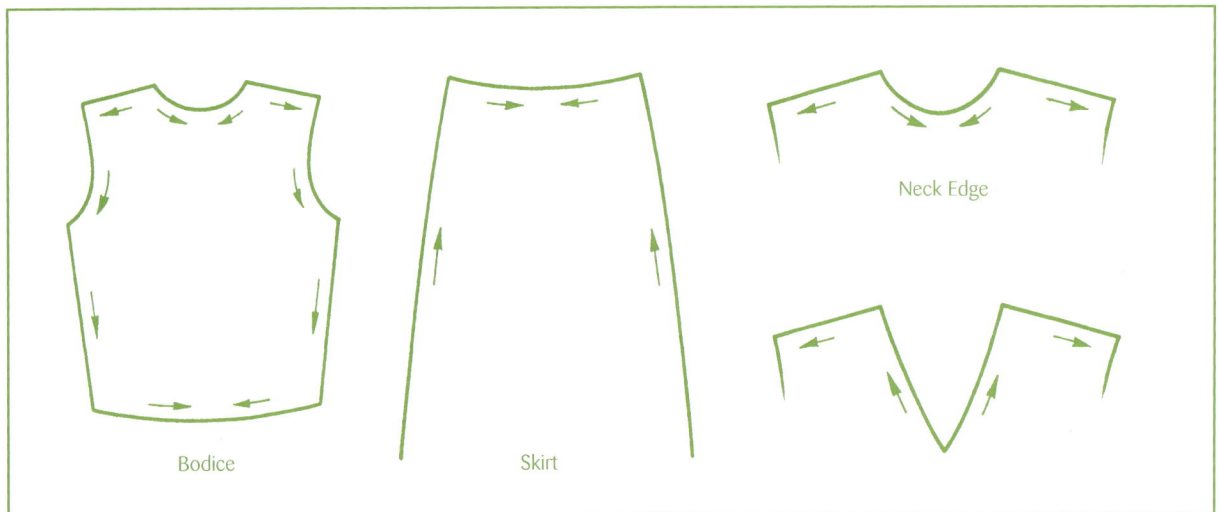

Figure 3.2—Staystitching Directions

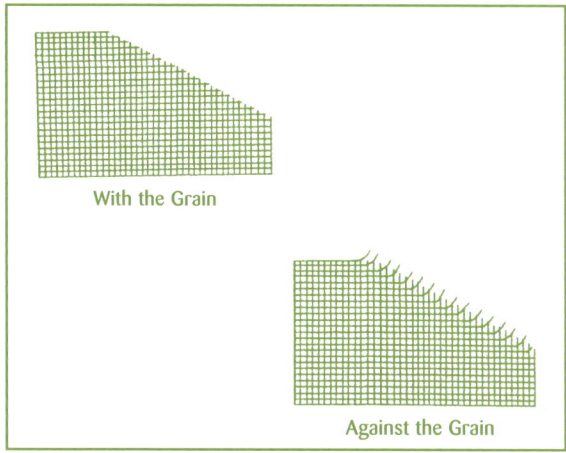

Figure 3.3—Finding the Grain Direction

to the fabric, this stitching will serve as staystitching.

Machine Basting

Machine basting is done with the longest stitch on the sewing machine. If needle holes show on your fabric, use machine basting only where it will *not* show on the finished garment. Hold the fabric securely behind and in front of the presser foot as you sew. Machine basting tends to pucker the fabric unless it is held taut as you sew. If you loosen the top tension slightly, the bobbin threads will be easier to remove. Use a different color bobbin thread to distinguish the machine basting from the finished stitching.

Machine basting can be used to sew basic seams before trying on a garment for fitting. A single row of machine basting, as in Figure 3.4, is used for easing, such as in sleeve caps. Pull up the bobbin thread, spreading and smoothing out gathers as you go, until the eased area is the proper size.

Two or more rows of machine basting are used for making gathers, as in Figure 3.5. To form gathers, pull up both bobbin threads and secure the ends by wrapping threads around a pin until ready to sew.

Figure 3.4—(Top) Using Machine Basting for Easing
Figure 3.5—(Bottom) Using Machine Basting for Gathering

Some machines have a speed basting stitch which is a very large stitch used for loose basting. It is good for making center front and center back lines. Try it on your fabric first; it may leave needle marks.

Another good stitch that is used for machine basting is the chain stitch, which utilizes only the top thread. Some machines can be set up to do this. Check your manual. The chain stitch is very easy to remove.

Straight Seams

Always line up your fabric straight in front of your needle. On most fabrics a straight stitch will do the job of sewing straight seams. On stretch knits a narrow zigzag will allow the fabric to stretch without "popping" the seams. Some machines are equipped with a special stretch for sewing seams on knits. If your machine will only straight-stitch, stretch the fabric as you sew when stitching knits.

Curved Seams

To make a nice, smooth line on a curved seam, slow down. Move your fabric continuously, at a steady pace, as you go around the curve. If you use a shorter stitch length, you will have better control of your stitching. This will also strengthen the seam and prevent it from pulling out after it is clipped and pressed. Your seam guide can be a great help on curved seams. Place it at an angle 5/8" from the needle hole, as in Figure 3.6.

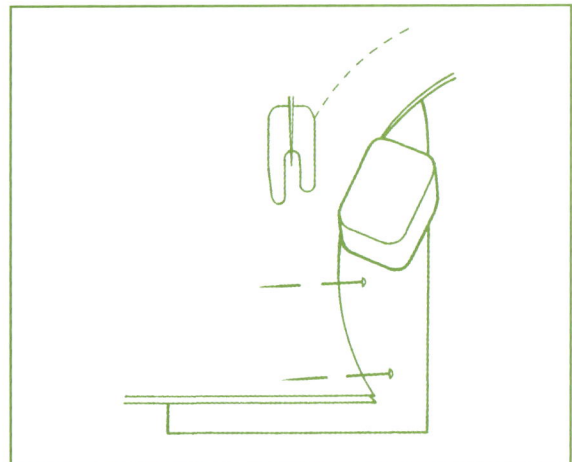

Figure 3.6–Positioning Seam Guide for a Curved Seam

Inside Curve to Outside Curve

This type of seam is found mostly on princess style dresses. Staystitch both seam edges just outside stitching line. Clip the inside curve and notch the outside curve, as in Figure 3.7. Sometimes the outside curve has a section to be eased. If so, make a row of ease-stitching in the curved area.

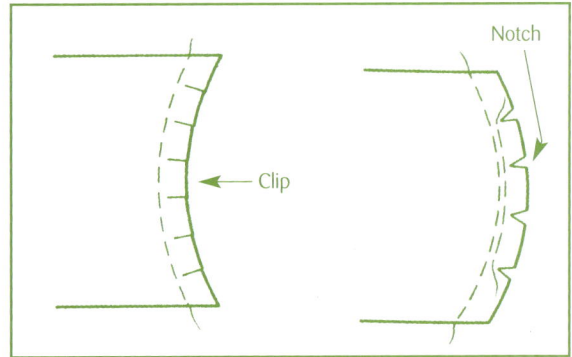

Figure 3.7–Staystitching a Seam with an Inside and an Outside Curve

Pin or baste the seams together, matching *seamlines*. Stitch on seamline, easing fabric as you sew. Do not allow tucks or gathers to form in the seam.

Bias Seams

Bias seams require special care because they have so much stretch. Use a thread with stretch such as polyester or cotton-covered polyester. Use a shorter stitch than usual on your machine or use a very narrow zigzag stitch. If seams are long, baste loosely, leaving a long thread end at the bottom. Allow garment to hang overnight. Smooth stretched seam along the basting thread, then stitch. When joining a bias edge to a straight edge, sew with bias edge on top. Pin together every 3" or 4" before sewing to hold bias in place.

Corner Seams

To make a strong corner seam, reduce the size of the stitch for 1" each side of the corner. Use a small stitch (15 to 20 per inch). Following the 5/8" seam allowance, sew to within 5/8" of the end of the fabric (use your crosswise seam allowance guide here). Leaving the needle in the fabric, raise the presser foot and pivot the fabric until the bottom edge has lined up with the 5/8" seam allowance guide to the right of the presser foot. Lower the presser foot and continue stitching, changing back to a regular stitch after 1". See Figure 3.8.

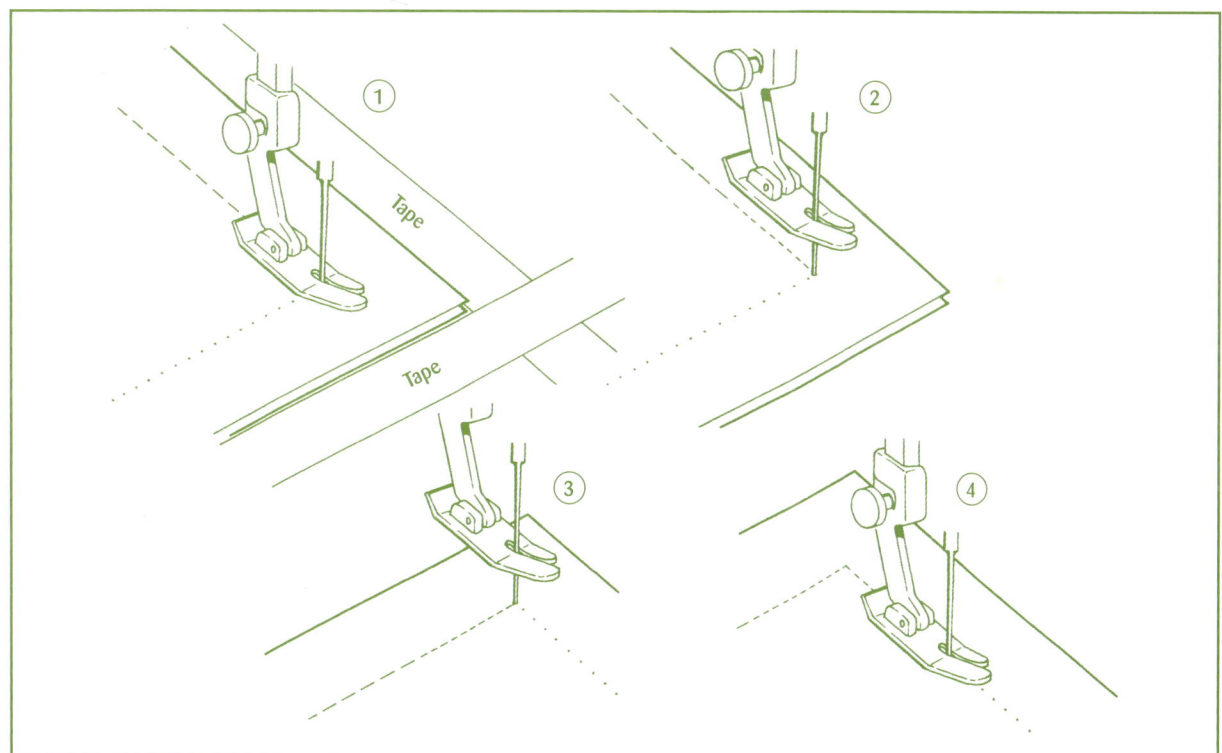

Figure 3.8—Making a Corner Seam

Take one or more diagonal stitches across the point on collars and other sharp corners—one stitch for lightweight fabrics, two for medium weight, and three for heavyweight. See Figure 3.9. This will ensure a sharp point when corner is turned.

To match an inside corner to a straight seam, first reinforce the inner corner, as in Figure 3.10. Stitch just inside the seamline for 1" each side of the corner, using a small stitch. Clip to the corner, being careful not to cut the stitching. Spread the corner open to fit the straight edge, as in Figure 3.11. With clipped side on top, stitch on the seamline, as in Figure 3.12. Use this same method for sewing an inside corner to an outside corner, pivoting at the corner.

Trimming and Clipping

All seams that are to be enclosed should be trimmed and clipped before turning. Seam allowances should be graded—

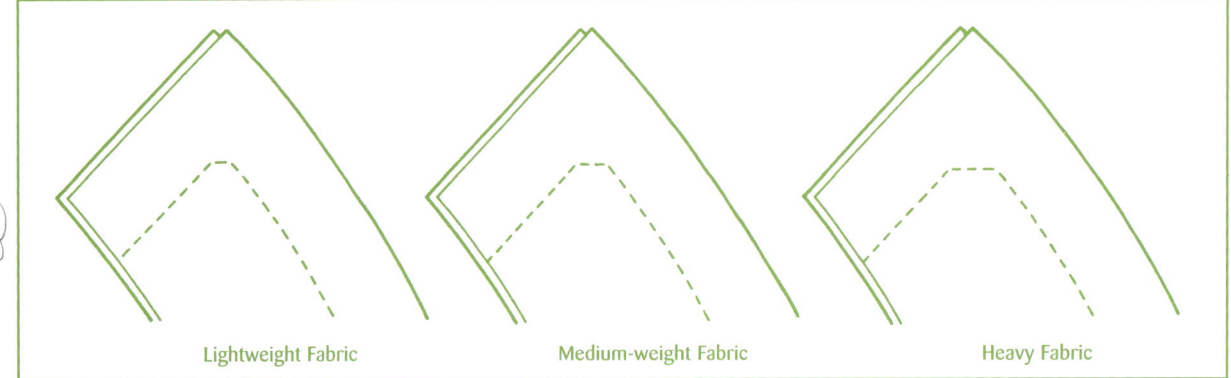

Lightweight Fabric   Medium-weight Fabric   Heavy Fabric

Figure 3.9—Stitching for Sharp Corners

Figure 3.10—(Left) Reinforcing Inside Corner
Figure 3.11—(Center) Stitching an Inside Corner to a Straight Seam
Figure 3.12—(Right) Stitching an Inside Corner to an Outside Corner

that is, each layer should be trimmed to a different width, as in Figure 3.13. The seam nearest the garment side should be the widest. This applies especially to collars, cuffs, and all other seams where a nice, flat finish is desired.

On curved seams, pinking shears can be used for trimming and notching at the same time. Corners must be trimmed as much as possible to reduce bulk—the sharper the point, the greater the trimming. Cut across the point, then trim on either side, as in Figure 3.14. Seam allowances should be trimmed so that they will not overlap and cause bulk when turned.

Understitching

Understitching is used primarily on facings. It helps them to roll to the underside of the garment and lie flat. It can also be used on undercollars, cuff facings, and waistbands.

After the facing has been sewn to the garment, lay fabric right side up and turn facing toward the seam allowance. If seam is curved, be sure seam allowance has been trimmed and clipped. Stitch close to the seam, on top of the facing, catching all layers of seam allowance. See Figure 3.15. Turn facing to inside.

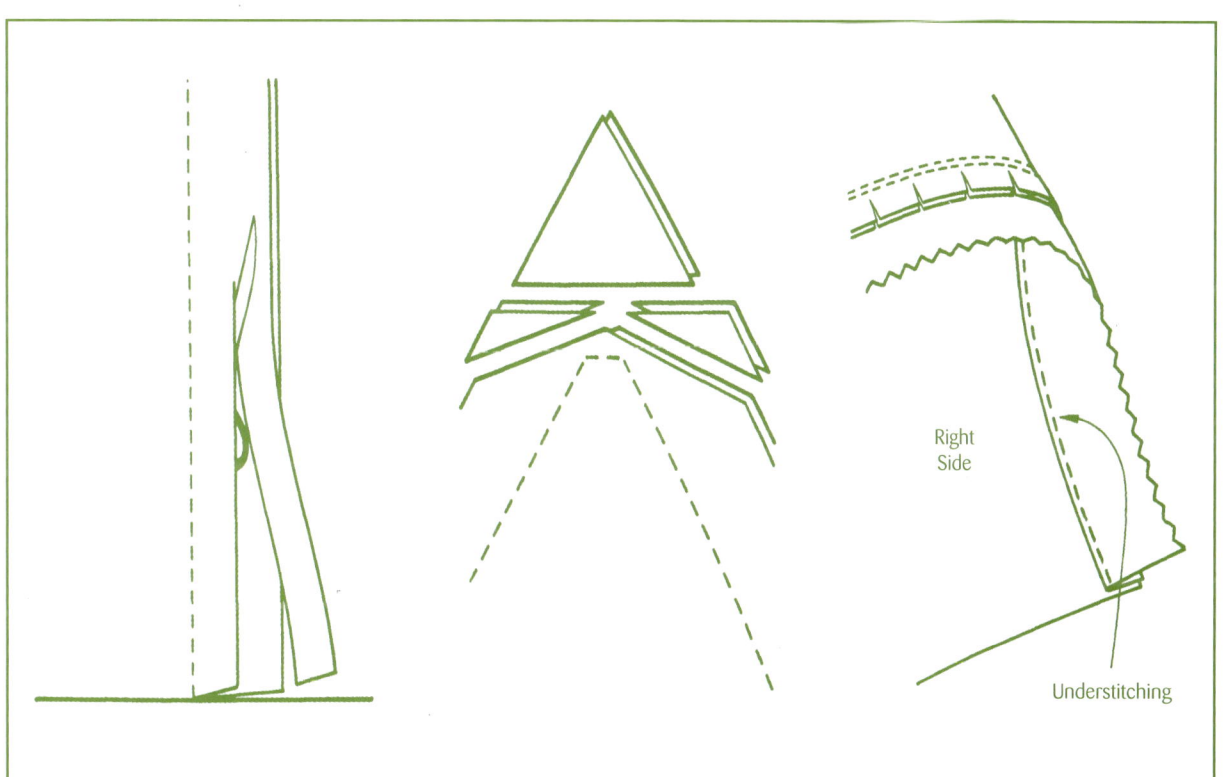

Figure 3.13—(Left) Trimming Seams
Figure 3.14—(Center) Trimming Corners
Figure 3.15—(Right) Understitching a Facing to Make It Lie Flat

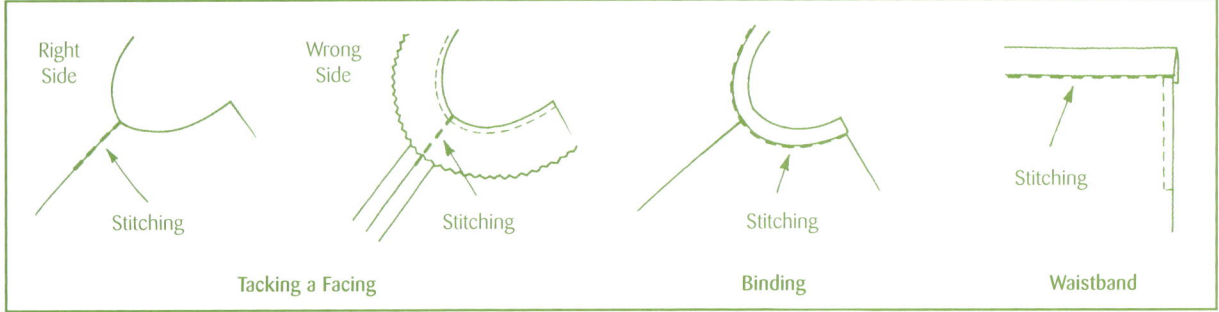

Figure 3.16—Stitching in the Ditch

Stitching in the Ditch

This finishing technique, shown in Figure 3.16, is used where you don't want the stitches to show on the right side. The stitching is done on the right side of the fabric, directly on top of the stitching of a previously sewn seam. It is useful for securing waistbands and bindings, and for tacking facings in place. A small stitch will disappear nicely into the fabric. A zipper foot is an aid in sewing close to a waistband or binding.

Topstitching

An attractive, decorative finish, shown in Figure 3.17, can be achieved with the use of topstitching. It is often done around collars, lapels, cuffs, and pockets. Topstitching is usually placed 1/4" from the garment edge, but this can vary with the garment and the effect desired.

Machine tension may need to be adjusted for topstitching. Sometimes a

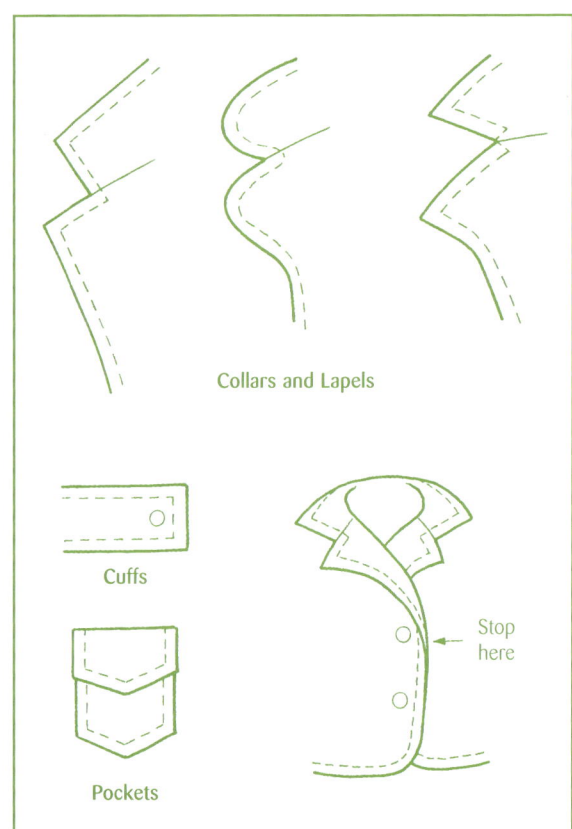

Figure 3.17—Topstitching

slightly looser tension will make a better-looking topstitching. It's a good idea to test top stitching on four to six layers of fabric before trying it on your garment.

Use a regular thread or, for a more pronounced topstitching, use a heavier thread, such as buttonhole twist. One word of caution, however: *silk* buttonhole twist will shrink. Do not use it on fabrics that will be washed. Use cotton-covered polyester thread instead.

A longer stitch is usually used for topstitching (6-8 stitches per inch). A double strand of regular thread can also be used if your machine can take it. If your machine has only one thread spindle, use two bobbins on the spindle instead of a spool of thread. Use a size 14 or 16 needle if it won't harm your fabric.

If you use topstitching on lapels, be sure to stop your stitching where the lapel rolls and start again on the facing side of the fabric for the lapels; or use your topstitching thread in the bobbin as well. Topstitching does not always look the same on both sides, especially if you have adjusted the tension or if a heavier thread is used on top. Leave long thread ends where stitching stops. Use a hand needle to sew these ends into the fabric between garment and facing.

Straight stitching is essential for topstitching with a professional look. Use your presser foot or seam gauge as a guide, or use self-stick sewing tape. When making two or more rows of topstitching, stitch all rows in the same direction to prevent puckering.

Hand Sewing

Although today's modern sewing methods have made it possible to do most sewing by machine, there is still a need for hand sewing. Finishing details are often done by hand, and other hand sewing techniques are useful in basic garment construction and in tailoring. Never substitute hand sewing for machine sewing on a job that can be done better and more quickly by machine, however. Use your knowledge of hand sewing to aid you in garment construction and to give your garment that finely finished custom look of a professionally made garment.

Needle Sizes

Hand sewing needles come in various sizes and types. The higher the number, the finer the needle. Choose the one that fits the job you will be doing. Sharps are the most commonly used needles. Sizes 6-10 are the most practical for most fabrics. Below is a listing of needle types and their uses:

Sharps: (Sizes 1-12) – Medium length, most commonly used.

Betweens: (Sizes 1-12) – Short, round-eyed needles, used for fine stitches in heavy fabric or quilting.

Ball-point: (Sizes 5-10) – Used for knits, will not harm fabric yarns.

Milliners: (Sizes 000-12) – Long and thin, good for basting, taking long stitches, and gathering.

Wedge-shaped: (Sizes 11-18) – For leather, vinyl, imitation leather, and suede.

Crewel: (Sizes 1-10) – Medium length needle with large eye for embroidery thread.

Calyx-eyed: (Sizes 4-8) – Same as sharps but open at top for easy threading.

The size of your needle should be correct for the fabric you are working on. Too large a needle will leave holes in delicate fabrics. Too small a needle will break or not penetrate easily when used on heavy fabrics. Here is a general guide for you to follow:

Sizes 8-10—*Lightweight fabrics* – chiffon, tricot, organdy, challis, crepe jersey

Sizes 6-8—*Medium-weight fabrics* – double knits, satin, velvet, denim, corduroy, ribbed sweater knits, quilted fabrics

Sizes 1-5—*Heavyweight fabrics* – heavy coat fabrics, upholstery fabrics, canvas, duck, sailcloth

Thread

Use the same thread for hand finishing that you use on the machine to stitch you garment. Use a single thread, except where you need extra strength, such as for buttons and hand-sewn zippers.

Thread has a definite direction as it comes off the spool. It should be drawn through the fabric in the same direction as it comes off the spool. This will prevent tangling. Unwind only 18" - 20" of thread. Cut it on an angle for easy threading. Thread your needle with this cut end and tie a knot in this same end, as in Figure 3.18. Your thread will be going in the right direction. If using bobbin thread, as in Figure 3.19, use it in the opposite direction.

Spool: Thread and Knot This End

Bobbin: Thread and Knot This End

Figure 3.18–(Top) Knotting Thread from Spool
Figure 3.19–(Bottom) Knotting Thread from Bobbin

If thread gets twisted while hand sewing, let the needle hang loose while the thread unwinds. If you run your thread through some beeswax, it will prevent it from tangling and getting tied up in knots.

Work from right to left unless otherwise stated. If you are left-handed, reverse all sewing directions. Secure ends of hand stitching with two or three short stitches.

For basting or marking, use white or a light color thread. Dark colors may leave permanent marks on light fabrics. Silk thread is good for basting: it will not leave marks in the fabric when pressed. For permanent hand sewing, use thread that matches the fabric. Buttonhole twist is strong and is used for sewing on buttons and for decorative hand sewing. For decorative hand finishing, use any color thread that will give the desired effect.

Uses for Hand Sewing

Here are a few of the operations you can perform with hand sewing.

Thread tracing—A basic running stitch used to transfer pattern markings from the wrong side to the right side of the garment.

Basting—Used to hold seams together for fittings; also where pin-basting is not sufficient.

Overcasting—For overcasting seams on fabrics that ravel extensively. Used only on very fine garments or where the machine does not do a satisfactory job.

Tacking—For hand tacking facings where machine tacking would show or be impractical (on sheers or delicate fabrics).

Hemming—For most garments, especially where an invisible hem is desired.

Are You Left-Handed?

As you progress through this book—and life—you'll find that most illustrations and instructions are written for right-handed people. Let's face it. We lefties are in the minority.

But there are a couple of things you can do to make sewing, especially hand sewing, easier for you. When you see an obvious right-handed illustration, such as that shown for the running stitch, you can hold it up to a mirror to reverse it to a left-handed diagram, as shown below. As you read, keep a mirror at hand to use whenever you meet a new stitch or process that needs to be "reversed" for you.

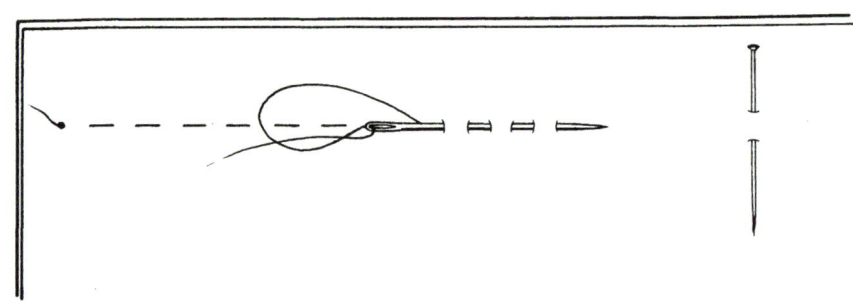

Left-handed running stitch (above) is the mirror image of a right-handed running stitch, as in Figure 3.20.

By now, you have probably understood, when reading printed material, to replace in your mind the words "right" with "left" and "left" with "right". If the instructions seem especially complex or difficult, you might actually want to cross out the words "right" and "left" and replace them with the *correct* words (for you): "left" and "right."

Good luck with your left-handed sewing!

Fastenings—For sewing hooks, eyes, and buttons; also for making thread loops.

Buttonholes—For finishing facings on bound buttonholes or for making hand-worked buttonholes.

Zippers—For hand finishing zippers on delicate fabrics (sheers, velvets) or for a custom look on any garment.

Decorative trimming—Hand finishing with any of the decorative stitches; gives your garment a custom look.

Types of Stitches

Practice the following stitches on scraps of fabric to enlarge your "stitching" vocabulary.

Running Stitch—Basic stitch used for easing, gathering, tucking, and mending. Take several small stitches, weaving the needle in and out of the fabric before pulling thread through. Use stitches 1/16" - 1/4" long. See Figure 3.20.

Basting Stitch—Basically a running stitch.

Even Basting—Used for temporarily holding seams together. Take even 1/4" stitches spaced 1/4" apart. See Figure 3.21.

Uneven Basting—Used for marking center fronts and backs. Take 1/4" stitches spaced 1/2" - 1" apart. See Figure 3.22.

Diagonal Basting—Used to hold underlining or interfacing to fabric before final stitching. Take horizontal stitches parallel to each other, leaving long floats in between. See Figure 3.23.

Backstitch—Strong, secure stitch, used mainly for repairing seams. Also used in hard-to-reach areas, or for understitching where machine stitching would be difficult.

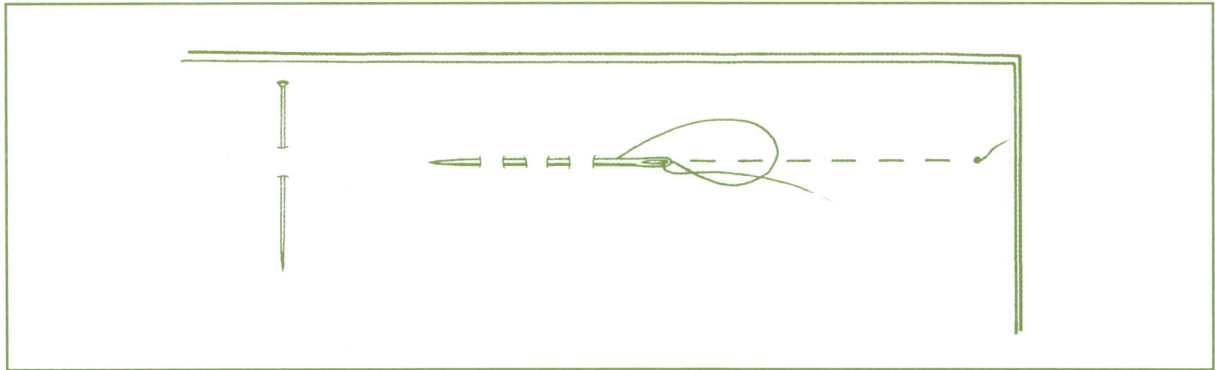

Figure 3.20–Running Stitch

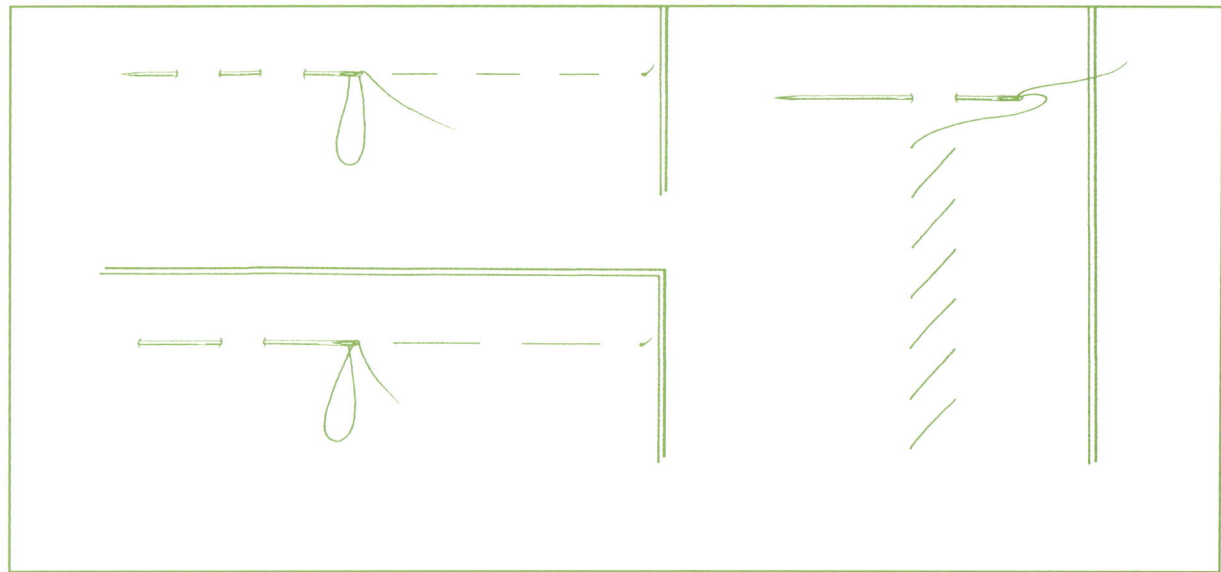

Figure 3.21 – (Top Left) Even Basting
Figure 3.22 – (Bottom Left) Uneven Basting
Figure 3.23 – (Right) Diagonal Basting

Even Backstitch—Stitches on right side look like machine stitching. Stitches overlap on underside. Bring needle up through fabric. Take stitch 1/8" behind thread and come up 1/8" in front of thread. Repeat, inserting needle at end of first stitch. Continue in this manner. See Figure 3.24.

Half Backstitch—Stitches have spaces between them on surface of fabric and overlap on underside. Bring needle up through fabric. Take stitch 1/8" behind thread and come up 1/4" in front of thread. Continue. See Figure 3.25.

Prickstitch—Variation of the half backstitch. Stitches on top are very short and have long spaces between them. Used mainly for decorative stitching and for hand insertion of zippers. Insert needle a few threads behind point where thread emerges. Bring needle up 1/4" in front of thread. See Figure 3.26.

Pickstitch—Same as the prickstitch except that bottom layer of fabric is not caught in the stitching. Any of the backstitches can be used as a pickstitch. Used as topstitching, especially where underneath layer would show. See Figure 3.27.

Slipstitch—An almost invisible stitch. Used for hemming, tacking facings, finishing waistbands, attaching linings, and matching seams on plaid and striped fabrics. Bring needle up through fabric. Slide needle through folded edge of upper layer of fabric for

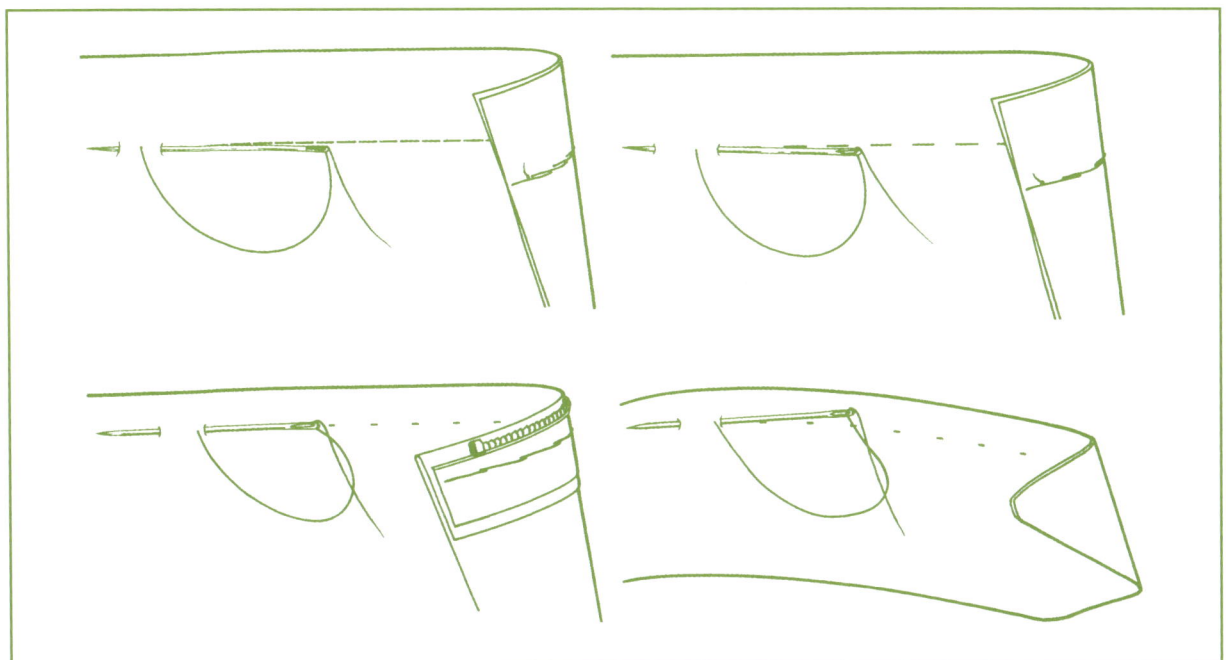

Figure 3.24 – (Top Left) Even Backstitch
Figure 3.25 – (Bottom Left) Half Backstitch
Figure 3.26 – (Right) Prickstitch
Figure 3.27 – (Right) Pickstitch

1/8" - 1/4". Pick up thread of under fabric and slide needle through folded edge again. Continue. See Figure 3.28.

Hemming Stitch—A slanted stitch used to secure hems. Used primarily on hems that have seam binding. Bring needle up through hem edge. Take a tiny stitch in garment 1/4" - 3/8" to the left. Catch only 1 or 2 threads in this stitch. Insert needle diagonally under hem edge and come up through hem. Repeat. See Figure 3.29.

Variation—Stitches can be made vertical instead of horizontal. Bring needle up through hem edge. Take a tiny stitch on garment opposite this spot. Insert needle diagonally under hem edge and come up through hem. Repeat. See Figure 3.30.

Blindstitch—A hemming stitch concealed by the hem. Used on hem edges that are prefinished, usually stitched or stitched and pinked. Fold back hem edge. Take a tiny stitch near hem edge. Take a tiny stitch in garment 1/4" to the left, then a tiny stitch in hem 1/4" to the left. Continue. See Figure 3.31.

Catchstitch—A good hemming stitch for knits because it has "give"; also good on bulky fabrics that don't ravel. Can be used in the same way as a blindstitch. Also used to hold edges of interfacing to garment fabric. It is worked from left to

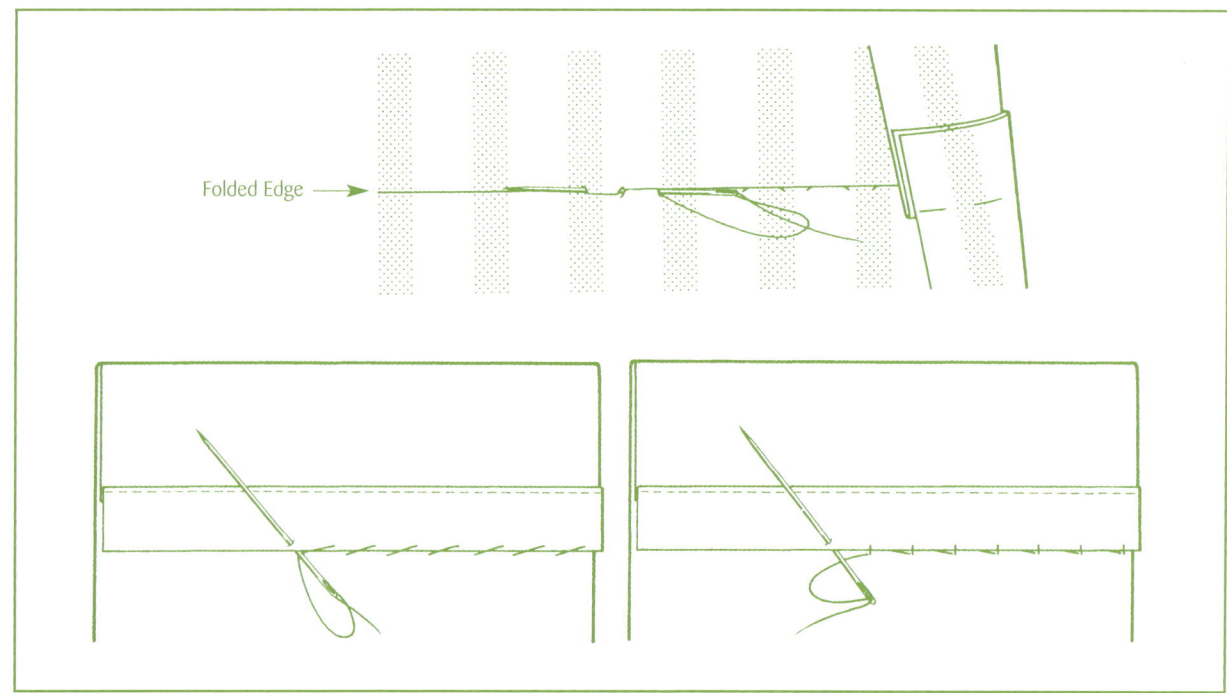

Folded Edge →

Figure 3.28—(Top Left) Slipstitch
Figure 3.29—(Bottom Left) Hemming Stitch—Horizontal
Figure 3.30—(Bottom Right) Hemming Stitch—Vertical

right, as in Figure 3.32. Bring needle up through hem edge. Take a tiny stitch in garment 1/4" - 3/8" to the *right*. Then take a small stitch in hem 1/4" - 3/8" to the *right*. Threads will cross. Continue, making sure stitches in garment are tiny. Do not pull stitches tight.

Overhand Stitch—Tiny stitch used to hold two edges together. Used for sewing items that have been turned, such as belts; also for closing edges in items that have been stuffed, such as pillows. Used for attaching lace or other trim to garment edge. Insert needle at

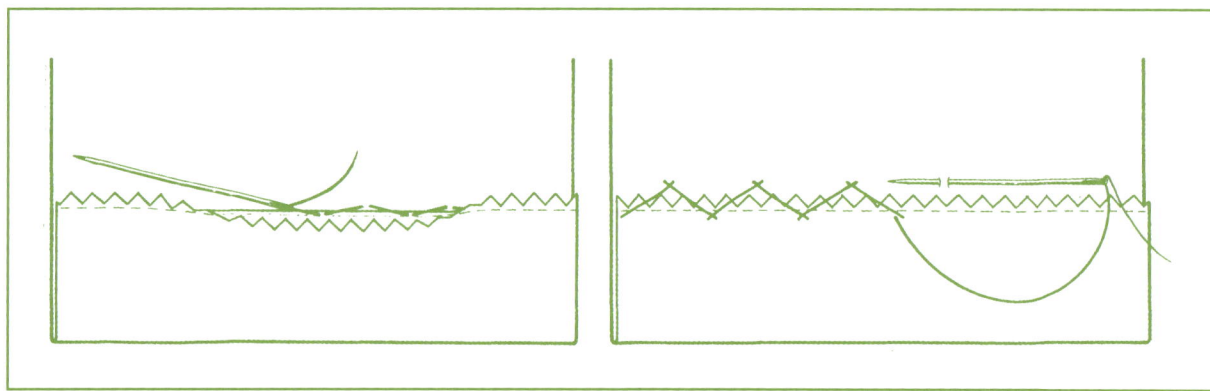

Figure 3.31—(Left) Blindstitch
Figure 3.32—(Right) Catchstitch

an angle from back edge to front edge, taking very shallow stitches close together. See Figure 3.33.

Whipstitch—Variation of the overhand stitch. Needle is inserted at right angles to the fabric instead of diagonally. Stitches are slightly slanted, as shown in Figure 3.34.

Overcast Stitch—Used to finish raw edges of seams on fine garments or fabrics that ravel a lot. Take diagonal stitches over the single edge of fabric, working from either direction, as in Figure 3.35.

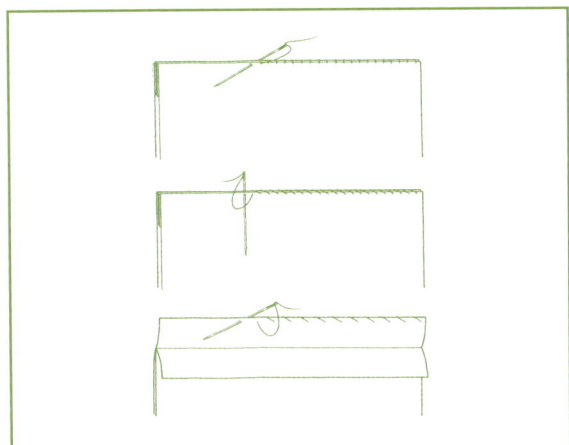

Figure 3.33 – (Top) Overhand Stitch
Figure 3.34 – (Center) Whipstitch
Figure 3.35 – (Bottom) Overcast Stitch

Blanket Stitch—Basically a decorative embroidery stitch. Used to finish raw edges on garments and blankets and as decorative trim on collars, lapels, and hems. Also used for sewing on hooks and eyes and for making thread belt loops. Work from left to right. If desired, make a row of

machine basting 1/2" (or desired distance) from garment edge to use as a guideline. Fasten thread to garment and bring out under edge. Insert needle into right side of garment and bring out under edge, keeping thread under the needle, as in Figure 3.36. Draw needle through to form stitch along edge of fabric. Remove machine basting when finished.

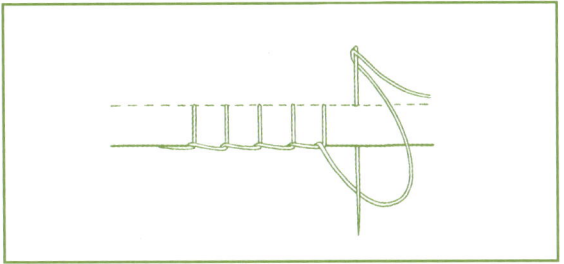

Figure 3.36 – Blanket Stitch

Stitch width can be varied for a decorative effect, as in Figure 3.37.

If fabric ravels easily or if more body is desired, turn raw edge under 1/4" before sewing, as shown in Figure 3.38.

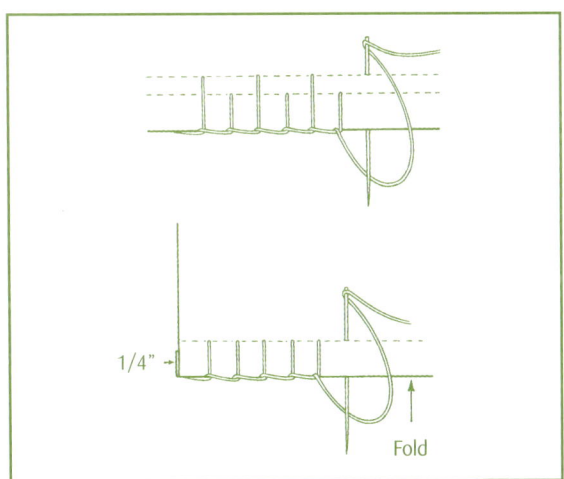

Figure 3.37 – (Top) Varied-width Blanket Stitch
Figure 3.38 – (Bottom) Turn under raw edge if fabric ravels or does not have enough body.

Seams and Seam Finishes

In deciding what kind of seam to use, your choice will be determined by the garment you are making and the type of fabric you are using. Most garments are constructed of plain seams, which may be finished in a number of ways, depending on the qualities of the fabric. Below is a list of several types of seams and seam finishes. Choose the one that is most compatible with your fabric. Pretest first on a scrap of fabric to be sure it will do the job well.

Basic Seams

Plain—The seam most commonly used for garment construction. It is usually finished to prevent raveling. Seams may be left unfinished on garments that will be lined or on any fabric that does not ravel. Most knits do not ravel, and seams may be left unfinished if desired. See Figure 3.39.

Crossed—Wherever two seams cross in a garment, there will be extra bulk. Whenever possible, seams should be finished and pressed open before being sewn together in a crossed seam. To aid in matching seamlines, fasten them together through the seams, using a hand sewing needle. Pin seam allowances to garment to hold them in place while stitching, as in Figure 3.40. To reduce bulk in crossed seams, trim

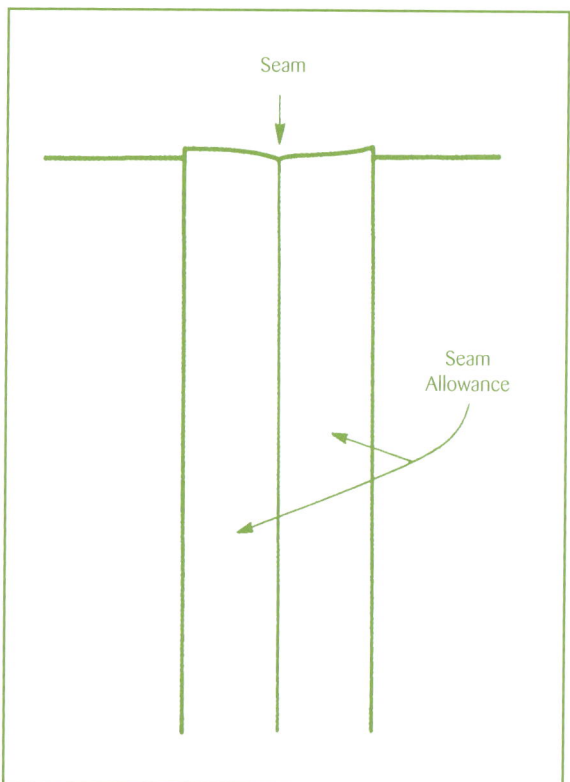

Figure 3.39–Plain Seam

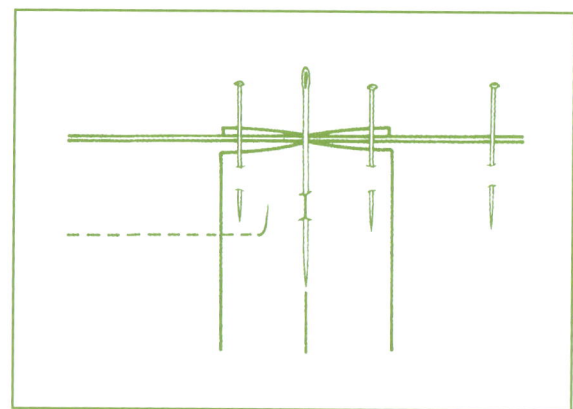

Figure 3.40–Crossed Seam

corners of seam allowances after stitching seams together. See Figure 3.41.

French—A narrow, enclosed seam used mainly on sheer fabrics to prevent raw seam allowances from showing

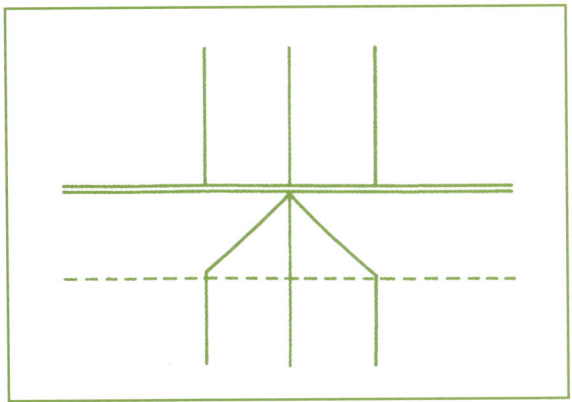

Figure 3.41—Trimming Crossed Seams

seam works well on straight edges only. For curved edges, use a *Mock French* seam. With *right* sides together, stitch a 5/8" seam. Trim seam to 1/2" as in Figure 3.43A. Turn edges of seam allowance 1/4" toward each other and press. Stitch edges together as in Figure 3.43B.

Double Stitched (mock flat-fell)—This is a good substitute for the French seam where a narrow seam is desired. It is especially good for soft knits, such as tricot or jersey, where edges have a tendency to curl. Make a row of stitching along seamline; make another row 1/8" from the first, toward the seam

through. With *wrong* sides of fabric together, stitch a 3/8" seam. Trim seam to 1/8", as in Figure 3.42A. Press to one side. Now fold fabric *right* sides together on stitching line. Sew 1/4" from folded edge as in Figure 3.42B. This

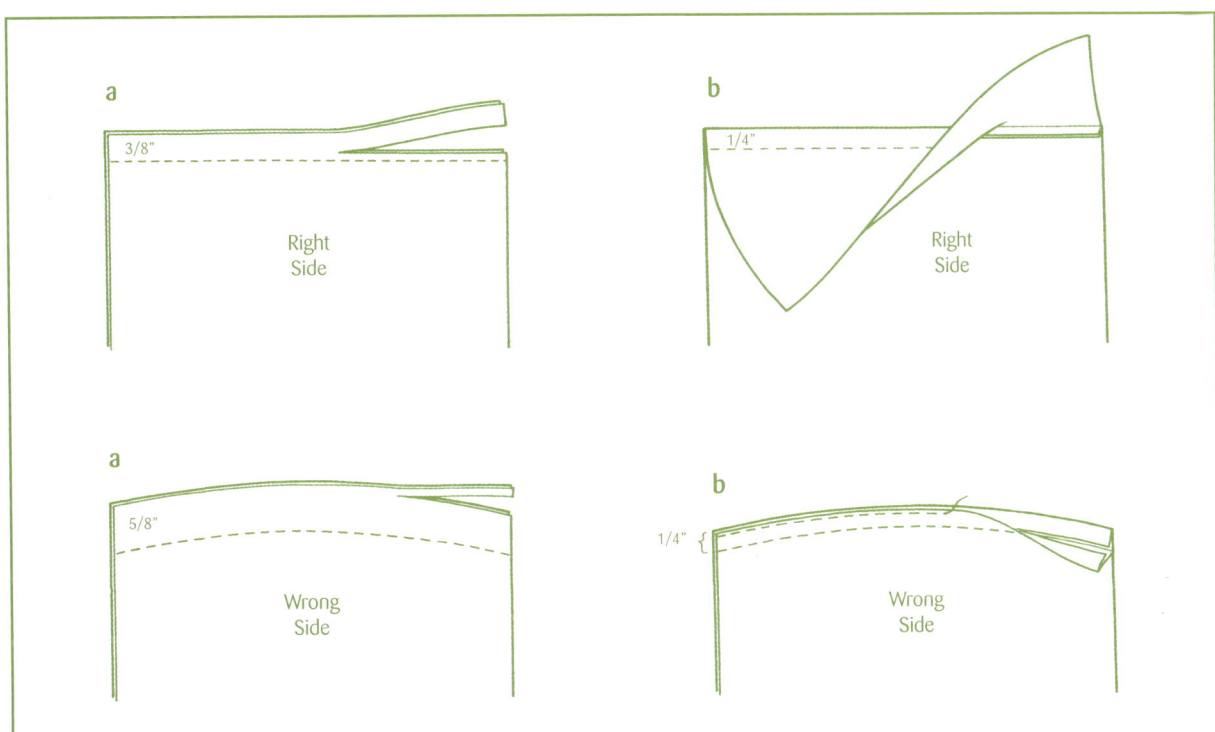

Figure 3.42A—(Top Left) French Seam, Right Side
Figure 3.42B—(Top Right) French Seam, Wrong Side
Figure 3.43A—(Bottom Left) Mock French Seam, Right Side
Figure 3.43B—(Bottom Left) Mock French Seam, Wrong Side

allowance, as in Figure 3.44. In place of plain stitching on the second row you can use zigzag or blindstitch. Trim seam allowance close to stitching.

seam. Stitch close to edge on top of seam. See Figure 3.45. If desired, this final stitching can be done by hand.

Figure 3.44—Double Stitching

Self-bound—This is another good substitute for the French seam. It works best on fabrics that do not ravel easily. Stitch a 5/8" seam. Trim top seam allowance to 1/8". Fold up edge of bottom seam allowance 1/8". Turn up and place folded edge on top of original

Figure 3.45—Self-Bound Seam

Flat-felled—A strong seam used mainly for menswear, jeans, sport clothes and children's clothes. It is a sturdy seam that holds up well after repeated washings. It can be used with the double row of stitching on either side of the garment, although the double row is usually on the outside. To make a flat-felled seam with both rows on the outside, make a plain seam with the wrong sides together. Press both seam allowances to one side. Trim underneath seam allowance to 1/8". Fold under edge of top seam allowance 1/4" and stitch down, covering narrow seam allowance. See Figure 3.46.

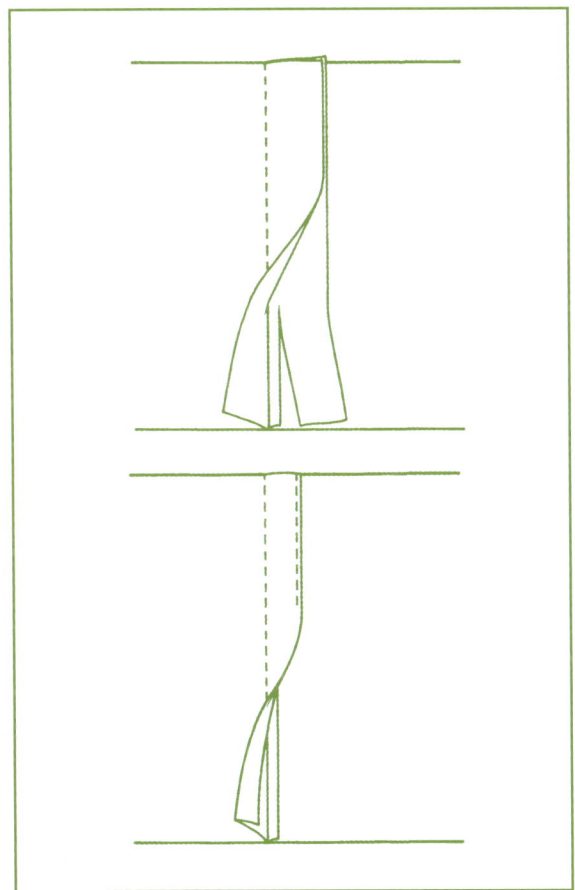

Figure 3.46—Flat-Felled Seam

Some Decorative Seams

Topstitched—A decorative seam used often on tailored garments. A plain seam can be either single topstitched or double topstitched. For single topstitching, make a 5/8" seam and press both seam allowances to one side. On the right side of the fabric, stitch through all thicknesses 1/4" (or desired width) from seamline. See Figure 3.47.

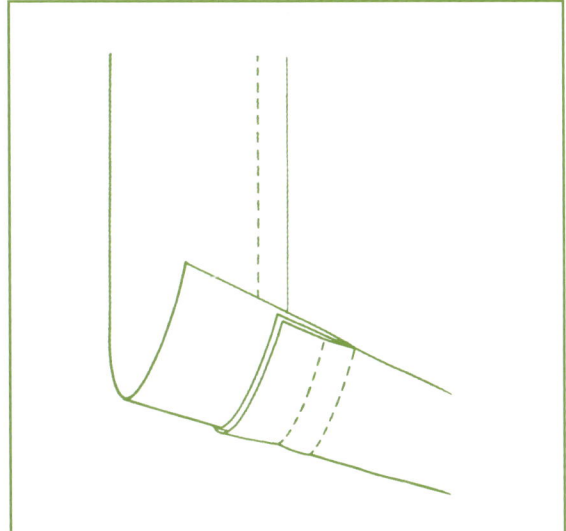

Figure 3.47—Topstitched Seam

For *double* topstitching, make a 5/8" seam and press open. From right side, stitch 1/4" (or desired width) from seamline on each side of the seam. Be sure to sew both rows of topstitching in the same direction. See Figure 3.48.

Welt—Similar in appearance to a single topstitched seam; it is used on bulky fabrics. Sew a plain 5/8" seam. Press seam allowances to one side. Trim underneath seam allowance to slightly

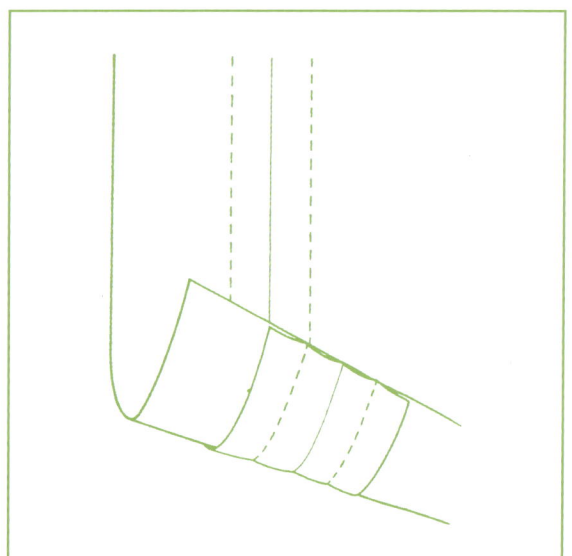

Figure 3.48—Double Topstitching

less than 1/4" from seamline, catching wide seam allowance. See Figure 3.49. For a double welt seam, add another row of stitching close to the seamline. This looks like a flat-felled seam.

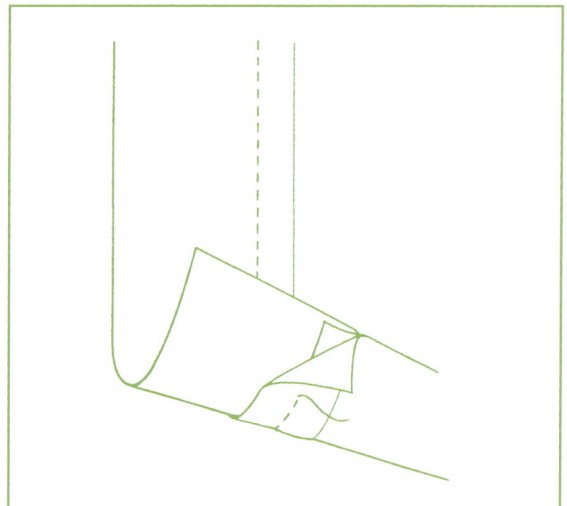

Figure 3.49—Welt Seam

Lapped or Tucked—Fold under and press seam allowance on one garment piece. On the right side, place folded edge along seamline of other garment piece. For lapped seam, stitch close to folded edge. See Figure 3.50.

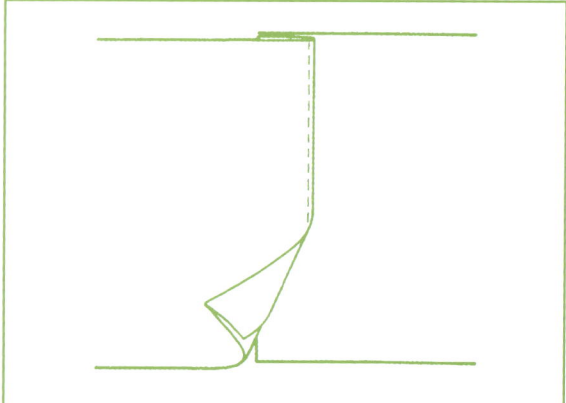

Figure 3.50—Lapped Seam

For tucked seam, stitch 1/4" from folded edge (or width of desired tuck). See Figure 3.51.

Lapped (for nonwoven fabrics)—Use this version of the lapped seam on bulky fabrics that do not ravel, such as felt, leather, and imitation suede. Trim seam allowance from one garment piece, as in Figure 3.52A. On the right side, place trimmed edged along seamline of other garment piece. Stitch close to trimmed edge. Make another row of stitching 1/4" from the first, as in Figure 3.52B. On underside, trim away any remaining seam allowance, close to stitching line.

Slot—A slot seam is made with an underlay of fabric. The underlay can be the same as the garment or a contrasting color for decorative effect. To make the slot seam, machine baste a 5/8" seam (for ease in removal, use a

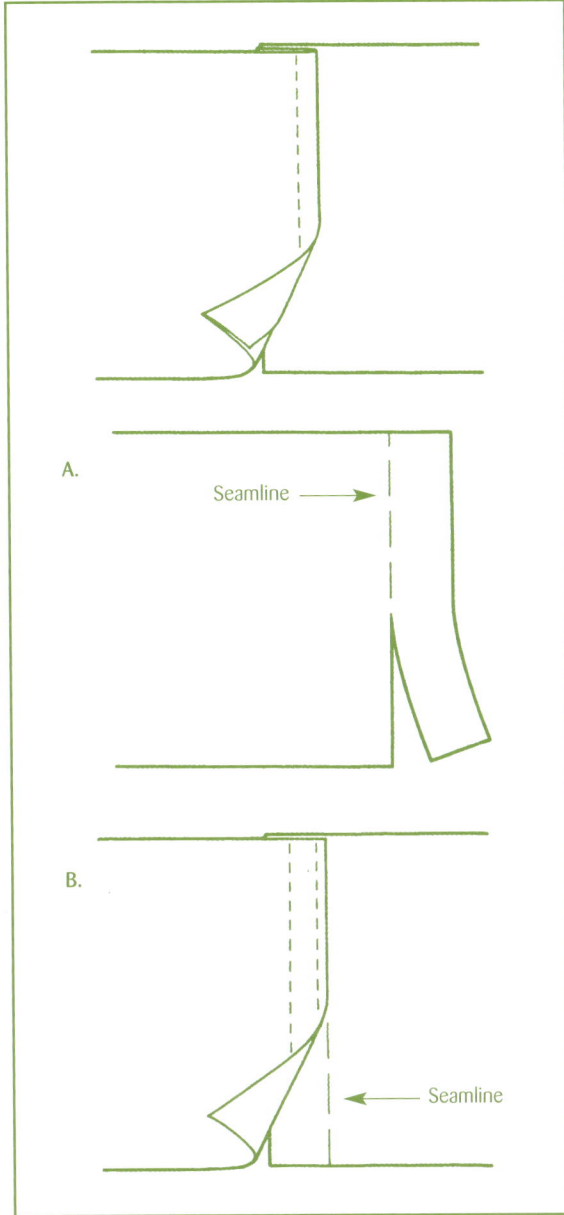

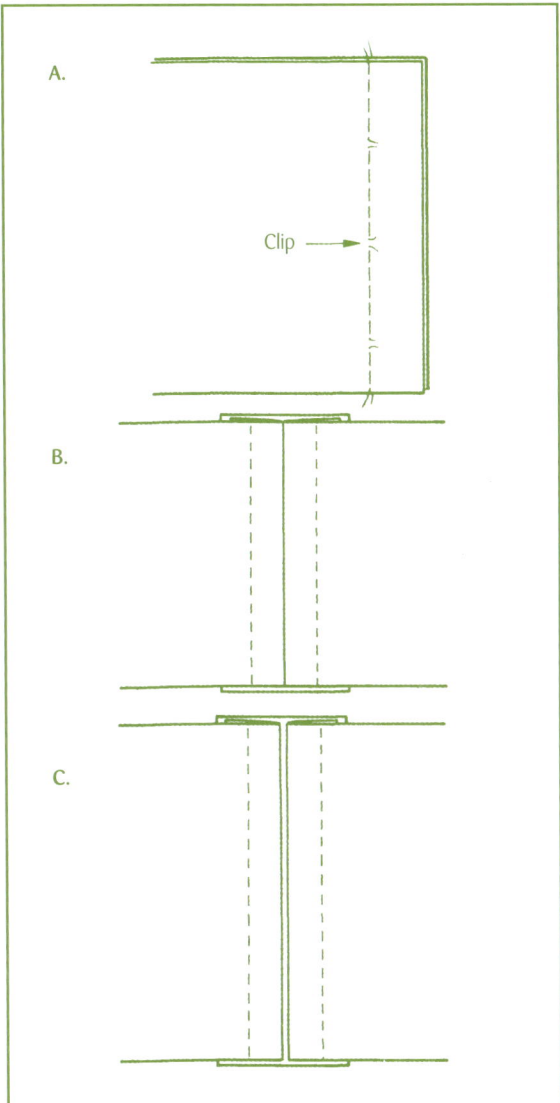

garment, topstitch 1/4" (or desired width) from each side of seamline. Remove machine basting. Seam will open slightly and underlay will show, as in Figure 3.53C.

Figure 3.51–(Top) Tucked Seam
Figure 3.52–(Bottom) Lapped Seam (for nonwoven fabrics)

Figure 3.53–Slot Seam

loose upper tension or clip bobbin threads every inch or so). See Figure 3.53A. Press seam open. Cut a 1-1/2" wide underlay the length of the seam. Center underlay under seam and pin or baste in place (try basting adhesive for this). See Figure 3.53B. On right side of

Piped or Corded—Piping is made from a folded bias strip of fabric. To insert piping in a seam, place folded edge of bias desired distance past seamline on right side of one garment piece. Clip seam allowance of piping on curves. Stitch in place on seamline, as in Figure 3.54A. Place right side of other garment piece over piping, as in Figure 3.54B. Turn garment over and stitch through all thicknesses following first stitching line, as in Figure 3.54C. When you turn the seam to the right side it will appear as in Figure 3.54D.

Cording is piping with a filler of cord. It can be purchased by the package in a variety of colors. Stitch cording along the seamline of one garment piece, using a zipper foot. Finish as for a piped seam, using a zipper foot to stitch close to cording.

Finishes for Plain Seams

Selvage—Needs no extra stitching. Used for straight seams. Requires adjusting pattern layout in order for seam to be cut on selvage.

Pinked or Scalloped—Use sharp pinking or scalloping shears to trim seam allowances before they are pressed open. See Figure 3.55. This method can be used on any firmly woven fabric that does not ravel extensively. If fabric is heavy, cut one seam allowance at a time.

Stitched and Pinked—Before pinking, sew a line of machine stitching 1/4" from the edge of each seam allowance. This gives greater stability to the seam finish and helps retard raveling. See Figure 3.56.

Zigzagged or Overedged—Use a medium width zigzag and a short stitch length. Use plain zigzag or multiple stitch zigzag. Stitch near the edge of each seam allowance. Trim away excess fabric, being careful not to cut stitching. See Figure 3.57. If your machine has an overedged stitch or blindstitch, use this in place of zigzag, as in Figure 3.58.

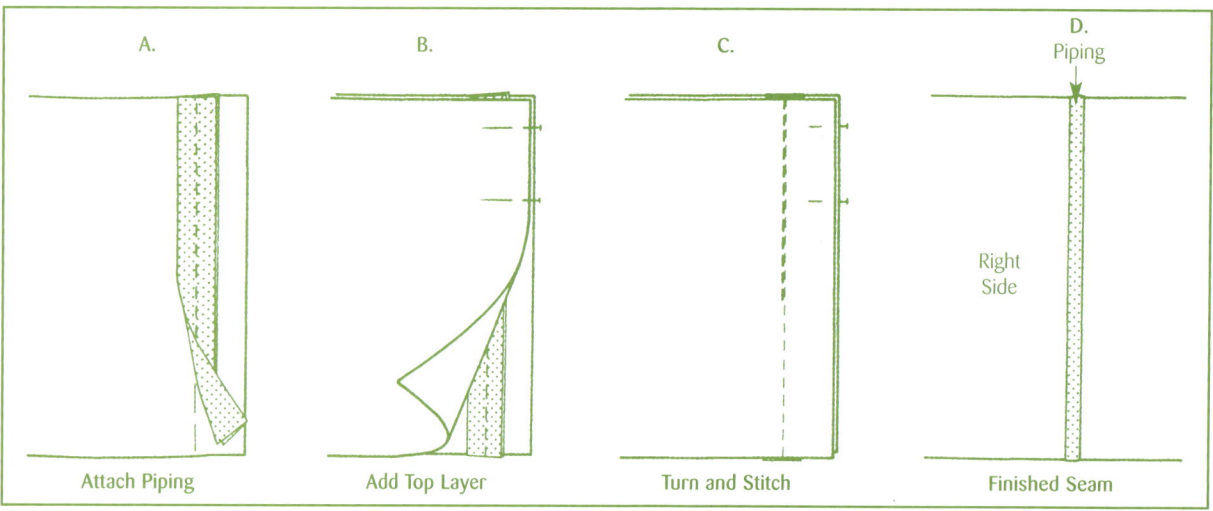

Figure 3.54—Piped, or Corded, Seam

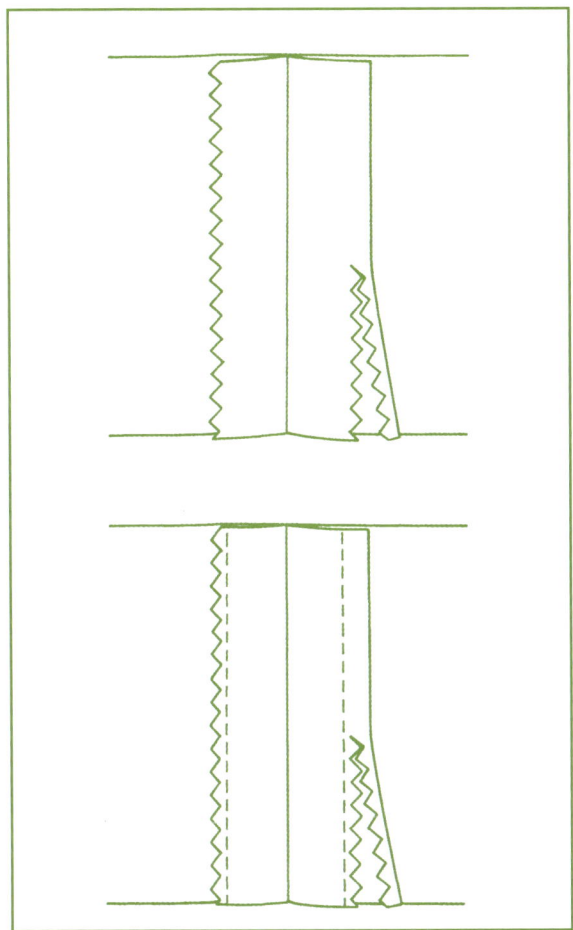

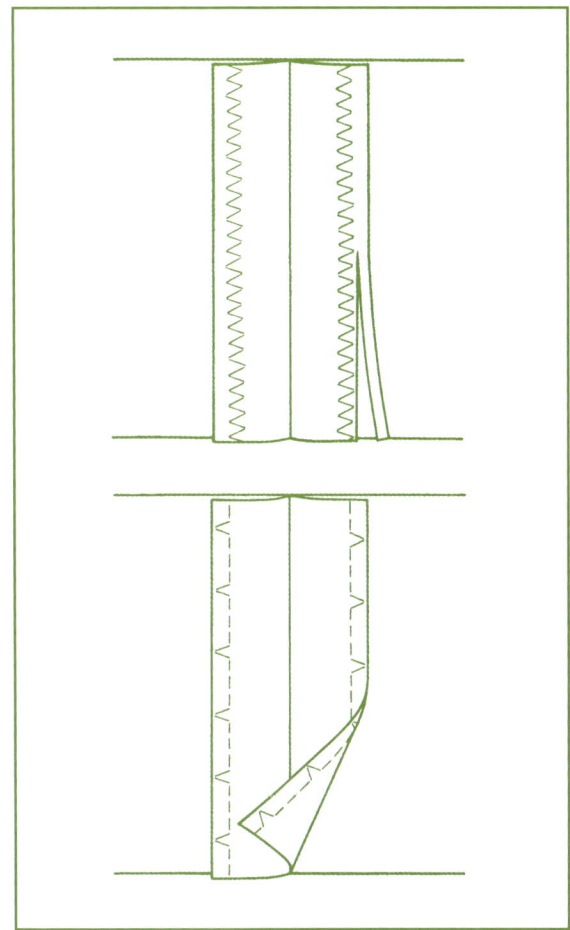

Figure 3.55 – (Top) Pinked, or Scalloped, Finish
Figure 3.56 – (Bottom) Stitched-and-Pinked Finish

Figure 3.57 – (Top) Zigzagged Finish
Figure 3.58 – (Bottom) Overedged or Blindstitched Finish

These first four seam finishes are the ones that are most commonly used. They can be used satisfactorily on most types of fabrics. Following are some additional seam finishes that can be used on special fabrics or for specific purposes:

Edgestitched (Clean-Finished)— Turn under edge of each seam allowance 1/8". Stitch close to fold, as shown in Figure 3.59. This finish works well with cottons and other lightweight fabrics. It is a neat, tailored finish and

is suitable for unlined jackets made of lightweight fabrics. This method is not suitable for bulky or heavy fabrics.

Bound— Use purchased double-fold bias tape and apply to each seam allowance edge. See Figure 3.60. Be sure to place narrower fold of binding on top. Stitch close to edge. This looks especially nice in an unlined jacket and is suitable for bulky fabrics.

Seams may also be bound with lace, tricot, or nylon net. Cut strips of net or

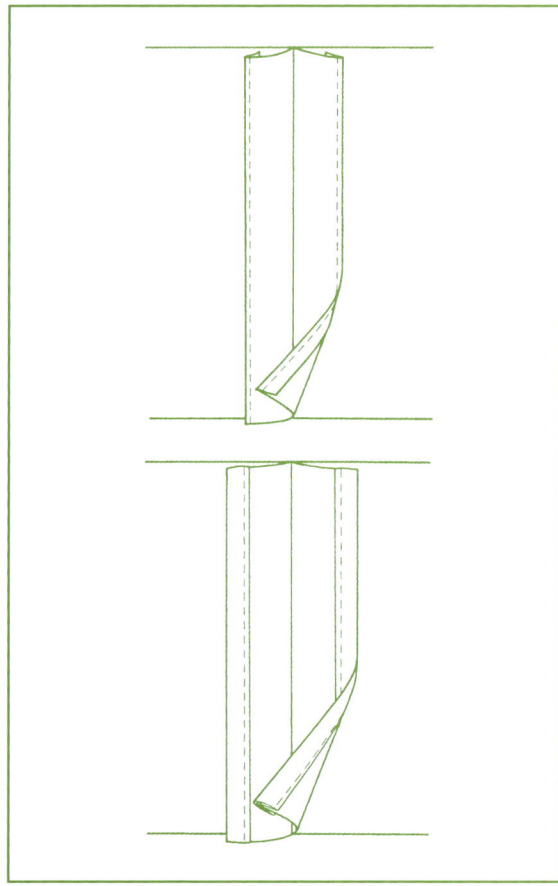

Figure 3.59–(Top) Edgestitched Finish
Figure 3.60–(Bottom) Bound Finish

with this method. Be careful, though: lace and net can be scratchy if they come in direct contact with the skin. Check before you sew them into areas that will be coming into direct contact with the body, such as armholes and sleeves. Remember that the nylon net must be cut on the bias and the tricot on the crosswise grain for maximum stretch.

Hong Kong—This is an elegant version of the bound finish used on designer clothing. It has become a favorite of home sewers since it is easy and gives a fine finish. Use lining fabric or a lightweight fabric that matches the garment fabric. If your garment is underlined, use a strip of underlining fabric. Cut 1-1/4" wide bias strips or use rayon bias tape and press it open. With right sides together, sew bias strip to the right side of seam allowance in a 1/4" seam, as in Figure 3.61A. Trim bulky fabrics' seam allowances to 1/8" (lightweight fabric does not need to be trimmed). Press. Turn bias over seam

lace 5/8" wide or use purchased 1/2" lace trimming. Chiffon, lace, velvet, and other elegant fabrics are often finished

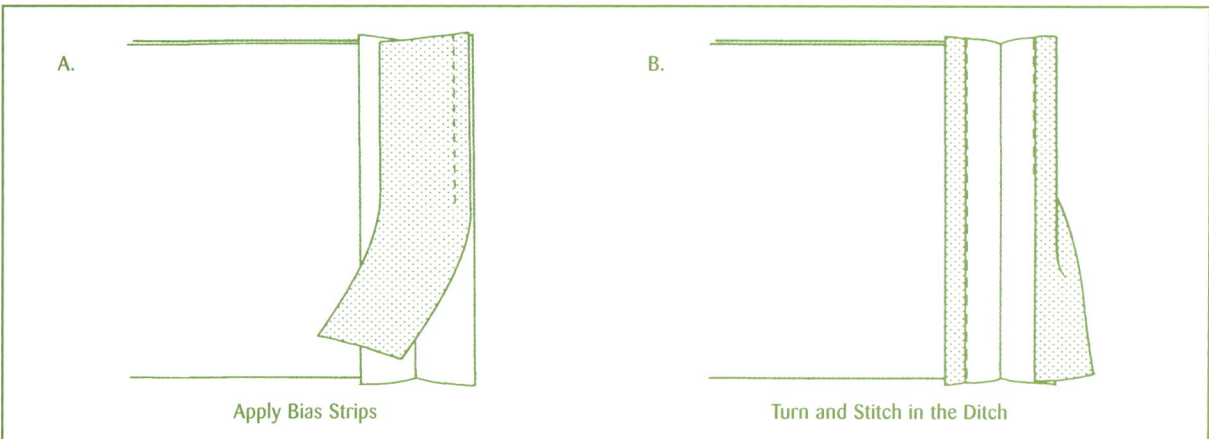

A. Apply Bias Strips

B. Turn and Stitch in the Ditch

Figure 3.61–Hong Kong Finish

edge to underside of seam allowance. Stitch in the ditch to secure bias strip, as in Figure 3.61B.

Hand-overcast—This is a time-consuming method but is sometimes preferred by those who like a custom finish. Use a single thread and overcast each seam edge with stitches 1/8" deep. A line of machine stitching 1/8" from edge of fabric is helpful as a guideline. Do not pull stitches too tight. This is a good finish for fabrics that ravel extensively. See Figure 3.62.

Figure 3.62–Hand-Overcast Finish

Before continuing with your reading, answer the following multiple-choice questions to check what you have already learned.

1. For best results, use _____ needles on knits.

    a. wedge-point
    b. ball-point
    c. sharp-point

2. _____ is used primarily on facings to help them roll to the underside of the garment and lie flat.

    a. Stitching in the ditch
    b. Stay stitching
    c. Understitching

3. The _____ is an almost invisible stitch used for hemming.

    a. slipstitch
    b. pickstitch
    c. pinning stitch

4. The _____ seam is most commonly used for garment construction.

    a. plain
    b. cross
    c. French

5. The _____ finish is an elegant version of the bound finish used on designer cloths.

    a. edgestitch
    b. Hong Kong
    c. hand-overcast

Check your answers with those provided on page 199.

FITTING AND SHORTCUTS

Garment Fitting

During the process of making your garment, there will be times when you will need to try it on to see how it fits. Loose-fitting garments, such as capes, robes, and caftans, generally require a fitting only to adjust the hem after completion of the garment. Garments that have intricate seaming or that are more closely fitted will need to be tried on at least once, perhaps twice, during construction.

When fitting your garment, be aware of the law of physics—for every *action* there is a *reaction*. Fitting produces a chain reaction. Each little change in one part of the garment will affect the garment somewhere else. Start at the top of your garment when fitting and make your adjustments from the top down, ending at the hemline. It's nice to have someone help you with your fitting, especially with adjustments on the back of the garment.

How to Fit

There are two methods of putting your garment together for the first try-on. You can either baste or you can pin. To save time, use machine basting wherever possible. Test on a scrap of fabric first to make sure the needles will not leave permanent marks on your fabric when stitching is removed. Baste the garment *right* sides together along major seamlines. If you use pin-basting, baste the garment *wrong* sides together. This will keep the pins on the outside of the garment and will save your skin from scratch marks. Face all the pins in the same direction, with their points down, wherever possible. Place 2" or 3" apart directly on the seamline parallel to the edge of the fabric. Keep in mind that these seam allowances will be turned to the inside of your finished

garment, so allow room for them when doing your fitting.

Always try your garment on right side out. Trying a garment on inside out reverses the right and left sides. You may not have the same contours on both sides—most people don't. If your garment is to be worn with a belt, put one on during your fitting, or tie a string around your waist to simulate a belt. If shoulder pads are called for, pin them in place.

First Fitting

The first fitting is usually done after the darts and basic seams are stitched. Side seams should be pin-basted or machine basted, since most seam adjustments are made at the side seams. Sleeves should not be sewn in until shoulder and side seams have been checked and corrected. Leave the neckline unfinished. Necklines and armholes will fit more snugly during a fitting than when finished, due to the untrimmed seam allowances that are still in place. If desired, place a row of staystitching on neck and armhole seamlines, and clip seam allowances. This will allow armhole and neckline to fit more correctly. If the garment has a collar, lay it around the neck of the garment to see if it fits the neck correctly. After side and shoulder seams are corrected, machine baste sleeve into

armhole. Try on garment again and check for ease of movement and correct hang of sleeve.

With your garment on, walk, sit, bend, and go up and down steps. Reach up, out, and forward with your arms. Stoop down, knee bent. You want your garment to be comfortable when you wear it, not just when you're standing in front of a mirror. Make any adjustments that are needed to obtain a perfect fit. Pin in loose areas, let out tight ones. Most changes made when fitting will be minor, since all major changes were made on your pattern before cutting. Once you're satisfied that it not only fits well but feels good, you're ready to make the permanent adjustments.

Adjustments

Following is a check list of some of the minor problems you may encounter and what to do about them:

Seamlines and grainlines off center—Garment may need to be raised on one side. Raise skirt at waistline, as in Figure 4.1, raise bodice at shoulder, as in Figure 4.2.

Wrinkles—Garment is either too loose or too tight. Diagonal wrinkles are sometimes caused by fabric creeping as you sew. Open seams and restitch.

Figure 4.1–(Top) Adjusting Off-Center Skirt at Waistline
Figure 4.2–(Bottom) Adjusting Off-Center Bodice at Shoulder

Figure 4.3–(Top) Correcting Wrinkles at Ends of Darts
Figure 4.4–(Bottom) Correcting Wrinkles at Sides of Darts

Wrinkles at ends of darts—Darts may be too short. Make darts longer. Sometimes wrinkling is caused by poor tapering of dart point. Restitch, tapering carefully. See Figure 4.3.

Wrinkles at sides of darts—Darts may be too straight or too tight. Restitch darts making them conform more to your body curves. See Figure 4.4.

Wrinkles from neck to armhole—Shoulders need adjusting. Sometimes only one needs adjusting. Raise shoulder and take in seam. Taper to neck or armhole, whichever is needed. Adjust collar or sleeve to fit. See Figure 4.5.

Figure 4.5–Correcting Wrinkles in Upper Bodice

Wrinkles below waistline in back—Waist needs to be raised in back. Raise skirt and widen seam allowance, as in Figure 4.6. Do not change seam allowance on bodice.

Shoulders too wide—Make wider seam allowance on bodice armhole at shoulder, tapering to underarm. See Figure 4.7. Do not change seam allowance on sleeve.

Figure 4.6–(Top) Correcting Wrinkles Below Back Waistline
Figure 4.7–(Bottom) Narrowing Shoulders

Tight neckline—Lower neckline seamline. See Figure 4.8. Don't overdo—remember, the facing will take up the seam allowance.

Gaping neckline—Raise bodice at shoulder, tapering from neckline to shoulder, as in Figure 4.9. Make change in neckline facing also.

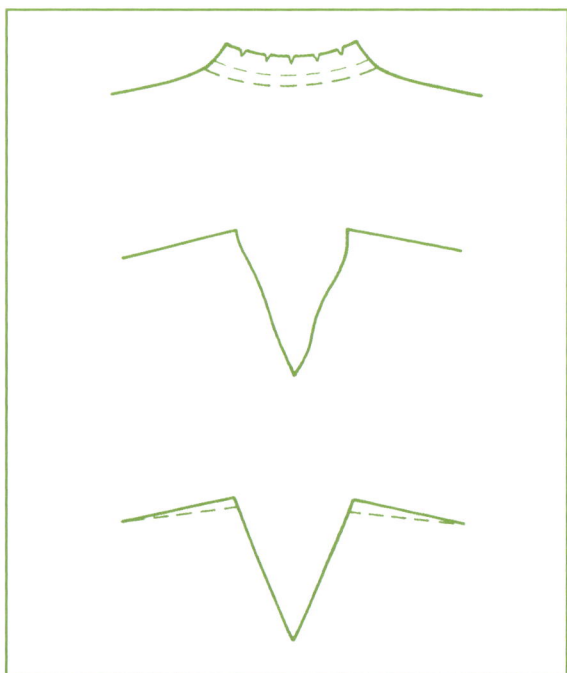

Figure 4.8–(Top) Lowering Neckline
Figure 4.9–(Center and Bottom) Correcting a Gaping Neckline

Stand-up collar too high—Make collar narrower. If collar is straight, reduce width of collar by increasing neckline seam allowance. See Figure 4.10A. If collar is shaped, reduce width by increasing top seam allowance. Do

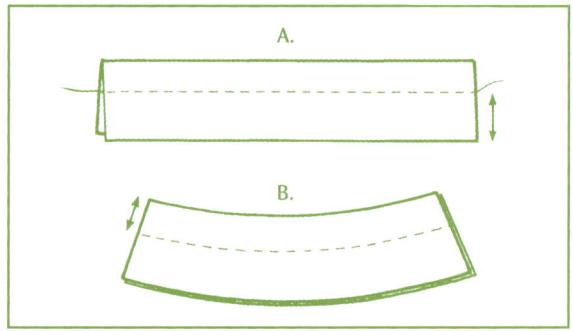

Figure 4.10–Lowering Stand-up Collar

not change the neckline on the bodice. See Figure 4.10B.

Gaping armhole on sleeveless bodice—Raise shoulders at armhole, tapering to neckline. See Figure 4.11A. Sometimes a large bust can cause armholes to gape. If needed, take small dart in armhole, as in Figure 4.11B. Facing will need to be adjusted to fit armhole.

Tight armhole in sleeveless bodice—Lower armhole seamline at underarm, as in Figure 4.12. Don't overdo—remember, the facing will take up the seam allowance.

Tight armholes with sleeves—Take less seam allowance when stitching underarm area, as in Figure 4.13. Contrary to what you may think, taking more seam allowance will restrict arm movement.

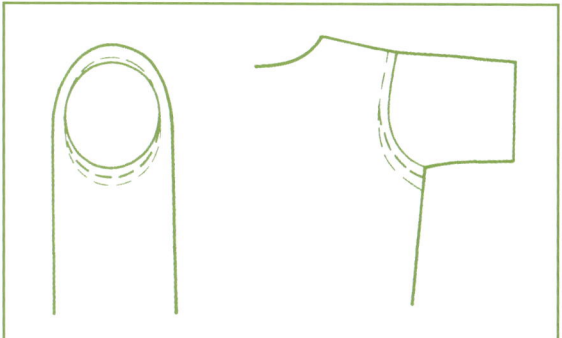

Figure 4.13—Correcting Tight Armhole with Sleeves

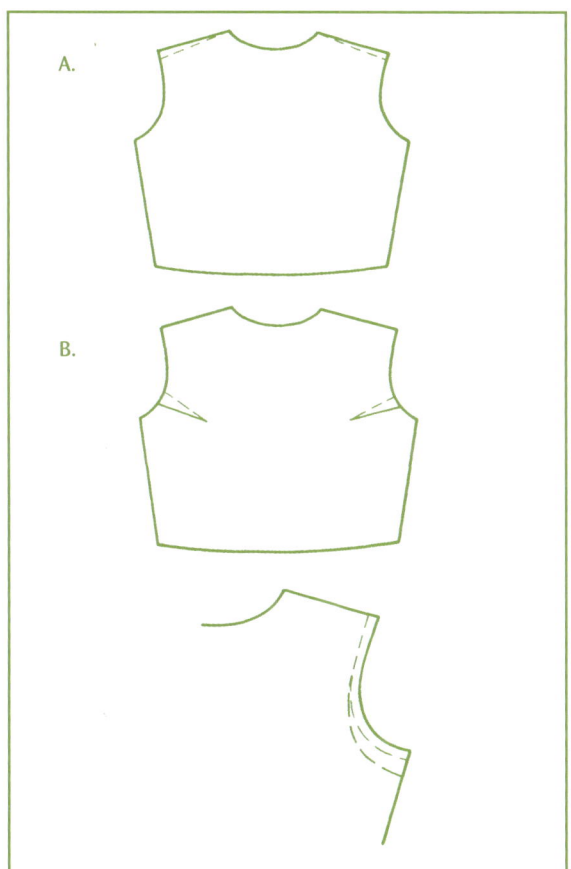

Figure 4.11—(Top and Center) Correcting a Gaping Armhole in a Sleeveless Bodice
Figure 4.12—(Bottom) Correcting a Tight Armhole in a Sleeveless Bodice

Rippling in sleeve cap—Too much fullness in the sleeve cap. Certain fabrics (such as permanent press) do not ease smoothly. Remove sleeve and restitch gathering line on sleeve 1/8" inside seamline. See Figure 4.14. If this doesn't do the trick, remove easestitching and trim sleeve cap each side of center point, as in Figure 4.15. Make new line of easestitching 1/2" from sleeve edge.

Diagonal wrinkles in sleeve cap—Distribution of ease is incorrect. Open armhole seam between notches and spread ease toward front or back until sleeve fits smoothly. See Figure 4.16.

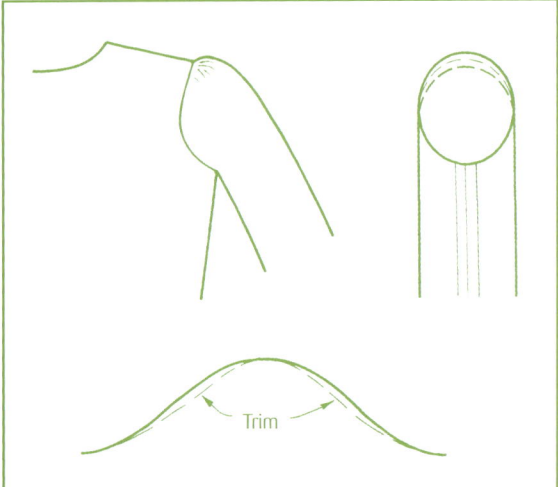

Figure 4.14 – (Top) Removing Too Much Fullness by restitching
Figure 4.15 – (Bottom) Removing Too Much Fullness by Trimming Sleeve Cap

Figure 4.16 – Redistributing Ease to Remove Diagonal Wrinkles

Waistline too low—Place string around waist and re-mark waistline on bodice. Do not change seam allowance on skirt. See Figure 4.17.

Waistline too high—Take smaller seam allowance on bodice at waistline. See Figure 4.18.

One-piece garment too big through body—Take in side seams tapering to nothing at each end. See Figure 4.19A.

Waistline Seam

Figure 4.17 – (Top) Correcting Low Waistline
Figure 4.18 – (Bottom) Correcting High Waistline

If alteration goes into armhole, be sure to take in sleeve seams also. See Figure 4.19B.

Pull-on pants or skirts—To establish the fit of an elasticized waistline, put garment on and place elastic around the waist over the garment. Adjust elastic to a comfortable fit, snug enough to hold the garment in place. Pin ends together. Pull up excess fabric above elastic until garment fits properly. Be sure pants crotch is in a comfortable position. Mark just above the elastic with pins or chalk all around the garment. This will be the foldline for the casing. See Figure 4.20.

Tightness in crotch—Let out leg seams. Raise waistline seam if necessary. See Figure 4.21.

Bagginess in front crotch—Deepen curve of crotch seam. Adjust side seams if needed. See Figure 4.22.

Bagginess in back crotch—Take shorter crotch seam in back. Lower back waistline seam. See Figure 4.23.

Final Fitting

When the construction of the garment is finished, the garment is tried on for the hem. Have someone mark the hem for you using a hem marker or a yardstick. Measure the same distance from the floor all the way around the hem. Be sure to wear a belt if it is called for, and wear the shoes you will be wearing with the outfit. If your garment

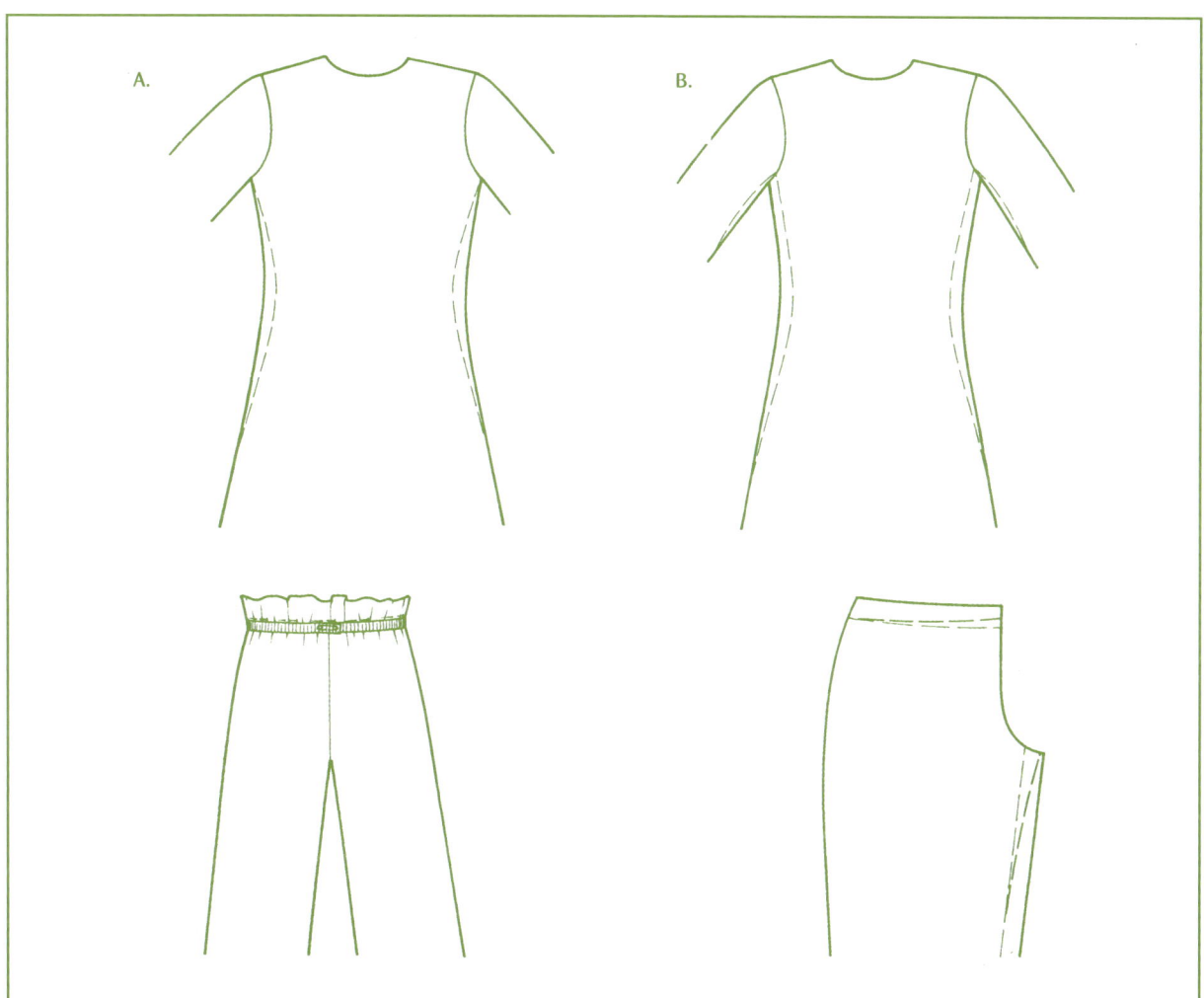

Figure 4.19 – (Top Left and Right) Taking in One-Piece Garment
Figure 4.20 – (Bottom Left) Establishing Waistline in Elasticized Garment
Figure 4.21 – (Bottom Right) Adjusting for Tightness in Crotch

Figure 4.22–(Top) Eliminating Bagginess in Front Crotch

Figure 4.23–(Bottom) Eliminating Bagginess in Back Crotch

contours of the body without pulling or wrinkling is a garment that has the mark of professional sewing.

Time-Saving Construction Methods

Putting a garment together is not difficult. Today's easy methods make sewing a breeze. Shortcuts abound in all phases of sewing, from shopping for patterns right on through cutting, marking, and stitching, to the final finishing details. Take advantage of these shortcuts and don't be afraid to try something you haven't done before. A new method may not seem like a time-saver on the first try, but once you get used to doing it, you may never go back to the old way.

Unit Construction

Smart sewers learn to do their sewing in units. It's easier to work on separate pieces than on a whole garment. If you finish each section as you go, you'll see the end product taking shape right from the very beginning. Good dressmakers sew as much as possible on each piece to reduce the amount of time spent handling fabric. Take advantage of production methods whenever possible. Less handling means less time spent on your sewing.

has a bias or circular skirt, or if the fabric is very stretchy, let the garment hang for 24 hours before marking the hem. Buttons and snaps can now be marked for the proper position on your garment. Be sure all top and bottom edges of garment are lined up before positioning buttons.

Remember one basic rule when doing any garment fitting: *A tight-fitting garment is neither attractive nor comfortable.* A garment that hangs straight and follows the natural

Do all your staystitching as soon as you remove the pattern pieces from the fabric. Sew all lines of machine basting (for marking, gathering, easing) while your machine is set for a large stitch. Apply all your interfacing at one time. If it's the fusible kind, that means one trip to the ironing board.

Start your sewing with the smallest pieces—collar, cuffs, pockets, facings, belts—using the factory method of continuous stitching. You can include sleeves in this stitching if you wish, or you may want to sew the sleeves to the garment before the underarm seam is sewn. Try each way and see which one works best for you. You may find that inserting the sleeve first works best for one style of garment while sewing the underarm seam first is more efficient for another style.

Clip apart all the small pieces after stitching and do all necessary trimming, clipping, and grading. Turn, press, and finish each piece as far as possible. Hems can be put in sleeves, outer edges of facings can be finished, and pocket edges can be pressed under. Once you've done everything you can on the small pieces, lay them aside.

Now start putting your main garment pieces together. Bound buttonholes should be made first. Zippers should be installed while garment is still flat, if this is possible (depending on the style of your garment). Skirts can be assembled, shoulder and underarm seams sewn. If your garment has a waistline seam, finish everything on the bodice—sleeves, collar, pockets—before sewing it to the skirt, as shown in Figure 4.24.

Figure 4.24–Assembling Main Garment Pieces

Then turn up your hem and your garment is finished.

Shortcuts and Timesavers

Everyone wants to learn to sew quickly and efficiently without sacrificing quality. Here are some timesavers that are worksavers as well. They will speed you along and help you turn out a professional-looking garment quickly and easily.

- Take advantage of "easy-to-sew" patterns. They have fewer construction lines and less detail to fuss over.

- Choose fabrics that are firm and easy to handle. Avoid slippery fabrics, plaids, and napped fabrics for beginning efforts. To save time and work, choose fabrics that don't require a lining or underlining. Printed fabrics will hide more mistakes than plain ones.

- Under-the-bed storage boxes are excellent for storing fabrics if you're short on closet or drawer space.

- Shoeboxes are a good size for storing patterns, trims, zippers, etc. and they stack easily.

- Buy all notions before starting your sewing project. You don't want to take time out for a trip to the store.

- Assemble all your supplies before you start cutting—fabric, pattern, shears, pins, tape measure, yardstick, etc. A silverware tray is handy for holding sewing supplies.

- As already mentioned, for left-handed sewers, a small mirror is handy for reversing the illustrations in your pattern instruction sheet.

- If your pattern has been used more than once and is showing signs of wear, repair it with transparent tape or reinforce it with a lightweight iron-on interfacing.

- Use time-saving methods for placing pattern on fabric (weights instead of pins, or simple items such as small ashtrays or table knives), or try spray adhesive to hold the pattern in place.

- If fabric is folded right sides together for cutting, seams will be ready to sew when you remove pattern pieces from fabric.

- Do all your cutting at one time— fabric, interfacing, lining, underlining, etc. No sense in making a mess more than once. Cut all notches or clips as you cut out in pattern pieces.

- Use selvages on straight grain edges of pattern pieces. This is especially useful for seams where zippers will be installed, since seams will need no finishing. Clip selvage every 6" or so to prevent puckering when fabric is washed.

- Stack all cut pieces neatly, small pieces on top, to keep them from getting lost. Roll up and tie with a strip of leftover fabric (you'll avoid creases this way). This is the factory method of bundling garment pieces.

- Do all your marking at one time, preferably just before sewing. Chalk marks don't stay forever and pins have a habit of falling out. Choose the marking method that is most suitable for your fabric. Check your pattern instructions to see which marks will be needed for the view you are making.

- To mark placement of pockets, buttonholes, and other details, place pattern on wrong side of a *single* layer of fabric (be sure it is the correct piece, right or left). Baste through pattern and fabric along marking line, taking *tiny* stitches on pattern side and longer stitches on fabric side, as in Figure 4.25. Remove pattern carefully. Thread will make only tiny holes in pattern.

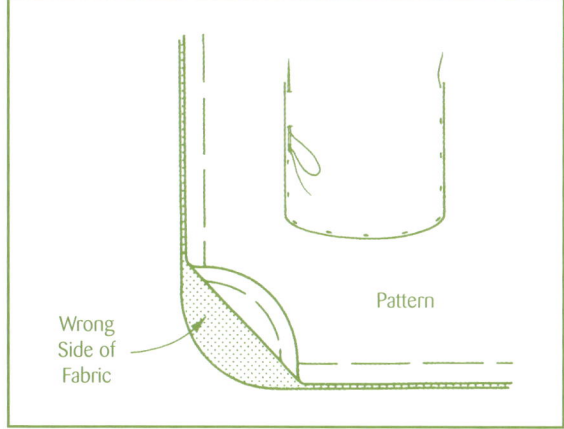

Figure 4.25–Marking Placement of Details

- Leave pattern pieces on fabric until you are ready to sew. Put each one back into the envelope as you remove it from the fabric. They get lost very easily—especially the small ones—and you may want to use them again.

- If fabric is the same on both sides, mark each piece on the wrong side with an X in chalk or basting thread. You will avoid mistakes such as sewing up two right sleeves.

- Have a wastebasket handy or tape a paper bag to your sewing machine. You'll have less mess to clean up.

- To keep threads from tangling in your sewing box, tape thread ends to spools with cellophane tape.

- Keep an artist's gum eraser near your sewing machine. This is handy for cleaning lightly soiled areas on your fabric.

- To keep small buttons, hooks, and snaps from getting lost, group them together on strips of cellophane tape.

- Here's a hint for quick removal of those tiny blood spots caused by pin pricks. Roll a piece of white thread into a ball and chew it for a minute or two (watch out for lipstick). Rub the spot hard with the damp thread until the spot disappears. Use this trick only on fabrics that won't spot.

- To remove a water spot from your fabric, let it dry, then rub the edges until the spot disappears.

- Use a small wire needle threader to repair snags on knit fabrics. Insert loop from wrong side of fabric, push snag through loop and pull to wrong side of fabric. Do not cut the snag.

- For a quick change of thread on your sewing machine, do it the factory way. Cut the thread near the spool. Place new spool on spindle and tie thread ends together in a square knot. Raise presser foot and pull thread toward the back. Thread will pull through tension discs, thread guides, and needle. See Figure 4.26. Cut off old thread and you're ready to sew.

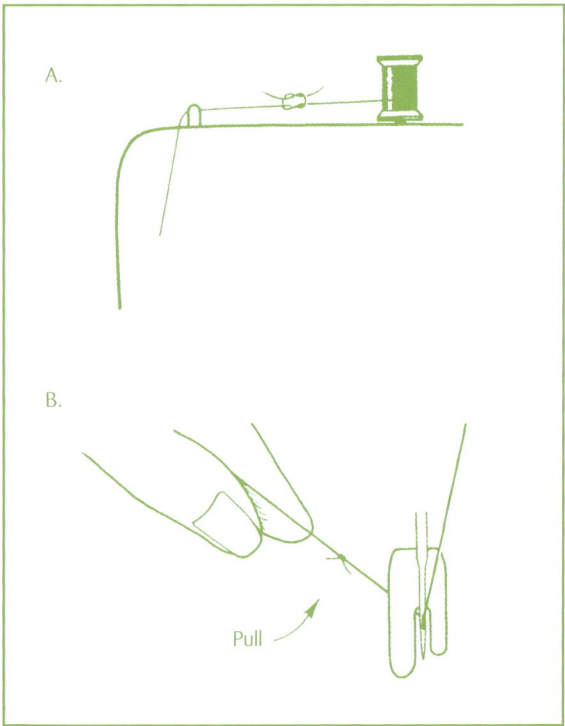

Figure 4.26–A quick change of thread. A. Knot thread ends. B. Pull knot through needle.

- Use pin-basting to hold pieces together as you sew. Place pins at right angles to the seamlines, heads slightly off the fabric. Remove pins as you come to them. You can sew over the pins if your machine has a hinged presser foot but if you hit one, you may blunt your needle.

- On small pieces you may not need to pin at all. Learn to handle fabric and sew without pins, keeping edges even, checking ends, and easing fabric as you sew to make ends come out even. Use your left hand to hold the fabric behind the needle and your right hand to hold the edges together and feed them into the machine in a straight line, as shown in Figure 4.27.

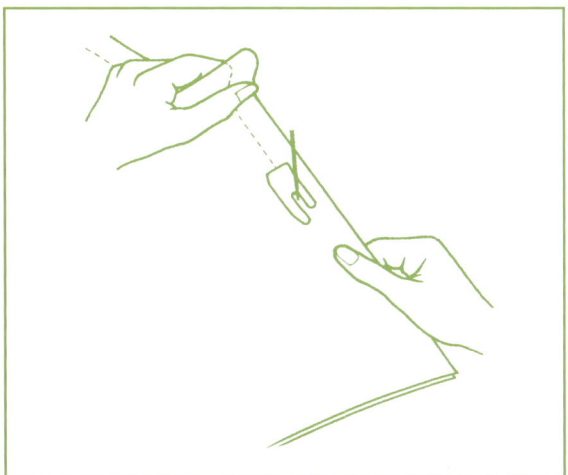

Figure 4.27—Sewing Without Pins

Much, much time can be saved by learning to sew without pinning or basting. Don't be afraid to try. Factory workers do it, and so can you.

- Learn to recognize standard seam allowance and topstitching widths. Let your seam guide be your teacher: you'll soon learn to sew without it.

- Take advantage of all time-saving sewing aids: adhesive sewing tape or quilting foot for guiding topstitching, double-faced tape for inserting zippers, fusible web for hems, pockets, appliqués, and for tacking facings.

- If garment is underlined, sew or fuse interfacing to underlining before sewing underlining to garment.

- If fabric will be underlined, transfer all markings to underlining instead of fabric.

- When sewing underlining to your fabric, use a zigzag stitch 1/8" from the edge. Seams will be pre-finished.

- When sewing seams on edges that are shaped differently, be sure to match *seamlines* at the end of each piece rather than the cutting lines. This is especially true at shoulder seams. See Figure 4.28.

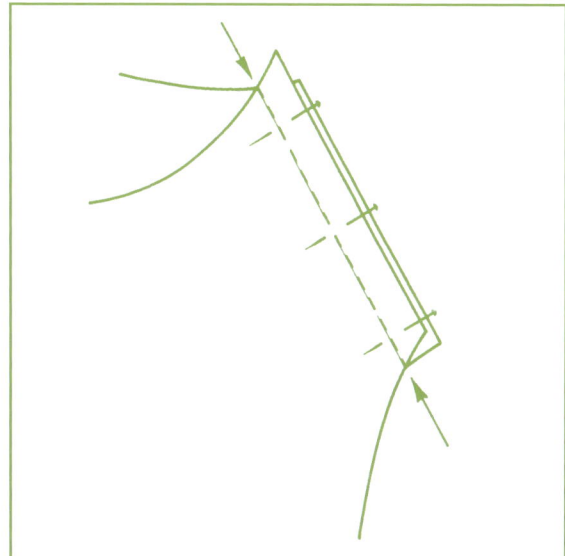

Figure 4.28—Match seamlines rather than cutting lines.

- Use the factory method of continuous sewing, feeding each piece into the machine without raising the presser foot. Clip the pieces apart when finished sewing, or as needed for further sewing.

- Do as much sewing as possible before making a trip to the ironing board. No sense in running back and forth each time a seam needs to be pressed open.

- Keep a supply of long, white envelopes or long strips of brown paper near your ironing board. Use them to slip under darts or seams to prevent an impression from showing on the right side of the fabric when you press.

- Most patterns follow the unit method of construction. Work on small pieces first—collar, cuffs, pockets, facings—and lay them aside when finished for quick application later.

- Do topstitching when needed. Sometimes topstitching is done *before* the garment is sewn together (on pockets, yokes, collars), and sometimes *after* the garment is finished (on lapels, collars, cuffs). Check your pattern instruction sheet. You might want to change thread for topstitching, so do as much of it as possible at one time.

- When changing sewing machine needles, put used needle into a scrap of felt. Use a marking pen to write needle type and size on the felt.

- On fabrics of more than one color such as prints and tweeds, you can use the main color for the top thread on your machine and a secondary color for the bobbin thread.

- To tie thread ends, make a single knot over a pin and pull thread close to garment to tighten. See Figure 4.29.

Figure 4.29–Tying Thread Ends over Pin

- When ripping a seam (even experts do this occasionally), clip top stitches every 1/2" or so. Pull out bobbin thread. Remove any remaining thread in the fabric with sticky cellophane tape or masking tape.

- Here's a good way to get an accurate corner. Sew the entire length of the seam along one side, then along the other side. The corner automatically falls where the stitches cross. Reinforce by stitching for 1" on either side of corner, taking one or two stitches diagonally across the corner.

- For pushing out turned corners, use an orangewood stick (the kind you use to take care of your fingernails).

- The eraser end of an unsharpened pencil makes a handy tool for turning narrow belts and straps.

- If you hold your shears at an angle when grading seam allowances, all layers can be cut at one time and each will be a different width. See Figure 4.30.

Figure 4.30–Grading Seam Allowances

- Reduce bulk in crossed seams by trimming corners of seams, darts, tucks, and folds.

- Sew zipper into seam while pieces are still flat. This can be one of the first seams you sew. Do this only if you are sure of the fit of your garment or if this is not one of the seams that will be altered.

- Machine baste main construction seams, then try on garment. Make fitting adjustments before final stitching. A different color bobbin thread will make it easier to find and remove basting stitches.

- When stitching sleeves into armholes, stitch with sleeve on top. Spread sleeve fabric slightly with fingers as

you sew to help ease fabric into seam without puckering, as shown in Figure 4.31.

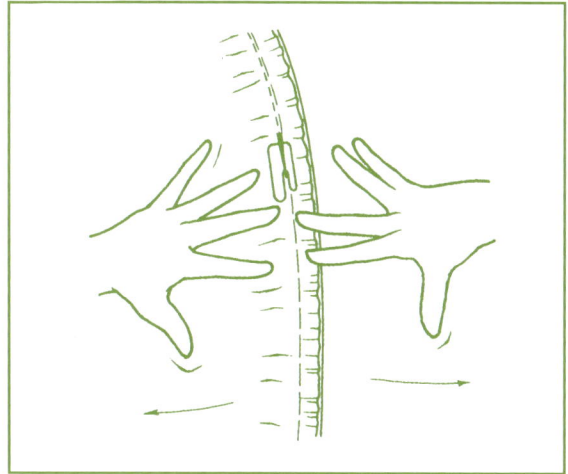

Figure 4.31–Easing Sleeve into Armhole

- When leaving an opening in a seam to allow for turning, turn and stitch to the edge of the fabric at each end of the opening. This will prevent the stitches from ripping during turning and will hold the seam allowance in place for hand finishing. See Figure 4.32.

Figure 4.32–Stitch to Edge of Fabric for Opening

- Stitch in the ditch to fasten facings and pants cuffs, and to finish collars, cuffs, and waistbands. Overcast raw edges of collars, cuffs, and waistbands instead of turning them under before the final stitching. The stitch in the ditch will hold them in place.

- To finish neck and armhole edges on knits that don't ravel, turn under seam allowance and topstitch close to fold. Add another row of stitching 1/4" from the first, as in Figure 4.33. A nice neat finish—no facings needed.

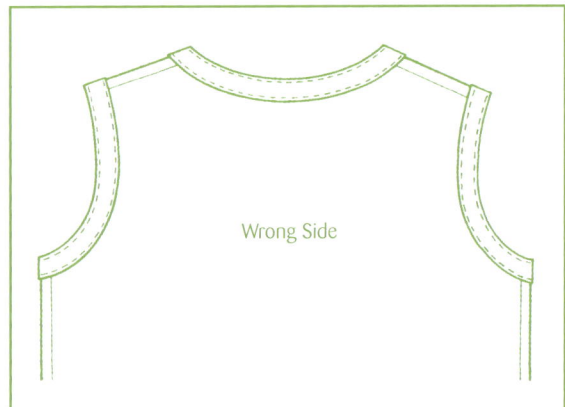

Wrong Side

Figure 4.33—A Neat Finish for Knit Edges

- To get a perfect curve on a shirttail hem, cut a piece of cardboard the exact shape of the shirttail hemline. Press hem allowance over cardboard before stitching. This is also a good trick for curved pockets.

- Before removing last piece of fabric from machine, sew onto a narrow strip of folded fabric. Machine is ready to sew into next piece of fabric when you are ready to start again. No worry about tangled threads at start of sewing.

- To keep your shears sharp, cut through fine sandpaper two or three times. This does not replace a professional sharpening, however.

- Put a drop of sewing machine oil on stubborn zippers to make them run more smoothly. Be careful not to get oil on your garment.

- When replacing worn out elastic in a casing, pin the new elastic to the old *before* pulling out the old elastic. New elastic will be pulled through casing in a jiffy.

Notions for Shortcut Sewing

On the market today you will find a wonderful supply of notions that can make your sewing as simple as ABC. Take advantage of them. New ones are being introduced all the time. Many of them are things that you have been seeing or using for years, such as buttons and zippers; but even these things change. New types and styles are being introduced all the time. Look around each time you go shopping and watch the ads in the sewing magazines. Keep an open mind to what's new. Old ways are not always the best ways.

How to Use Them

Always follow the package directions when trying out something new. If it doesn't work right, there must be a reason. Most of these products have been pretested to give the customer satisfaction. Practice on scraps of fabric before trying something new on your fabric or finished garment. Remember to preshrink all notions to be used unless the package says "preshrunk." Check to be sure you are using only washable notions and trims on fabrics that you will be washing. Below are some items that we think are worth trying. Experiment. Have fun.

Basting Adhesive

This is a handy adhesive for basting items such as trims, zippers, pockets, and appliqués. It comes in a tube and is easy to use. It will not harm needles or fabric. It washes out of washable fabrics, but do not use it on dry-cleanable ones.

Belting

There are several kinds of belting on the market. Choose the one that fits the job. *Regular belting* is washable and is used as a backing for fabric belts. It comes in black and white in 1/2" to 3" widths. It is also available as iron-on belting. *Grosgrain belting* is stiff grosgrain ribbon used as filling or backing on waistbands of skirts and pants. *Soft grosgrain ribbon* may be used as a facing in skirts and pants that don't have a waistband. *Waistband stiffening* is a non-roll strip used inside waistbands for a firm band that won't crush. It is available in widths from 1/2" to 2". *Men's waistbanding* is a pre-assembled band of facing and stiffener used in men's pants.

Bias Tapes

These are used most often as bindings and endings. They are made from cotton or polyester/cotton in a wide variety of colors. They range in width from 1/2" to 1" and have pre-folded edges, as shown in Figure 4.34. The *double-fold bias* tape is folded lengthwise slightly off-center for ease in application. It is sewn to the edge of the

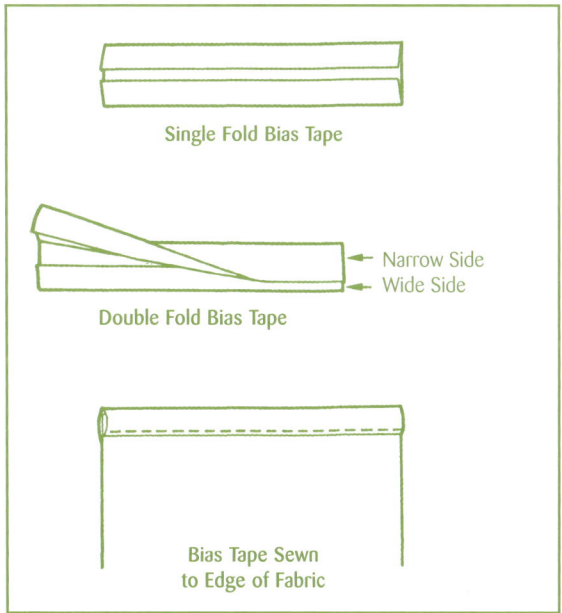

Figure 4.34—Bias Tapes

fabric with the narrower side on top so that the wider side will be caught in the stitching underneath. *Single-fold bias tape* also comes in rayon for use on finer fabrics.

Braids

There is an infinite variety of braids and decorative trims on the market today, a few of which are shown in Figure 4.35. Your imagination can come up with a multitude of uses for many of them. *Fold-over braid* is finished on both edges and is folded in half, slightly off-center. It has a fairly heavy look but is very flexible for ease in trimming curved edges on pockets, collars, and jackets. It is not difficult to use and gives a very elegant, tailored finish. Other braids are *soutache* (a herringbone), *middy* (very narrow), and *knit braid* for use on knit fabrics. *Rickrack braid*, with pointed edges, comes in many colors and in sizes from baby to jumbo. To apply it by machine, sew right down the middle. The

polyester rickrack is softer than the cotton and needs no ironing. Points will not curl up after washing.

Buckles

There is a wide variety of types and styles of buckles to accent any garment. Several types of closures are available. The way your belt fastens will be determined by the kind of buckle you use. Be as decorative as you like. If you plan to use buttons as well, be sure they are keeping with the design of the belt buckle.

Buttons

You will find an almost limitless array of buttons in any notions department or fabric store. They come in all sizes, shapes, and colors. Be sure to have a swatch of fabric with you when you pick out your buttons. Check the back of your pattern envelope for the correct size. Remember to purchase your buttons *before* you make your

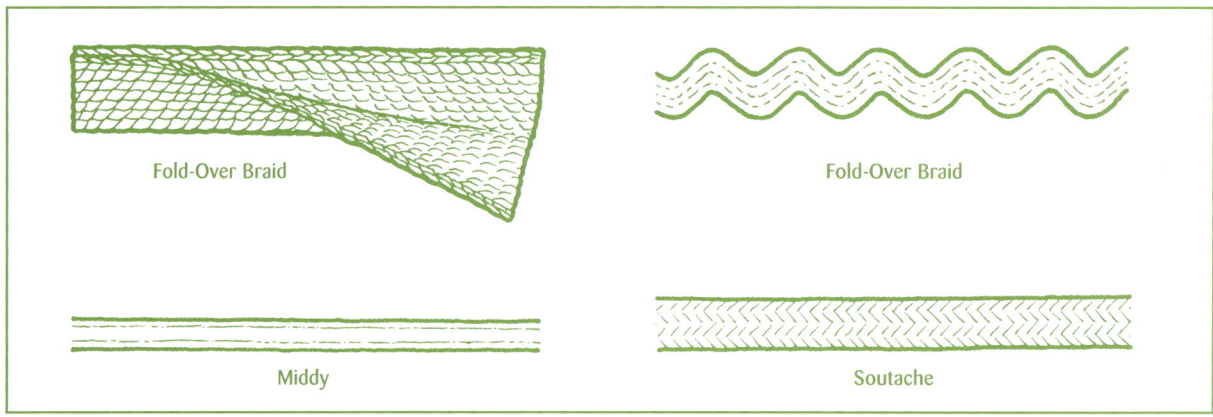

Figure 4.35—Types of Braids and Trims

buttonholes. You don't want to end up being unbuttoned because the button wouldn't fit through the hole.

Don't overlook the possibility of covered buttons and buckles for a really custom look. These can be sent out to be done by a professional—usually through the services of a fabric store—or you can choose to cover your own with leftover scraps of fabric. Uncovered buttons and buckles can be purchased in the fabric store. How-to directions are included.

Double-Faced Tape

Double-faced tape is a narrow tape with adhesive on both sides. It is used to hold a zipper in place for sewing. It can also be used to hold pockets in place. It's easy to use and worth a try. *However, you must not sew over the tape.* The tape is to be removed after the zipper is inserted. It can also be used to hold seams together before sewing. Again, remove the tape after sewing.

Elastic

Elastic thread is a thin, single strand of elastic that can be used on the bobbin when shirring by machine. It can also be used for hat bands and for making loop closings for buttons. *Braided elastic* is used in casings and has lots of stretch and "snap." *Woven elastics* are softer and do not curl; they can be stitched to a garment, such as pajamas. Be sure to suit the type of

elastic to the garment it will be used on; this will assure you the right amount of stretch. Elastics are available for everything from lingerie to swimsuits. Even wide, decorative elastic is available—it can be used as a belt with the addition of a suitable buckle.

Eyelets

Eyelets are round, metal rings used to reinforce holes for lacings and belt buckles. They can be bought in several different colors and are applied with a special tool. The tool can be purchased with the eyelets and will usually apply gripper snaps as well.

Fastener Tape

Fastener tape, shown in Figure 4.36, can be used in any opening that has an overlap. One layer of the tape has tiny nylon or polyester hooks; the other layer has tiny loops. When pressed together, they mesh and form a firm fastening. This tape can be purchased in strips or in small button-sized dots. There are two types: iron-on and sew-on. It is a good substitute for zippers, snaps, or buttons. The trade name is Velcro.

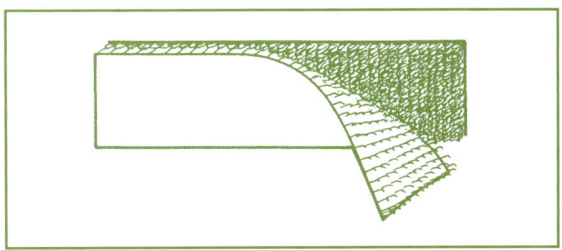

Figure 4.36—Velcro Nylon Fastener Tape

Fusible Web

Don't overlook fusible web, an ingenious invention. It is a thin web used between two layers of fabric to hold them together. It's indispensable in applying appliqués, whether or not you plan to topstitch them later. It's also marvelous for holding hems, facings, and trims in place. It will eliminate lots of hand sewing. Be sure to read the directions before fusing, and test it on a scrap of fabric first. It can be used on any fabric that can be steam-pressed. The exceptions are sheers and a few synthetics, so test first. It comes in strips or by the yard. It is not to be used as an interfacing, although it does give a slight stiffness to the fabric after fusing.

Hem Facing

When fabric is very heavy or when a hem allowance is very small, hem facing, shown in Figure 4.37, is used. It is usually 2" wide and acts as a substitute hem. It comes in a variety of colors as well as in lace.

Figure 4.37—Hem Facing

Hooks and Eyes

These are strong fasteners used where there will be some strain, such as at the top of a zipper opening. They come in several sizes. There are black ones for dark fabrics and nickel for light fabrics. Large, covered hooks and eyes are used for coats, furs, and deep-pile fabrics. Flat hooks and eyes can be used for waistbands on skirts and pant.

Horsehair Braid

This is a stiff, woven braid made of nylon. It is used to stiffen and flare the hem of a skirt. It is usually used on long gowns.

Labels

This is where you get to do a little showing off. Once you've become adept at creating your own masterpieces, go ahead and indulge yourself. Have some labels made up with your name on them. Many attractive styles are on display in your fabric store and can be ordered very inexpensively. You *want*

people to know it's your creation when you take off your jacket or coat at the theater or restaurant. You'll need some anyway when you start sewing for other people.

Laces

Here there is a variety from wide to narrow, from heavy to delicate, from plain to fancy. *Lace edgings* have one straight edge and one decorative edge. They can be flat or gathered and are applied along the edge of a garment. *Insertion* has two straight edges and is used as a band within a garment. Sometimes the fabric underneath is cut away for an openwork effect. *Galloon* has two decorative edges and is used like insertion. *Beading* has a row of openings for threading ribbon. See Figure 4.38. Laces give a delicate, feminine, dressy look to any garment.

Needle Conditioner

This is a pad used to sharpen blunt or snagged sewing machine needles. Run the pad through the *unthreaded* machine 5 or 6 times. It can be used with all types of machine needles. It's especially handy for renewing needles dulled by synthetic fabrics.

Reflective Fabric

This fabric is used as decorative trim on outdoor clothing. It can be sewn on by hand or machine. The fabric reflects in auto headlights. This is a great safety item for nighttime pedestrians, cyclists and outdoor sports enthusiasts.

Ribbing

Ribbings are knitted bands that stretch. They are used for sleeve cuffs

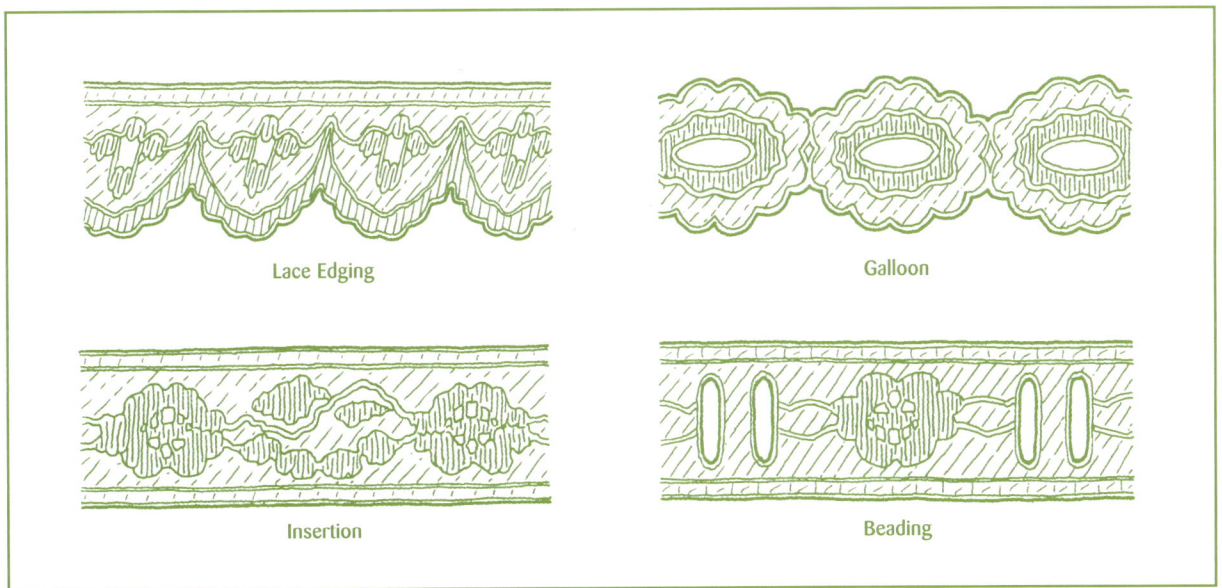

Lace Edging

Galloon

Insertion

Beading

Figure 4.38—Types of Laces

and neckbands—also for the bottom edges of jackets. Be sure to get one with the right amount of stretch for the job you want it to do. Measure the area where it will be used to determine how much will be needed, or buy whatever your pattern calls for.

Seam Binding

A straight rayon or polyester tape, seam binding is usually used as a hem finish. It is also valuable as a stay (reinforcement) to prevent stretching in seams. *Stretch lace seam binding* is a good choice for hems on knit fabrics. *Iron-on seam binding* is also used for hems. Test it on a sample first to make sure it will stick.

Self-Stick Sewing Tape

Self-stick tape has adhesive on one side and measured markings of various widths on the other, as shown in Figure 4.39. It is used as a stitching guide when sewing on the right side of a fabric. It's especially handy for topstitching.

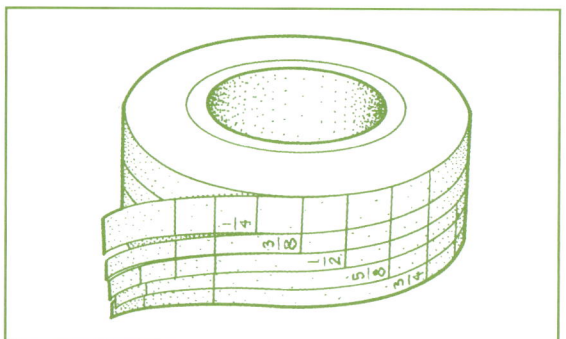

Figure 4.39–Self-Stick Sewing Guide

Shaping Aids

Shaping aids, shown in Figure 4.40, include shoulder pads, chest pieces, and sleeve heads. They can be purchased in kits and are a great aid in the construction of menswear. They are used in tailoring to give a better shape and fit to men's suits.

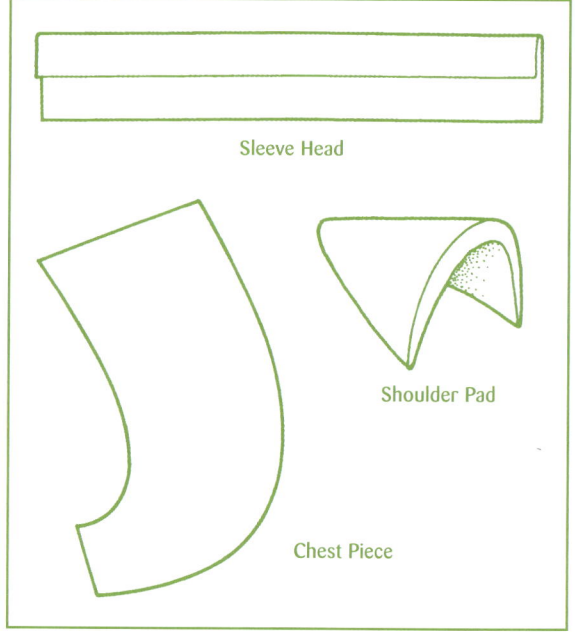

Sleeve Head

Shoulder Pad

Chest Piece

Figure 4.40–Shaping Aids

Snaps

Sew-on snaps are used where there is little strain. *Fabric-covered snaps* can be purchased for use on sheer fabrics, or where they will show, as on coats. *Gripper snaps* are sturdy and are used on work clothes, pajamas, and children's clothing. They are hammered into place; instructions come with the snappers. Decorative ones are often used on sportswear. Both kinds of snaps can be purchased by the yard on woven or knit tape. These are handy for use on children's clothing or slipcovers.

Spray Adhesive

This is a handy item that aids in holding the paper pattern to the fabric for cutting. It eliminates the need for pinning. The pattern is easily removed and no residue remains on the fabric.

Trims

It is impossible to tell you about all the different decorative trims that are on the market. These include the laces and braids as well as fringe, sequins, beads, ribbons, appliqués, and any other decorative items used to trim a garment. The variety is limitless. Each year new designs are brought out, inspiring new ideas. Your imagination is your best friend in this department.

Tubing Tape

Tubing tape is used when making narrow bias tubing for button loops, ties, etc. It is applied to bias strips before stitching. Bias strips are turned right side out quickly and easily by pulling on the tape. Good for anything that needs turning.

Twill Tape

This woven tape is strong and will not stretch. It is used as a stay to prevent seams from stretching. It is used also in tailoring. Widths vary from 1/4" to 1". It is available in either cotton or polyester and comes in black or white only.

Weights

Weights, shown in Figure 4.41, are heavy little gadgets to add weight and body to garments and draperies. They are usually sewn into the hem. *Round lead weights* look like coins and come in two sizes. Lead weights can also be purchased by the yard. encased in twill tape 1/2" wide. *Gold chain* is sometimes used as a weight where it will show, such as at the bottom of a jacket lining.

Zippers

When buying a zipper, be sure you get the one that is right for the article

Figure 4.41—Weights for Garments and Draperies

you are making. Zippers come in many sizes, types, and colors. *Regular zippers* have metal teeth and are very sturdy. *Synthetic coil zippers* have teeth that can be pulled apart and zipped back together in case fabric gets caught. Zipper tapes vary, too. Some are cotton and some are a softer, woven, synthetic which will not curl up when washed. There is also a lightweight knit polyester tape that has an adhesive basting strip for "sew-easy" application.

Separating zippers are used in jackets or in any open-front garment. Some zippers have pull-tabs on both sides for use in reversible garments. Others have pull-tabs at both ends and can be opened from either the bottom or the top. These are used in jumpsuits. *Ring-pull zippers* are used for decorative openings. *Trouser zippers* come in one length and are trimmed to size after application. *Blue jeans zippers* are made of metal in a 6" or 7" length. *Slipcover zippers* are extra heavy and come only in beige.

Invisible zippers are coil zippers which are concealed in a seam. They require a special zipper foot—inexpensive and adaptable to any machine—and are inserted by a different method of application. Be sure to follow directions that come with the zipper and zipper foot.

These are some of the notions you will find when you go shopping. There are others which are used for special purposes. You can buy pocket replacement kits to repair those nasty holes in men's trousers pockets. There's a snap-on plate for your steam iron that will eliminate the need for a press cloth. You can even buy non-slip material for the soles of children's pajama feet. There are gadgets galore—some you'll want and some you won't. Look around and keep in touch with new things as they come out. You may find they'll save you time and money and make your sewing a lot easier.

Before continuing, answer the questions. True or False?

1. Never try on your garment right side out.

2. Wrinkles below the waistline in the back require you to raise the skirt in the back and widen the seam allowance.

3. Do all your staystitching before you remove the pattern pieces.

4. Zippers should be installed while the garment is still flat, if possible.

5. Buy all notions before starting your sewing project.

6. The eraser end of an unsharpened pencil makes a handy tool for turning narrow belts and straps.

7. Stitch in the ditch to fasten facings and pant cuffs, and to finish collars, cuffs, and waistbands.

8. To keep your shears sharp, always send them to a professional.

9. Always follow the package directions when trying out something new.

10. Eyelets are round, metal rings used to reinforce holes for lacings and belt buckles.

Check your answers with those provided on page 199.

PART THREE

DARTS, PLEATS, AND PLACKETS

Overview

The previous parts covered what some would consider the "basics" involved in clothing construction. The remaining parts, beginning with this one, will cover details of perfecting the different techniques involved in garment construction.

This third part will cover the methods of constructing darts, tucks, gathers, pleats, and plackets. Upon completion of this part, you will be able to

- List the types of darts and explain their importance to a well-constructed garment

- Explain the methods used for gathering fabric by machine

- Define shirring and its use

- Explain the use of tucks

- List and describe the different types of pleats and their construction

- Explain plackets—their types and construction

DARTS AND GATHERS

Darts

Darts, tucks, gathers, and pleats are used for shaping a garment to fit the contours of the body. A dart or tuck must be placed correctly and sewn accurately in order to do its job of controlling fullness. A dart should end approximately 1" from the fullest part of the figure toward which it is directed. Its point should lie smoothly and not pucker. Pleats can be soft or tailored. Gathers are used to control fullness in a garment and to create soft folds in the fabric. Since all these techniques build

shape, they can be interchanged in some cases. As you gain experience, you may wish to experiment with substituting one for another.

Types of Darts

Darts can be straight, convex, or concave, as in Figure 5.1, depending on the area in which they are used. *Straight darts* are used at bustline, neckline, elbow, and waistline. *Convex darts* give curve to a hipline and are usually used in skirts without side seams. *Concave darts* give a fitted look

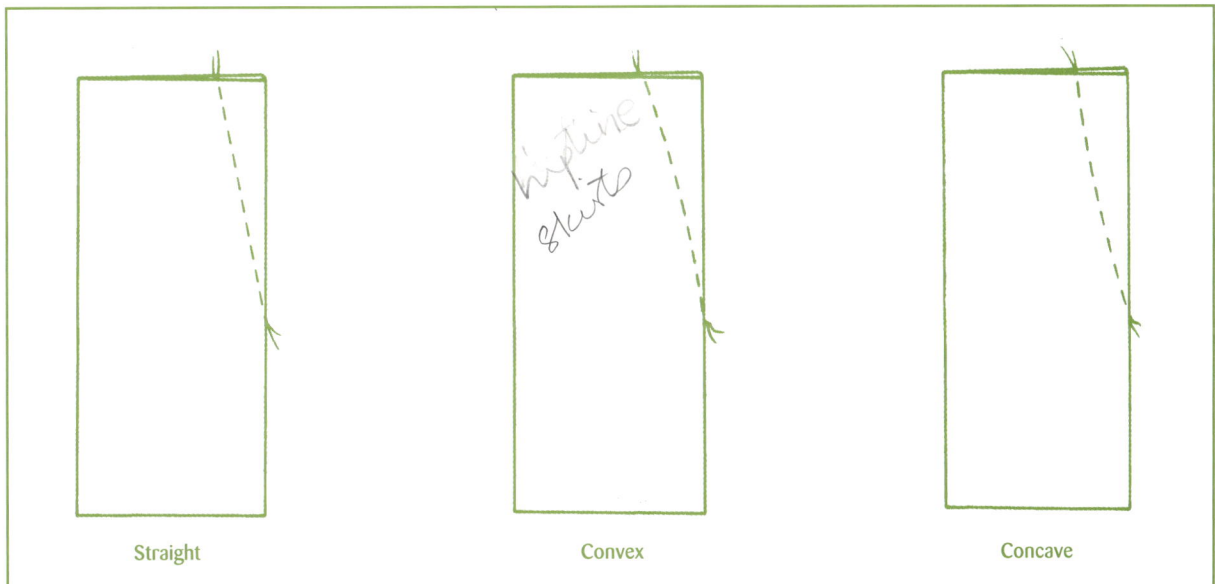

Straight   Convex   Concave

Figure 5.1—Types of Darts

between bust and waist in the front midriff area, as in Figure 5.2.

Contour darts, Figure 5.3, are tapered at both ends and are usually found at waistlines in garments without a waistline seam. Figure 5.4, *French darts*, are long darts that extend diagonally from the hip or waistline to the bustline.

Darts should be carefully marked to follow the stitching line exactly.

Stitching

If garment is underlined, machine baste center of darts through fabric and underlining before darts are sewn. This will hold fabric in place while darts are being stitched. See Figure 5.5.

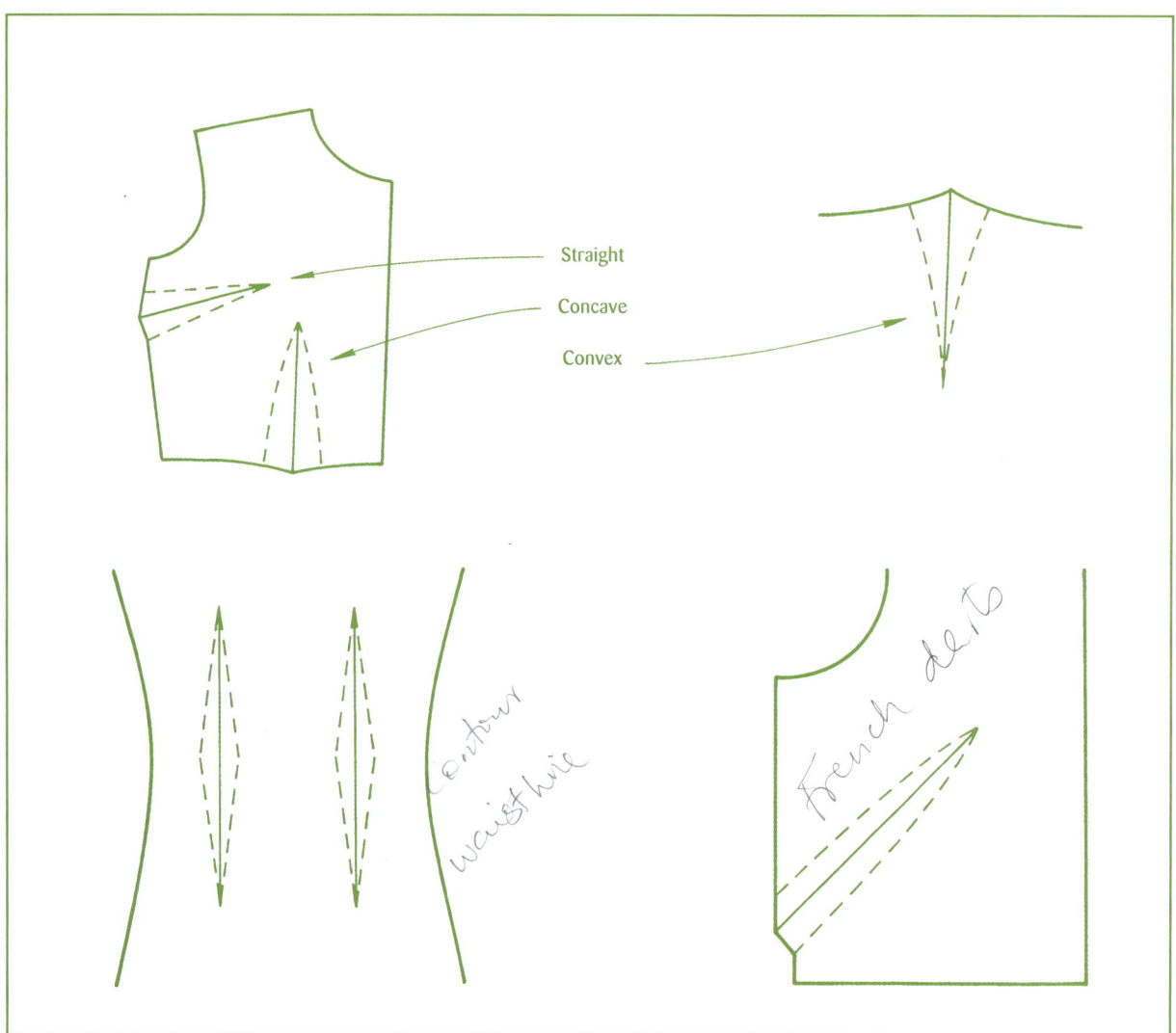

Figure 5.2 – (Top) Types of Darts Shown in a Garment
Figure 5.3 – (Bottom Left) Contour Darts
Figure 5.4 – (Bottom Right) A French Dart

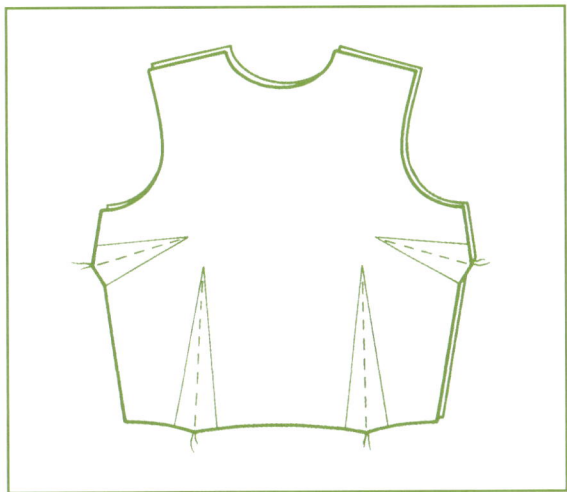

Figure 5.5—Machine baste fabric and underlining before darts.

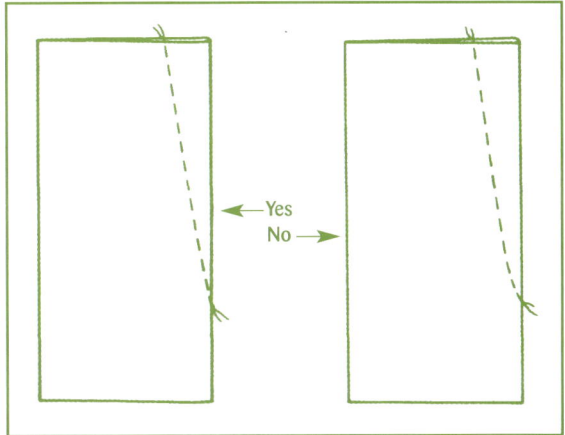

Figure 5.6—Do not curve the point of a dart.

Fold dart on center line. Match all dots or other matching points. Match notches at cutting line. Place pins horizontally across dart at matching points and at bottom point. With practice, you will be able to sew darts accurately without pinning.

Start at the wide edge and stitch to the point. Place the last two or three stitches right on the fold, then stitch off the fabric edge. If you sew all darts on the back and front pieces at the same time, you can sew continuously from one to the next without breaking the thread. Clip threads in between darts when finished. Do not backstitch at the points of darts. Since there will be no strain on the seam at the dart point, you don't have to tie the thread ends. Be sure to sew in a straight line off the edge of the fabric, as in Figure 5.6 on the following page. Do not curve the point—this will make an unattractive dart.

Here's a quick and easy way to make a perfectly stitched straight dart, as shown in Figure 5.7 and 5.8:

Step 1. Mark darts by making two clip marks at garment edge and a dot or an X at the point of the dart (Figure 5.7).

Step 2. Make a line on your sewing machine straight out from the needle to the edge of the machine (use chalk or tape).

Step 3. Fold dart in center, matching clips and having point of dart on fold.

Step 4. Place fabric under presser foot and line up point of dart with line on sewing machine.

Step 5. Stitch dart, keeping point of dart on marked line as you stitch. A straight dart every time!

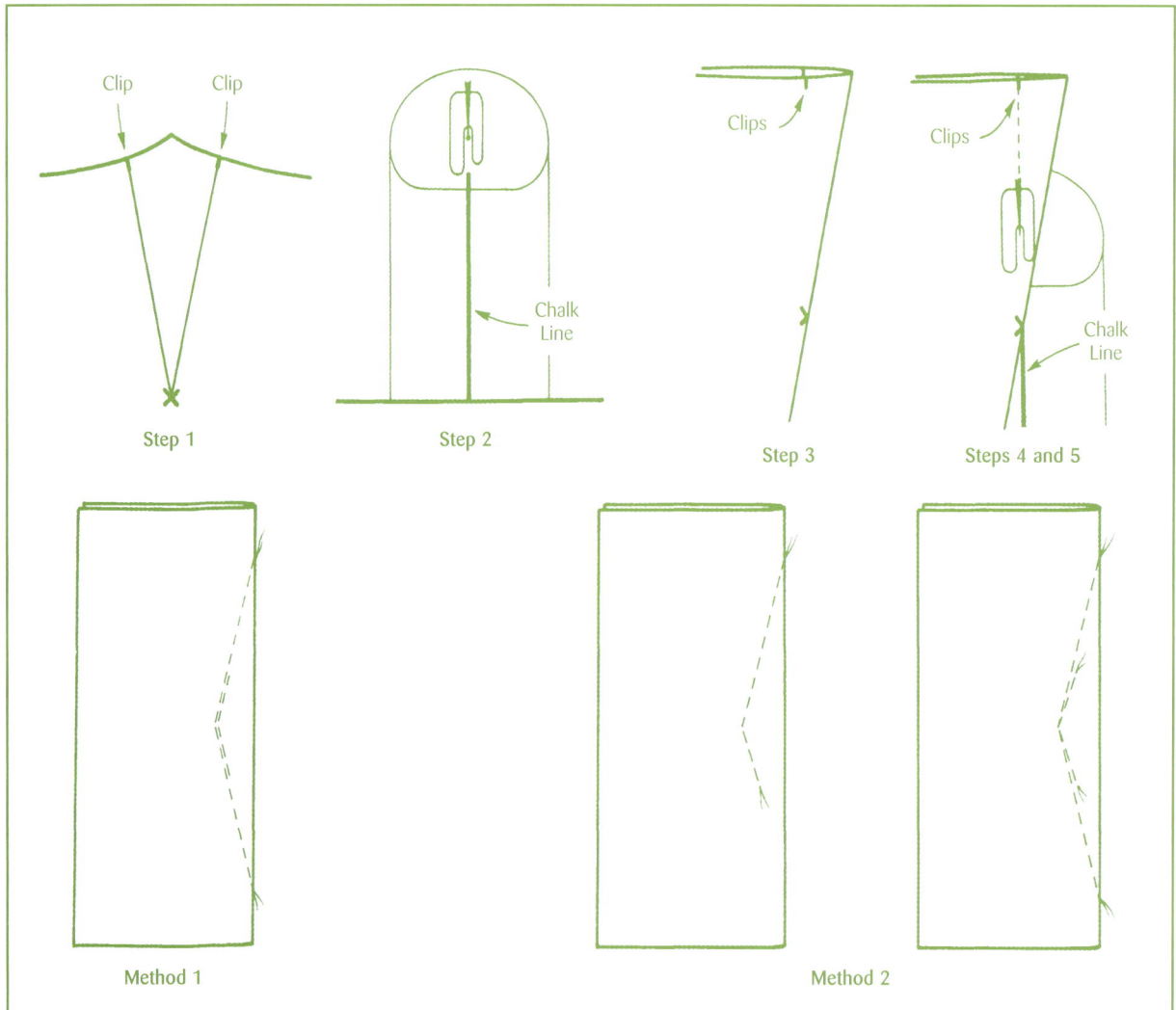

Figure 5.7–(Top) Making a Perfect Straight Dart
Figure 5.8–(Bottom) Contour Darts

For contour darts, use either of the following methods:

Method 1. Start at one pointed end and stitch to the other. Reinforce stitching at the center point where dart curves.

Method 2. Start stitching just before the center point and sew to the opposite end of dart. Repeat for other end, overlapping stitching at the center point. This will serve as reinforcing at the center.

Trimming

Darts are usually left untrimmed. However, in heavy or bulky fabrics, darts should be split open down the center to within 1/2" - 1" of the point. Extra-wide darts should also be treated in this way and then trimmed. Press dart open, pressing point flat. See Figure 5.9.

On sheer fabrics, make a second row of stitching 1/8" inside the first and trim close to the stitching. See Figure 5.10.

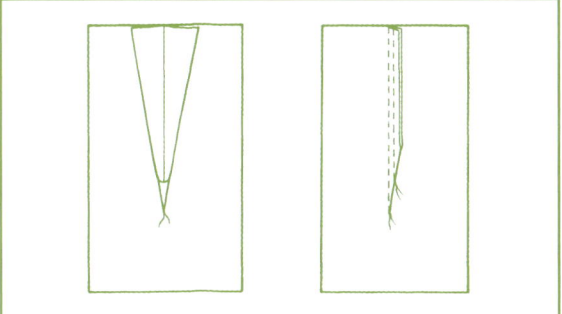

Figure 5.9 – (Left) Split and Press a Dart
Figure 5.10 – (Right) Dart on Sheer Fabric

Contour darts must be clipped in several places, particularly at the center, to allow them to conform to the body when turned (Figure 5.11).

To reduce bulk in seam allowances, trim diagonally across wide end of dart (Figure 5.12).

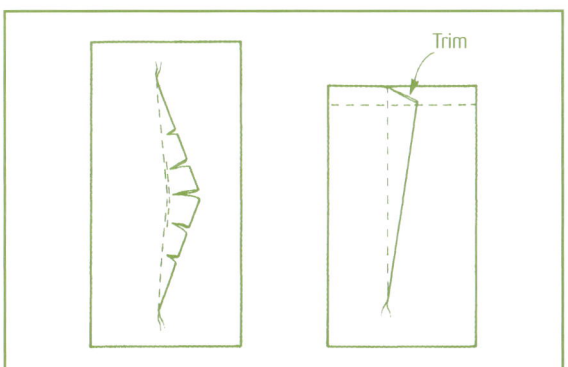

Figure 5.11 – (Left) Clipping a Contour Dart
Figure 5.12 – (Right) Trimming a Dart to Reduce Bulk

French darts should be cut on the center line to within 1" of the point *before* stitching, as in Figure 5.13. Seam together, matching markings. One side may need to be eased slightly into the other, as in Figure 5.14. Next, clip seam allowances to allow dart to curve. See Figure 5.15.

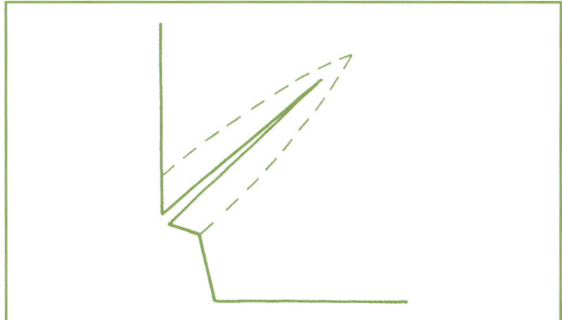

Figure 5.13 – Cutting a French Dart

Figure 5.14 – (Top) Seaming a French Dart
Figure 5.15 – (Bottom) Clipping a French Dart

Pressing

Press darts flat, then press to one side over curved surface, such as a tailor's ham or the end of the ironing board. If fabric marks easily, place brown paper or an envelope under dart before pressing to prevent ridge from forming on fabric. Press vertical darts toward the center of garment; press horizontal darts down. Press across the dart with the side of the iron, not toward the point.

Gathering and Shirring

Gathering is used to control fullness in a garment and to create soft folds in the fabric. *Easing* is a single line of gathering used where a slight amount of fullness must be eased into the seam without any gathering or puckering. *Gathering* is done with two or more rows of stitching, depending on the amount of gathering to be done and the

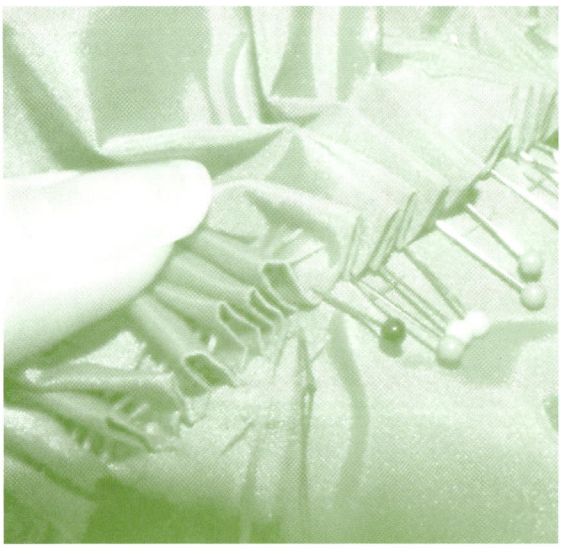

size of the area involved. *Shirring* is decorative gathering done with three or more rows of stitching. It shows on the outside of the garment. Gathering can be done either by hand or by machine. To gather by hand, use a small, even running stitch.

Gathering

Gathers may be found at waistline, cuffs, yokes, necklines, or sleeve caps, wherever a soft look is desired. Gathers start with two stitching lines on a long piece of fabric.

Gathering by machine is the quickest and easiest way to make uniform gathers. For gathering large areas such as the top of a full skirt, divide the gathering into sections, stopping at each seam. Leave long thread ends at the beginning and end of all stitching lines. These will be used to pull up the gathers. An extra heavy thread in the bobbin will help prevent breakage when pulling up gathers, especially in heavy or bulky fabrics. Use nylon, silk, or buttonhole twist for the bobbin thread.

For machine gathering, follow these steps:

Step 1. Set the machine for the largest stitch. On sheer or lightweight fabrics, use a slightly smaller stitch.

Step 2. Loosen top tension slightly. This will make it easier to pull up the bobbin thread.

Step 3. Make a row of stitching in the seam allowance on the right side of the fabric outside the seamline.

Step 4. Make a second row of stitching in the seam allowance 1/4" from the first row, as in Figure 5.16.

Step 5. Holding both bobbin threads at one end of stitching, pull up threads, pushing fabric along bobbin threads. Continue until one half of fabric is gathered.

Step 6. Repeat for other half of fabric. Adjust to correct size.

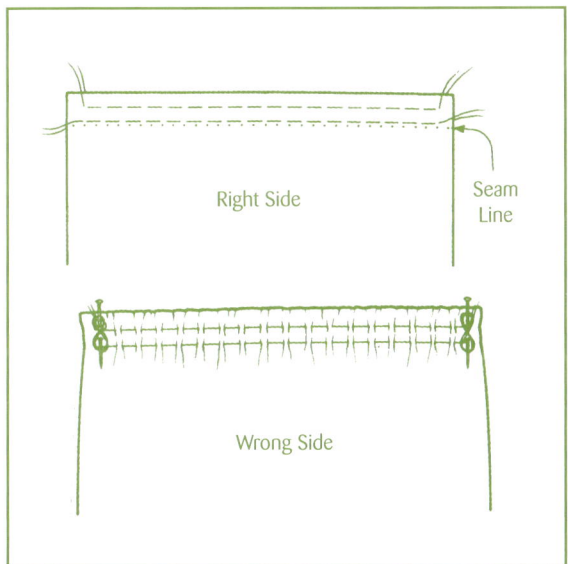

Figure 5.16–(Top) Stitching for Gathering
Figure 5.17–(Bottom) Pulling and Tying Bobbin Threads

Step 7. Fasten each end by tying threads or winding threads figure-eight fashion around a pin, as in Figure 5.17.

Alternate Methods

For small areas or short stitching lines, try one of these alternate methods:

Method 1. Make one continuous line of stitching instead of two lines. Start at one end of gathering line and sew to opposite end. With needle in fabric, raise presser foot and pivot fabric. Take on stitch and pivot again. Now sew back to starting point parallel to first stitching line. See Figure 5.18.

Method 2. Use one row of zigzag stitch instead of two rows of regular stitching. Set machine for medium stitch length and width. Sew on *wrong* side of fabric. Place fabric in machine and take one stitch, bringing bobbin thread up to top side of fabric. Pull both threads toward you for the length of the gathering line, plus several inches. Lay these threads on the seam allowance and zigzag over them, being careful not to catch them in the stitching. Use these two threads to pull up the gathers to the desired length.

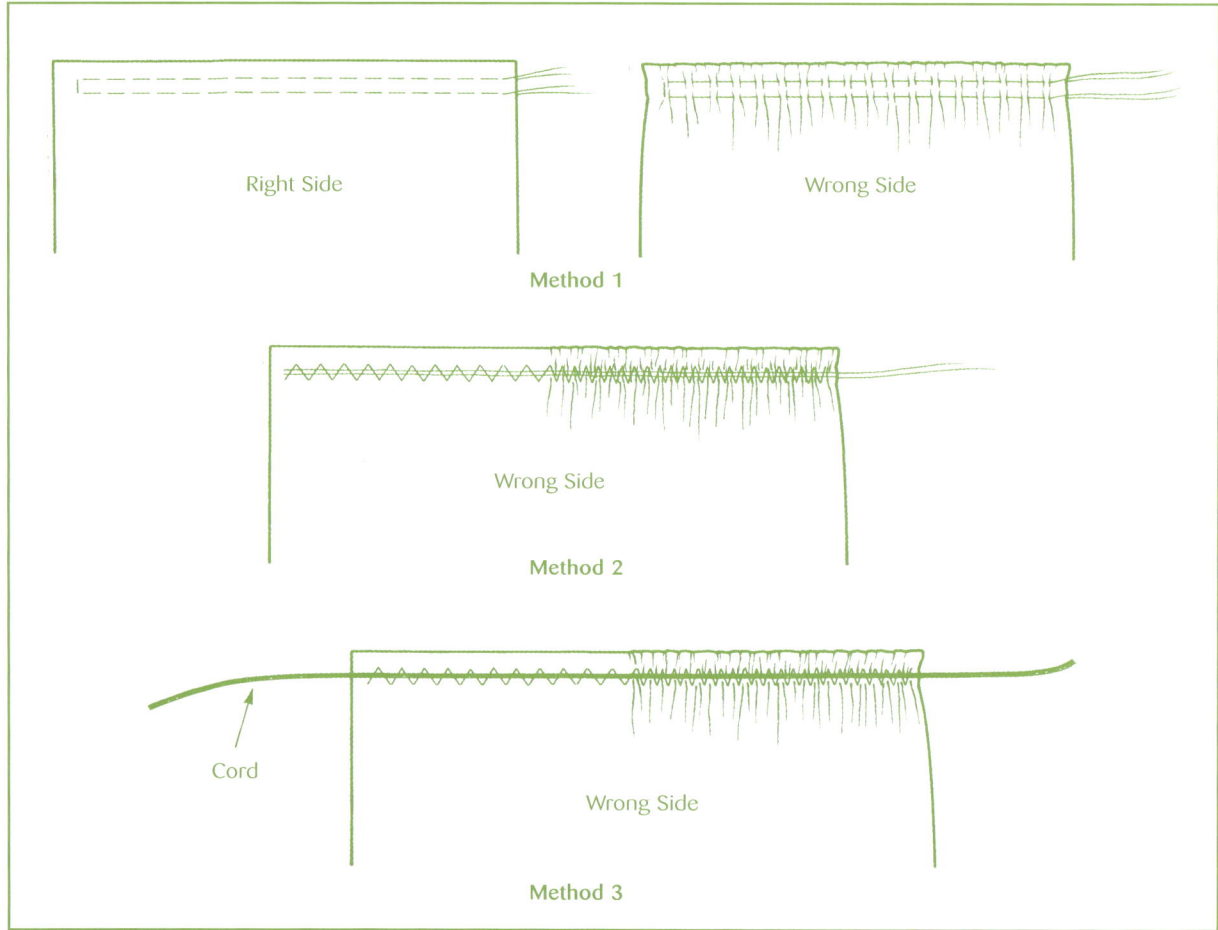

Right Side

Wrong Side

Method 1

Wrong Side

Method 2

Cord

Wrong Side

Method 3

Figure 5.18—Alternate Methods for Gathering Small Areas

Method 3. Make one row of zigzag stitching over a length of strong cord. Leave several inches of cord at each end. Be careful not to catch stitches in cord. This works well on heavy fabrics or where there are several rows of gathering.

Sewing Gathered Edge to Straight Edge

To sew a gathered edge to a straight edge, place the two layers of fabric right sides together. See Figure 5.19.

Step 1. Match all notches, seams, etc., and pin at these points.

Step 2. Pull up gathers between each point and adjust them evenly. Pin in place (remove any pins that are holding thread ends).

Step 3. Using regular length stitch, sew along seamline with gathers on top, keeping bottom layer flat.

Step 4. To reinforce seam, sew a length of seam binding over gathers just outside seamline.

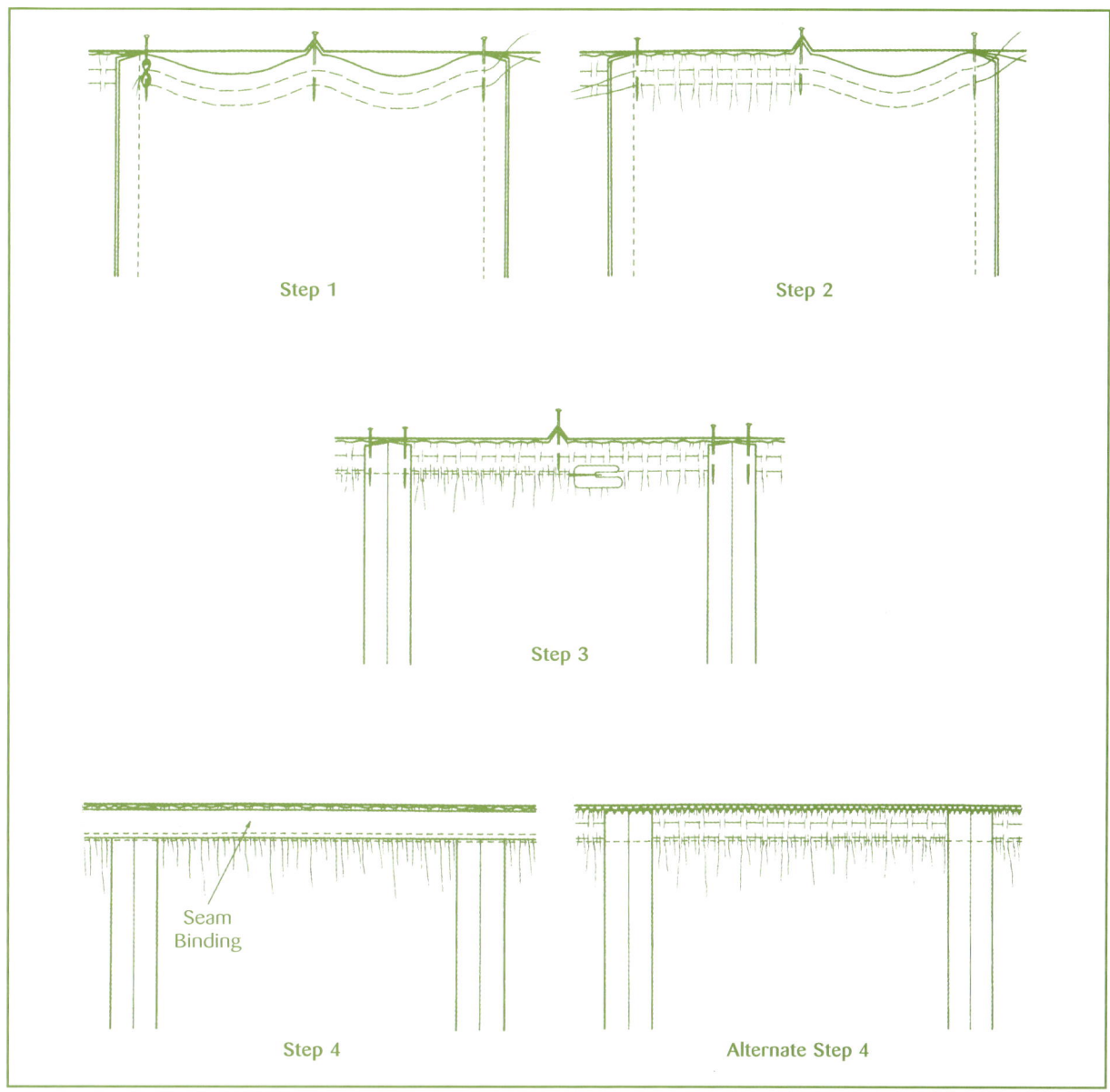

Step 1

Step 2

Step 3

Seam
Binding

Step 4

Alternate Step 4

Figure 5.19—Sewing a Gathered Edge to a Straight Edge

Alternate Step 4. If material ravels easily, trim edges and overcast with zigzag stitch.

Shirring

Several rows of gathers are used to make shirring, which is decorative gathering. Accuracy in stitching is very important in order to achieve the desired effect. Stitches should line up, one under the other, and rows should be an equal distance apart. Shirring works best on soft or lightweight fabrics.

After sewing all rows of stitching, pull thread at *one* end of the shirring until shirring is desired width. See Figure 5.20. Pull thread ends to wrong side and tie each row separately. If ends of rows will not be sewn into a seam, fold fabric and stitch a tiny pin tuck at each end of stitching lines to hold them securely. See Figure 5.21.

To hold shirring and keep it from pulling out, you might want to add a stay. Cut a piece of fabric the size of shirred area plus 1/2" all around. Fold under each edge 1/2" and slipstitch in place on wrong side of shirring (Figure 5.22).

Elasticized Shirring

Shirring with elastic thread gives stretch to the fabric and enables it to conform to the body. It is used especially for cuffs and waistlines, where it is comfortable and attractive. It's a good idea to try this out on a sample piece of

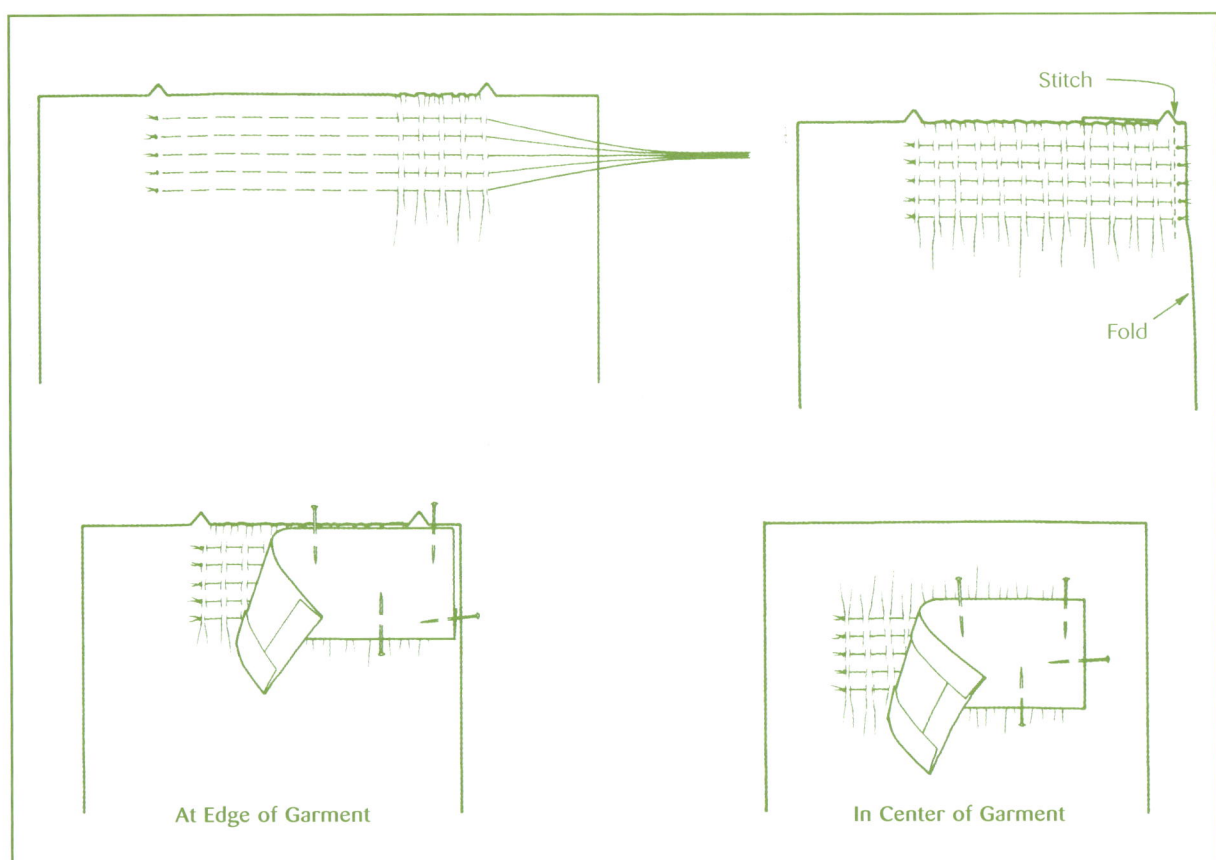

At Edge of Garment

In Center of Garment

Figure 5.20—(Top Left) Pulling Thread Ends to Shirr
Figure 5.21—(Top Right) Pulling Thread Ends to Shirr
Figure 5.22—(Bottom Left and Right) Adding a Stay to Hold Shirring

fabric first. You may have to adjust the stitch length or tension to get the desired shirred effect.

Elastic thread is used only on the bobbin. Wind it onto the bobbin by hand, stretching it slightly. Use regular thread on the machine. Set the machine for the largest stitch. Place a piece of paper between the fabric and feed dog. This will help the fabric to lie flat and not pull up into gathers as you sew.

Holding the fabric taut, stitch on the right side of the fabric. Make as many rows as desired, keeping them even and holding the fabric *taut* as you sew each row. After stitching is completed, peel paper off the back of the fabric to allow gathers to form.

If gathers need to be tighter, pull up elastic threads after stitching is completed. Pull thread ends to wrong side and knot each row separately. If ends of shirring will be caught in a seam, stitch across ends to hold in place. If shirring will not be sewn into a seam, fasten with a pin tuck on wrong side of fabric.

Pressing Gathers

In order to retain their fullness and attractiveness, gathers should never be pressed flat. The *seam allowance* of a gathered area can be pressed flat with

the tip or side of the iron. The seam of a gathered area should not be pressed open. Turn the seam to one side, toward the flat garment piece. Press only on the seam allowance and the flat garment piece, not on the gathers. On the wrong side of the fabric, press *into* the gathers, toward the seam, with the point of the iron. Be careful not to press creases into the gathers. These processes are illustrated in Figure 5.23.

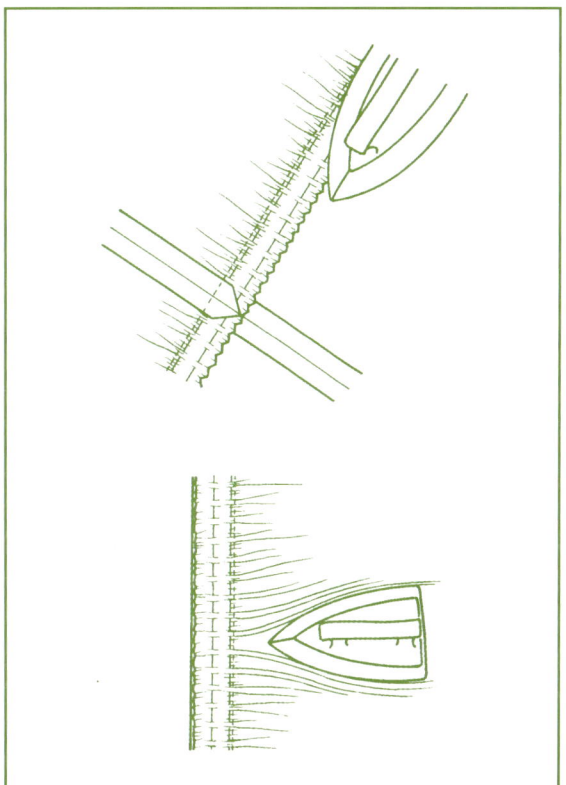

Figure 5.23–Pressing a Gathered Seam, at Top, and Pressing the Gathers, at Bottom.

Tucks

Tucks, which are used to control fullness, are sewn on the inside of the garment and serve the same purpose as darts. Tucks do not come to a point; the fullness is released at one or both ends of the stitching line. They are usually used at the waistline or shoulder (Figure 5.24).

Stitching

Fold the tuck on the foldline. Starting at edge of fabric, stitch along stitching line to end of tuck. Pivot and stitch to edge of fold. For tucks in the center of fabric, start at edge of fold and stitch across to end of tuck. Pivot and stitch the length of tuck along stitching line. Pivot again an stitch to folded edge of fabric. Stitching to edge of fold eliminates the need for backstitching or tying thread ends (Figure 5.25).

Pressing

Press tucks as sewn, then press to one side in the direction they are to be worn. Do not press past end of tuck where fullness is released.

Decorative Tucks

Decorative tucks are stitched on the outside of a garment. Use a thread that exactly matches the fabric or, for interesting effects, choose a thread of a contrasting color.

There are three kinds of decorative tucks, as shown in Figure 5.26:

1. *Blind tucks*—tucks that meet or overlap at the stitching line.

2. *Spaced tucks*—tucks with equal spaces between each one.

3. *Pin tucks*—tiny spaced tucks.

Decorative tucks must be very evenly spaced. A cardboard gauge, similar to your hem gauge, can be very useful for spacing tucks. Patterns that call for tucks have foldlines and stitching lines already marked on them. Follow stitching lines carefully for nice, straight tucks. To hold tucks in place, stay-stitch across ends in seam allowance, as in Figure 5.27.

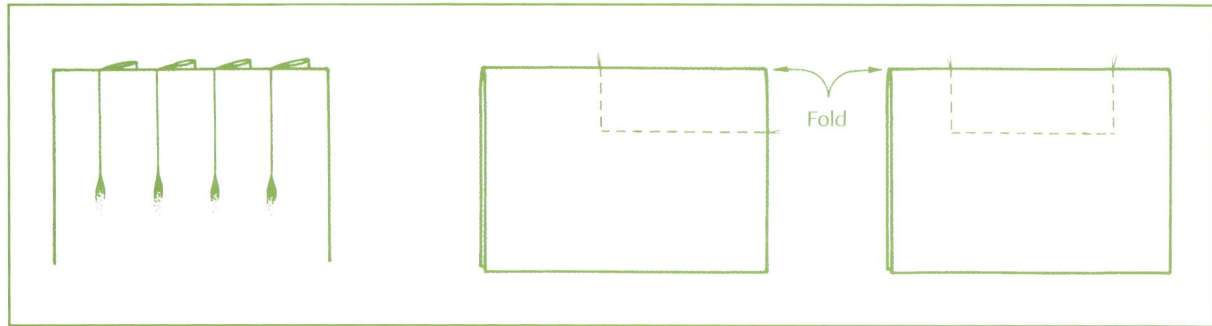

Figure 5.24–(Left) Example of Tucks
Figure 5.25–(Right) Stitching Tucks at End of Fabric (Center) or in Center of Fabric (Right)

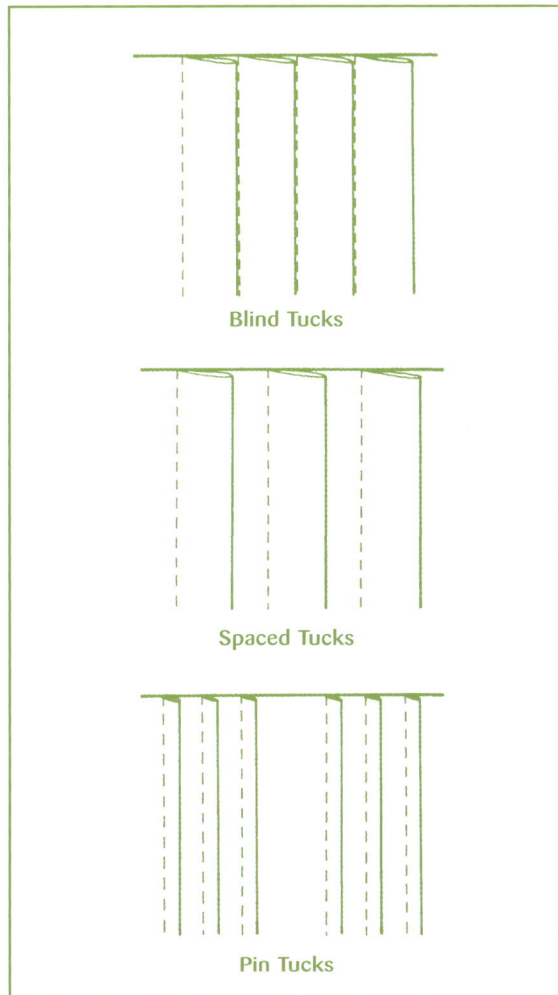

Figure 5.26–Decorative Tucks

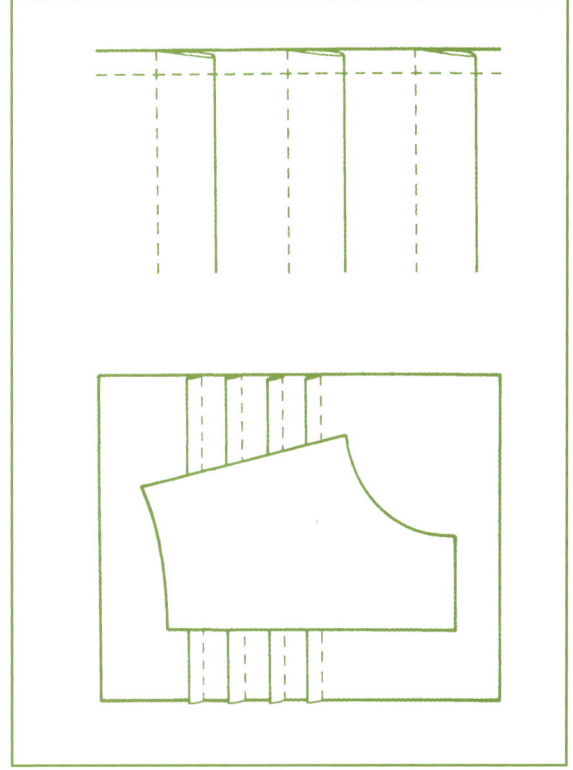

Figure 5.27–(Top) Staystitching to Hold Tucks in Place
Figure 5.28–(Bottom) Adding Tucks When They Are Not in the Pattern

If you wish to add decorative tucks to a pattern that does not call for them, stitch them into the fabric before cutting out the pattern piece. Be sure to allow extra fabric for tucks, as in Figure 5.28.

Twin-needle tucks can be made on machines that use two needles. These are not really tucks, but give the effect of tucks by drawing up the fabric between two close rows of stitching. The tighter the tension, the more raised the effect. Your machine manual will tell you how it's done.

Before continuing, answer the questions. True or False?

1. Straight darts are used at the bustline and neckline.

2. It is not necessary to backstitch at the points of a dart.

3. Easing is a single line of gathering used where a large amount of fullness must be put into a seam.

4. Machine gathering is the quickest and easiest way to make neat, even gathers.

5. Shirring is a form of decorative gathering.

Check your answers with those provided on page 199.

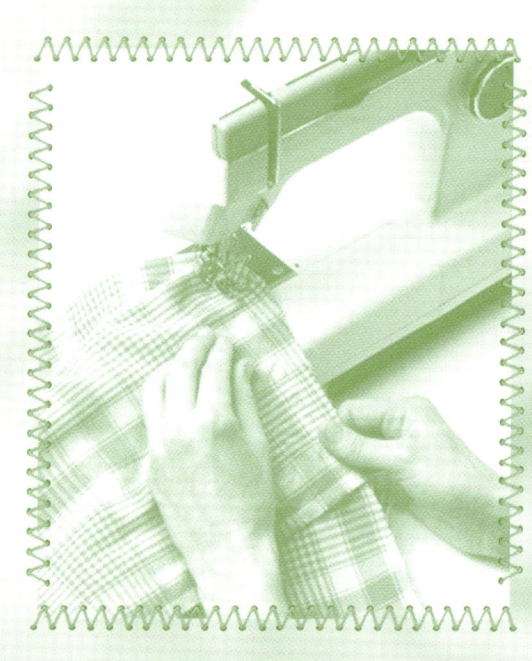

PLEATS AND PLACKETS

Pleats

Pleats are folds of fabric, always vertical, which provide controlled fullness. There are four basic types of pleats, as shown in Figure 6.1:

1. *Knife pleats*—These have folds that are all turned to the side in one direction. They usually lap from right to left.

2. *Box pleats*—These are created by two folds that meet in the center on the underside of the garment.

3. *Inverted pleats*—These have the two folds turned toward each other and meet on the outside of the garment rather than on the underside.

4. *Accordion pleats*—These are inverted folds that meet underneath when

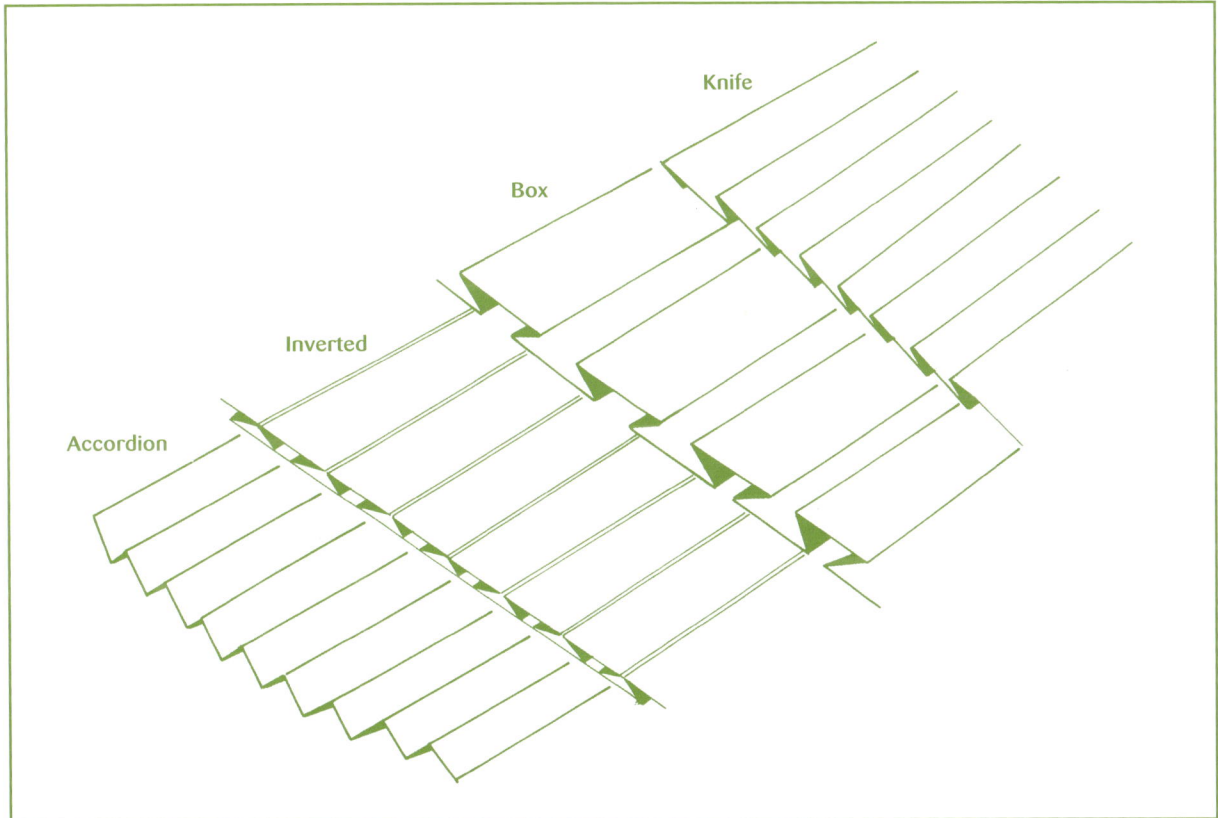

Figure 6.1—Basic Types of Pleats

pressed together. They resemble the bellows of an accordion.

5. *Sunburst pleats*—These are accordion pleats that are wide at the bottom and taper to nothing at the top.

Unpressed pleats and pressed pleats are the same; only the appearance is different. *Unpressed pleats* may be used in any soft fabric, as in Figure 6.2. *Pressed pleats* work best in fabrics that will take a crease well, as in Figure 6.3. Firmly woven fabrics that have a smooth, hard finish hold pleats well. A light to medium weight fabric works better than a heavy one. Heavy, bulky fabrics, especially knits, can be difficult to crease.

Figure 6.2–(Top) Unpressed Pleats
Figure 6.3–(Bottom) Pressed Pleats

Underlining is generally not used in pleated garments. The extra bulk of the underlining makes it difficult to crease the fabric. A lining may by used but should not be pleated. A full-length lining can have slits in the sides to allow for movement. Sometimes a pleated skirt is lined only from the waist to just below the hips.

Marking and Folding Pleats

Pleats are marked on patterns by two lines—a foldline and a placement line, as in Figure 6.4. Marking is done on a single layer of fabric. Use two different colors of thread or chalk when marking these lines so as not to confuse them when you do your pleating. Accuracy is very important in making these markings.

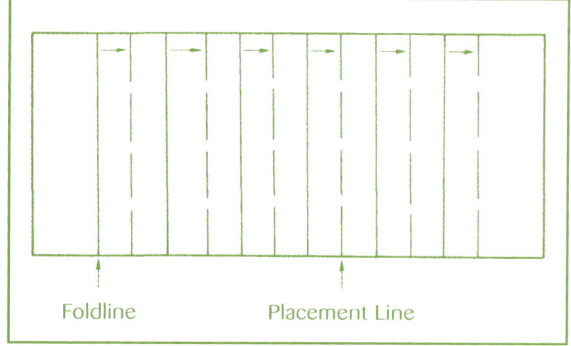

Figure 6.4–Foldline, Placement Line

Pleats can be formed on either the right or the wrong side of the garment. The zipper seam of the garment is usually left unsewn until after the pleats are formed. This enables you to work on a flat surface while doing your pleating. To form pleats on the right side, the pleat is folded on the foldline and the edge of this fold is brought to the placement line (Figure 6.5). To form pleats on the wrong side of the fabric, bring both marked lines together (foldline and placement line) and baste them along the marked lines. Turn pleats in the right direction. Machine baste top of pleats to hold them in place (Figure 6.6). All pleats should be basted in place the full length of the pleat to keep them in place until the garment is finished (Figure 6.7). If pleats are to be pressed, they should not be pressed until the hem has been finished.

Accordion Pleats

These narrow pleats are not folded or stitched. They are pressed into the fabric and stand away from the body. They are usually put into a garment by a professional pleater. Sometimes they are put into the fabric before a garment is made. The top of the pleated area is not folded—it is eased into the garment. Sunburst pleats are sewn flat to the garment and flare out to the hemline, as in Figure 6.8. It is wise not to fool with accordion pleats. Best results are achieved by using the services of a commercial pleater. To find a professional pleater, check the Yellow Pages of your telephone book, or ask at your fabric store, or local dry cleaner's.

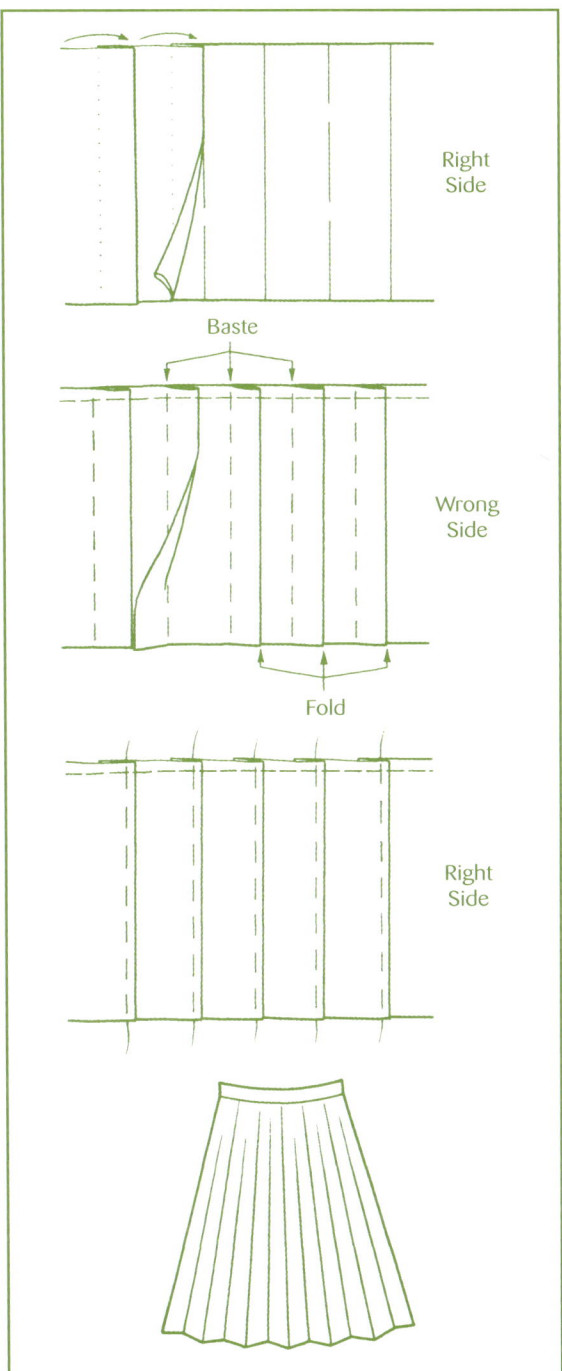

Figure 6.5–(Top) Forming Pleats on the Right Side
Figure 6.6–(Center) Forming Pleats on the Wrong Side
Figure 6.7–(Center) Basting Pleats on the Right Side
Figure 6.8–(Bottom) Example of Accordion Pleats

Fashion magazines sometimes have advertisements for this service. Professional pleaters can put any kind of permanently pressed pleats into any garment. Fabric can sometimes be purchased already pleated.

Pleat with Separate Underlay

Sometimes a single pleat is formed with a separate piece of fabric as an underlay, as in Figure 6.9.

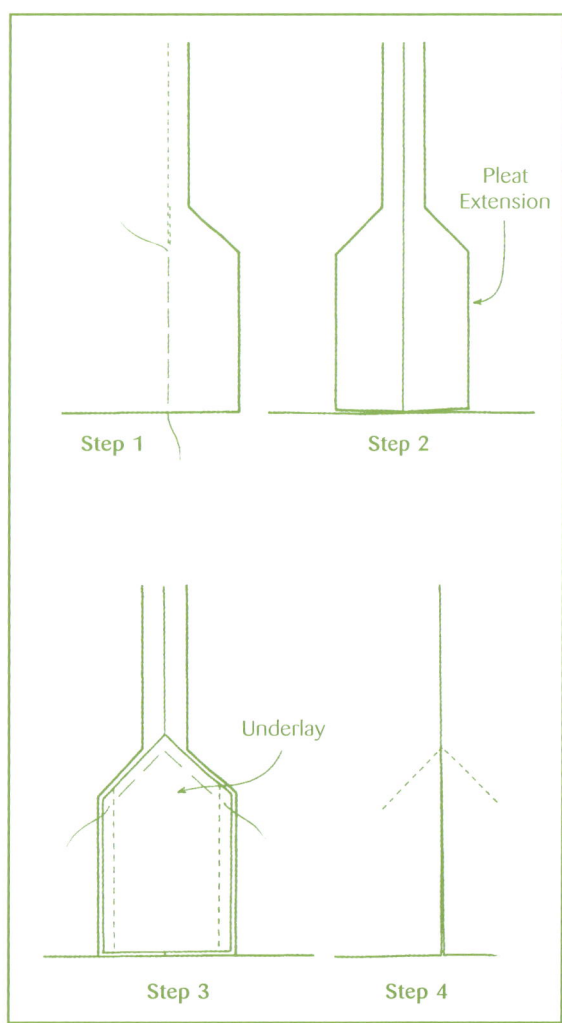

Figure 6.9–Sewing a Pleat with Underlay

Step 1. Stitch seam as required to top of pleat or marking on pattern. Backstitch at end of stitching to prevent pleat from pulling out. Baste pleat together along foldline.

Step 2. Press open the pleat extensions.

Step 3. Place underlay on top of pleat extensions, right sides together, lining up edges. Stitch seams along both sides through underlay and extension, but not through garment. Baste in place along top edge.

Step 4. On right side, stitch across top of pleat to hold it in place, following contour of pleat. Remove basting along pleat foldline and finish hem. If fabric is bulky, it would be wise to finish hems separately on garment and underlay before stitching pleat.

Zippers in Pleated Skirts

When a skirt has box pleats or inverted box pleats, the skirt seam will usually fall where two folds of the pleat come together. Use this seam for your zipper. If pleats meet at seam, zipper will be covered by folds after insertion is completed (Figure 6.10). If pleats do not meet at seam, zipper will be the same as in any other garment.

You can use either lapped or centered application in this case (Figure 6.11).

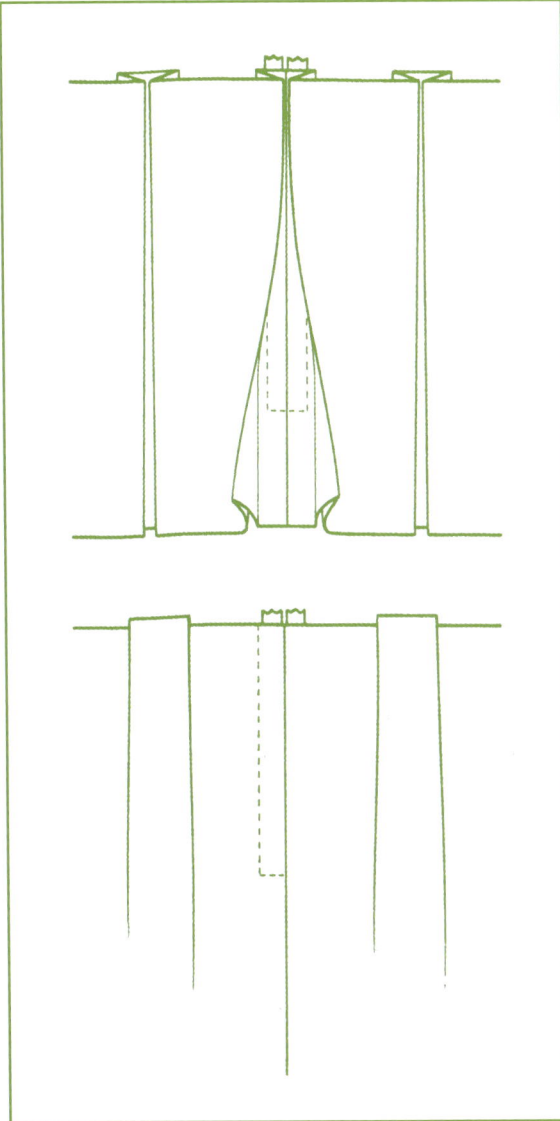

Figure 6.10 – (Top) Applying Zipper where Pleats Meet at Seam
Figure 6.11 – (Bottom) Applying a Zipper where Pleats Do Not Meet at Seam

In a knife-pleated skirt, the zipper is usually inserted in the side or back seam with this special lapped application:

Step 1. Stitch seam to zipper opening.

Step 2. Clip *left* seam allowance at bottom of opening. Turn back seam allowance and press or baste in place on wrong side (Figure 6.12).

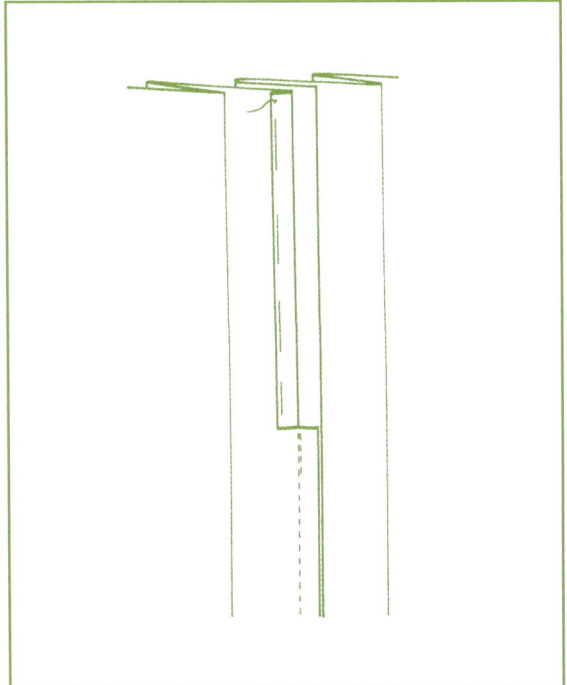

Figure 6.12

Step 3. From right side, stitch zipper in place along folded edge of seam allowance (Figure 6.13).

Step 4. From wrong side of garment, place other half of zipper along edge of unclipped seam allowance, with teeth just over seamline. Baste or tape in place.

Step 5. Stitch zipper to seam allowance (Figure 6.14).

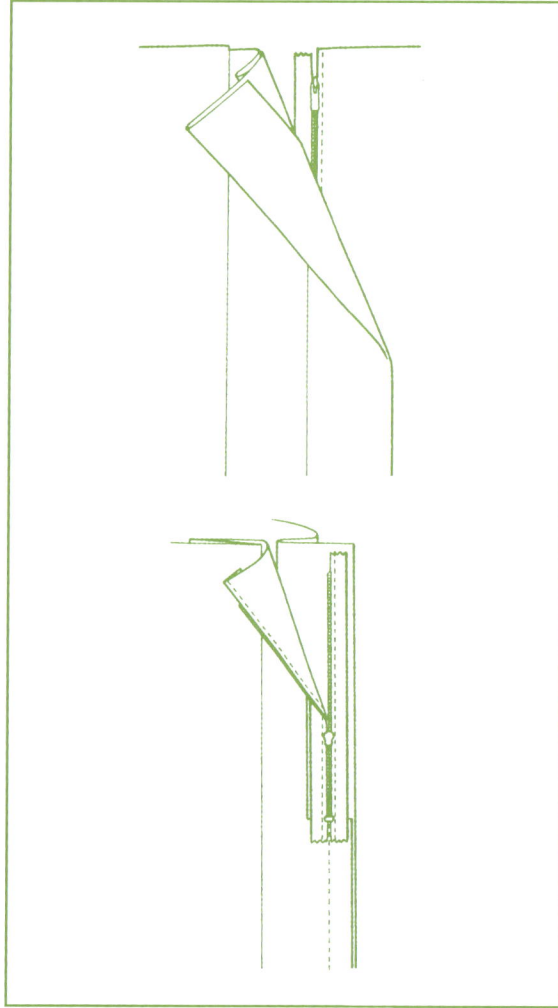

Figure 6.13—(Top)
Figure 6.14—(Bottom)

Hems in Pleated Garments

Hems in pleated garments should always be finished before the pleats are pressed or edgestitched. For heavy fabrics, it is best to finish the hem before the last seam is sewn. Sew the last seam through the finished hem, starting at the bottom edge of the skirt. Trim bottom edge of seam allowance on an angle and overcast the edges of the seam allowances together (Figure 6.15).

If the seam is to be pressed open, overcast the edges separately. See Figure 6.16.

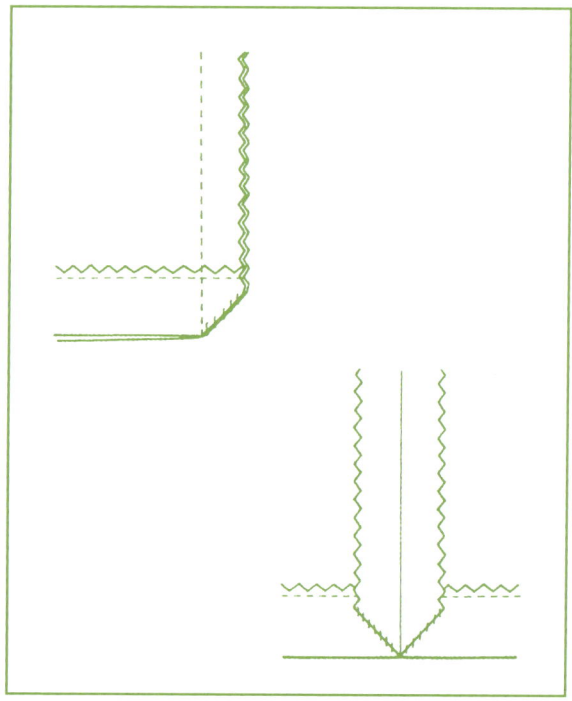

Figure 6.15—(Top)
Figure 6.16—(Bottom)

On lighter weight fabrics, the hem can be finished after the last seam is sewn. Press seam open and grade seam allowance in hem area to reduce bulk (Figure 6.17). Turn up hem and sew in place. If this seam is at the back fold of a pleat, make a clip in seam allowance at top of hem (Figure 6.18). Fold hem on seamline, right sides together. Press seam allowance together. Starting at bottom of hem, stitch through all thicknesses close to seam, tapering stitching into seam above hem (Figure 6.19). Tie thread ends or backstitch at bottom edge of hem.

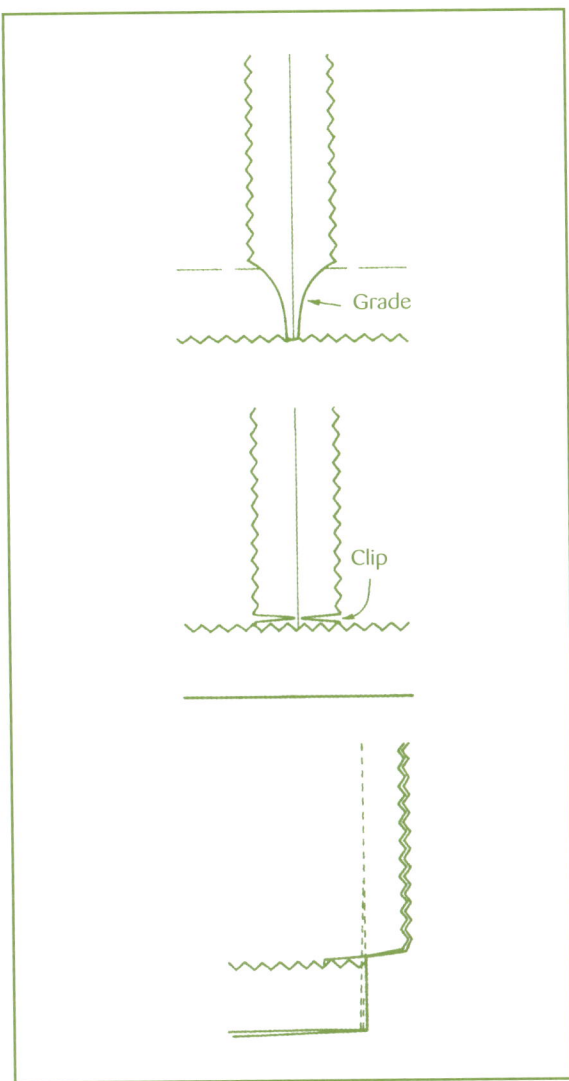

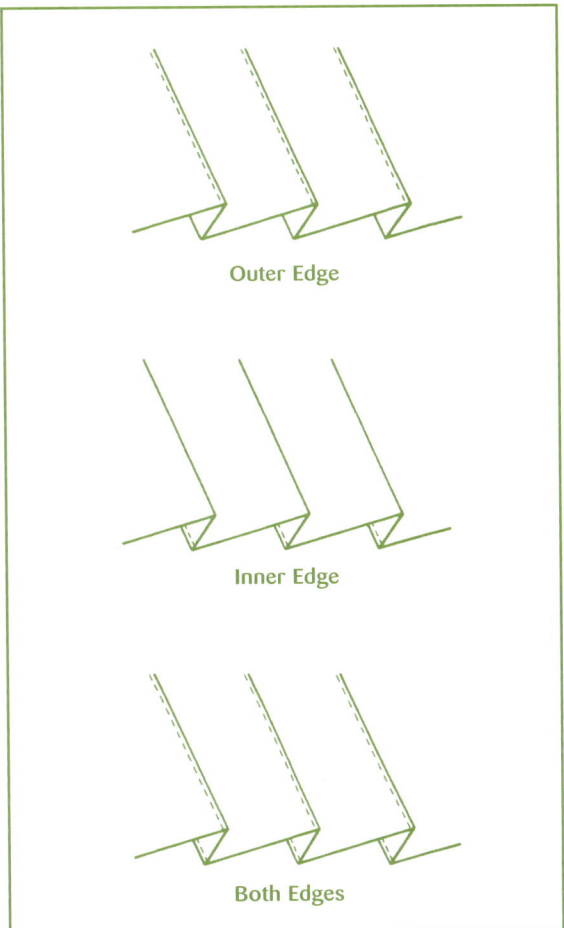

Figure 6.20–Edgestitching Pleats

Figure 6.17–(Top)
Figure 6.18–(Center)
Figure 6.19–(Bottom)

Edgestitched or Topstitched

Finished pleats may be edgestitched, if desired, to hold them in proper position. This edgestitching can be done on the outer edge of the fold, the inner edge of the fold, or both (Figure 6.20). The hem of the garment should be completed before any edgestitching is done. Edgestitching will hold pleats in place during laundering and will eliminate the need to repress them after each washing. If your garment is to be dry cleaned, the cleaner will press the pleats each time the garment is cleaned.

Sometimes pleats are topstitched in the hip area to give the garment a nice appearance and to hold the pleats in place. To topstitch pleats evenly, mark each pleat at the hipline with a pin. Stitch from pin to top of garment. Pull thread ends to wrong side at bottom of pleats and tie securely (Figure 6.21).

For inverted box pleats, stitch along folded edge on each side of pleat. Topstitching can be placed 1/4" from fold desired, for an attractive finish. Start at center of pleat, take two or three stitches across bottom of pleat, then pivot and sew along fold to top of pleat. Repeat for other side. Pull thread ends to wrong side and tie securely (Figure 6.22).

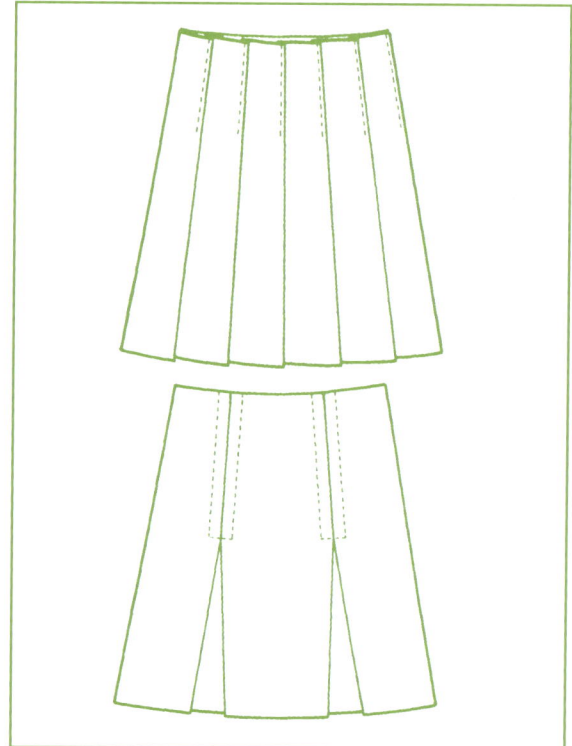

Figure 6.21–(Top) Topstitching Pleats
Figure 6.22–(Bottom) Topstitching Inverted Box Pleats

Plackets

Although most garment openings today are finished with zippers, there is still a need for knowing how to make plackets.

A placket is a finished opening in a garment that allows room for the garment to be put on. A placket can be made in a slash cut in the garment.

There are several types of plackets. Here are four that you should know how to make:

1. *Extension placket*—Sometimes used in a zipper opening when the seam allowance is not wide enough to accommodate the zipper. Can also have snaps, hooks, or nylon tape fasteners (Figure 6.23).

2. *Continuous lap placket*—A placket finished with a continuous lap of fabric. Used most often on sleeves with cuffs (Figure 6.24).

3. *Faced placket*—Usually used at necklines. Can also be used on sleeves with cuffs (Figure 6.25).

4. *Tab placket*—Commonly seen on sportswear for both men and women. Decorative as well as functional. Used frequently on knit fabrics (Figure 6.26).

When making plackets, remember that openings in men's garments lap left over right, and in women's garments, right over left. When plackets are used in the back of a woman's garment, the left back will usually lap over the right back. In side seams and in sleeves, plackets lap front

In a Slash

In a Seam

Figure 6.23–(Left) Extension Placket
Figure 6.24–(Right) Continuous Lap Placket

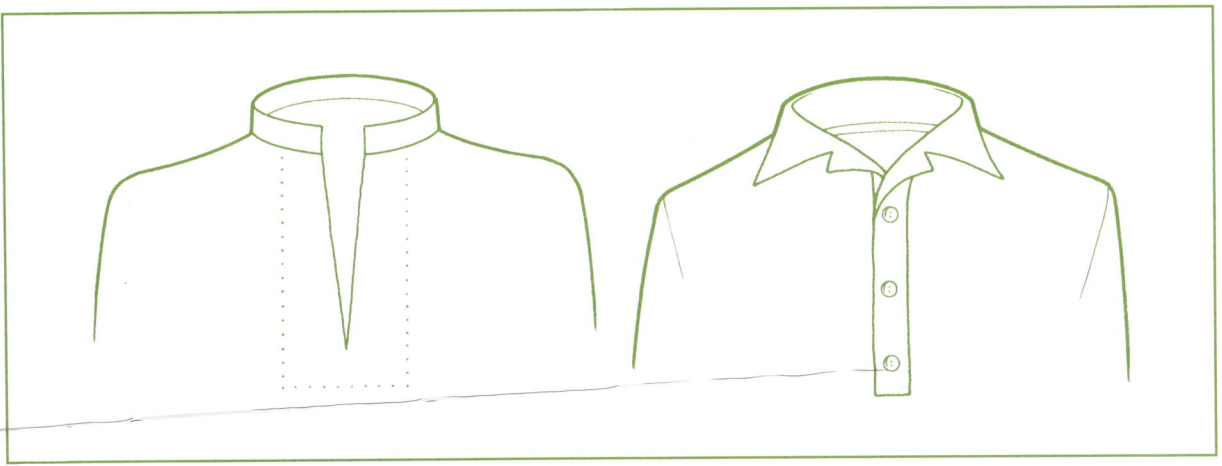

Figure 6.25–(Left) Faced Placket
Figure 6.26–(Right) Tab Placket

over back. Occasional variations may occur due to the styling of the garment.

A well-made placket should be flat and inconspicuous. The overlap should completely cover the underlap. A tab placket should have neat, square corners; it should lie flat and not pucker or bulge when the garment is fastened. Accuracy in slashing and stitching will make it easy for you to obtain a professional look in your plackets.

Extension Placket

This is a simple placket to make. It consists of two strips of fabric sewn to the seam allowance on each side of the placket opening. The strips are usually cut from the garment fabric. If the garment fabric is heavy or bulky, use a lighter weight fabric in a matching color. These extensions can be attached before the seam is sewn.

For a lapped zipper application, you will need an extension only on the edge that will overlap the zipper. The extension strips can be cut on the bias if the placket is curved and will be used with a zipper, as in the side seam of a skirt or pants. This will make it easier for you to sew the strips to the garment fabric and obtain a smooth, flat finish.

Where the opening is straight, the extension strips can be cut on the lengthwise grain of the fabric.

There are several ways of applying the extensions. Follow the method that is best for your fabric and garment.

Method 1

The extensions in this method are made from a single layer of fabric, as shown in Figure 6.27. Use this method on heavy, bulky fabrics; use it also when making an extension for a zipper opening.

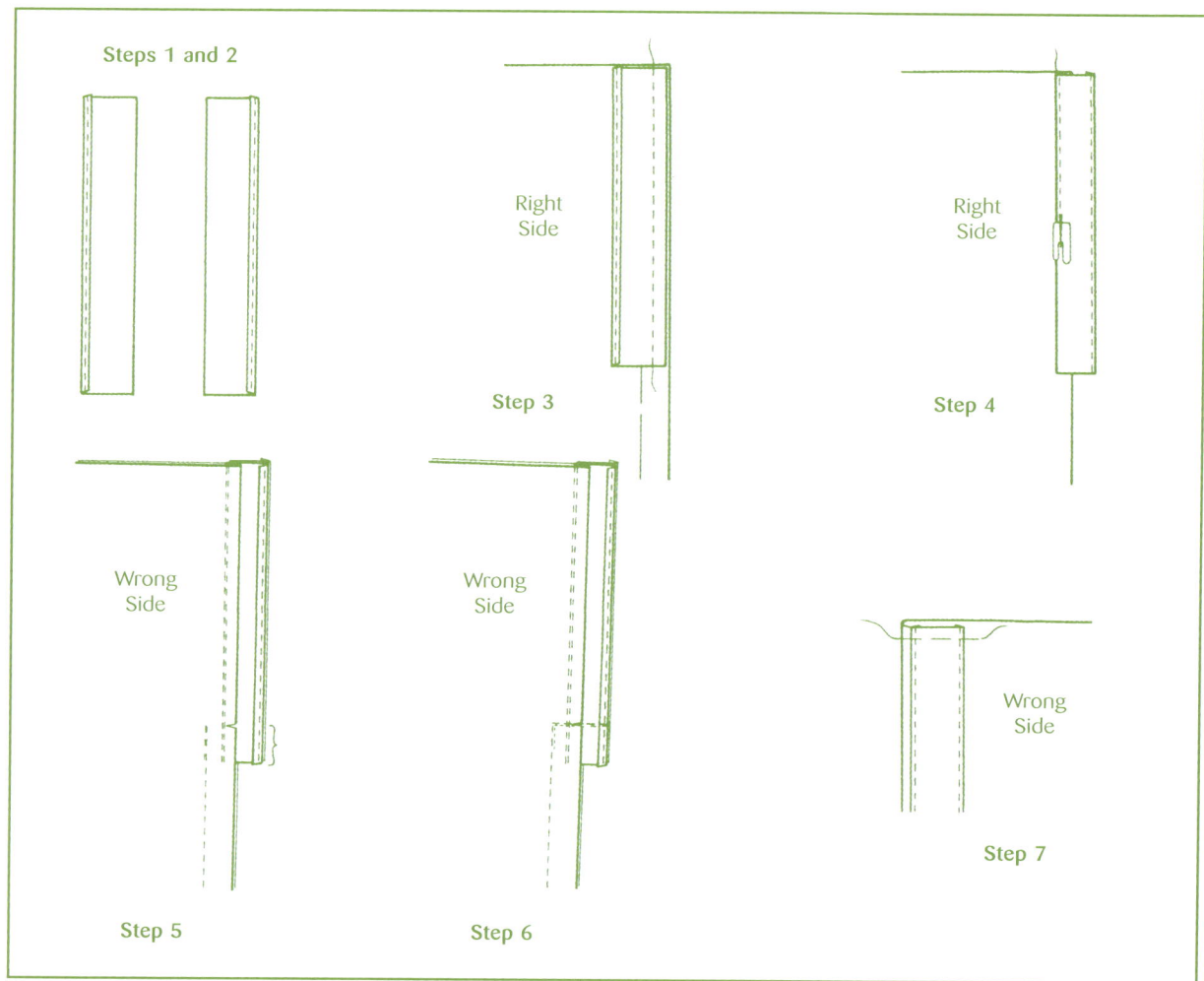

Figure 6.27–Extension Placket–Method 1

Step 1. Cut two strips of fabric 1-1/2" wide and 1" longer than placket opening.

Step 2. Finish one long edge of each extension strip in any manner suitable to your fabric (clean-finish, zigzag, or overcast). If fabric does not ravel, leave edge unfinished.

Step 3. With right sides together, lay one extension strip in one seam allowance of placket opening, matching raw edges at top and side. Sew 3/8" seam.

Step 4. Turn extension strip away from garment. Understitch close to seamed edge.

Step 5. Apply second extension to other seam allowance in the same way. If zipper is to be inserted, stitch seam below placket, using regular 5/8" seam allowance. Backstitch at bottom of opening. If zipper will not be used, finish seam and bottom of placket in the following manner:

Step 6. Stitch seam to bottom of placket opening, pivot and stitch to edge of extension strips, backstitching at end of stitching. To reinforce corner, use small stitch for 1/2" each side of corner or make a second row of stitching just outside the first.

Step 7. Turn extensions to one side, making sure garment opening laps in the right direction. Press seam in the same direction as the placket extensions. To hold overlap in place, machine baste through garment and overlap in garment seam allowance at top of opening.

Method 2

These extensions are made from a folded strip of fabric, as in Figure 6.28. This is a stronger extension for snaps or hooks and eyes since it is a double layer of fabric. Use this method on lighter weight fabrics.

Step 1. Cut two strips of fabric 2-1/2" wide and 1" longer than placket opening.

Step 2. Fold each strip in half lengthwise, wrong sides together, and press. Unfold strips. Fold under and press 1/4" on one long edge of each strip.

Step 3. Lay *right* side of strip on *wrong* side of garment, matching top and side edges of strip and garment seam allowance. Sew 3/8" seam.

Step 4. Press strip away from garment.

Step 5. Apply second strip to other seam allowance in the same manner.

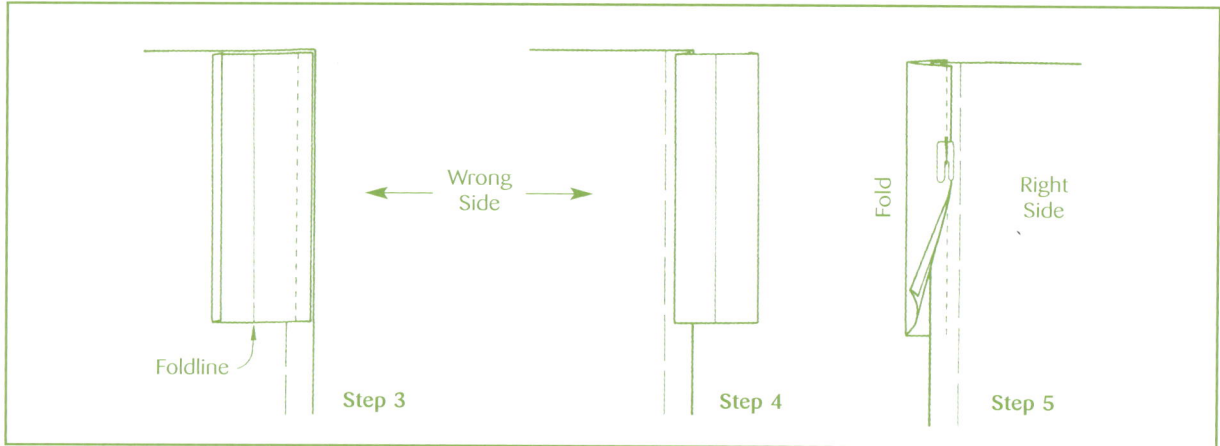

Figure 6.28–Extension Placket–Method 2

Step 6. Turn strips to right side of fabric on foldlines, covering previous stitching. Topstitch in place. Finish seam as in Method 1, Steps 6 and 7.

Method 3

This is a quicker method for applying a folded extension. The raw edges will not be enclosed as they are in Method 2. Use this method on closely woven fabrics that crease well and do not ravel easily, such as gingham and other lightweight fabrics.

Step 1. Cut two strips of fabric 2-1/2" wide and 1" longer than placket opening.

Step 2. Fold strips in half lengthwise, wrong sides together, and press.

Step 3. Place folded strip on right side of garment, raw edges even with edge of garment seam allowance. Sew 3/8" seam (Figure 6.29). Repeat for other strip.

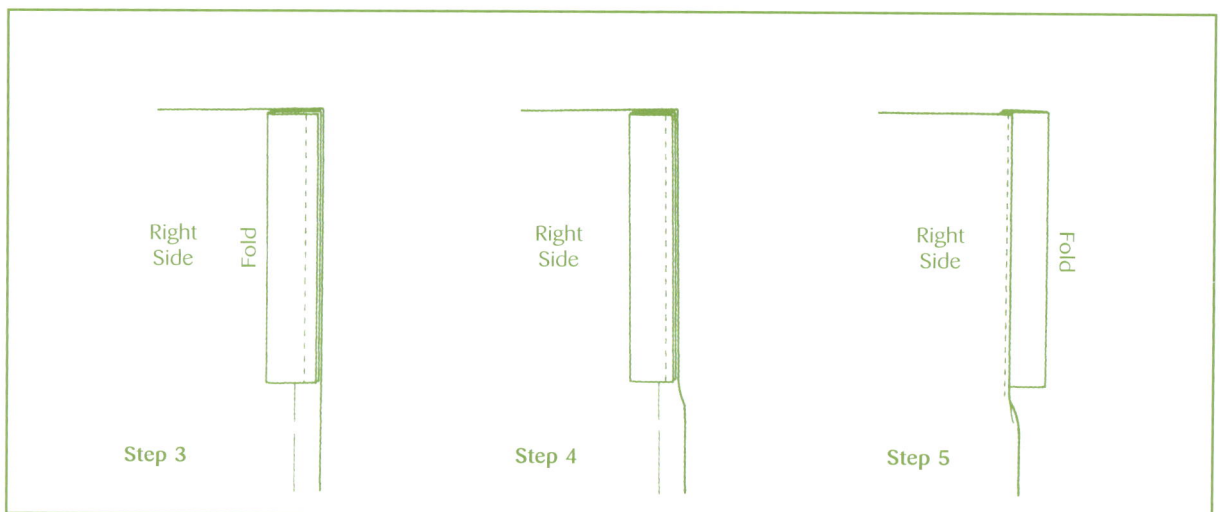

Figure 6.29–Extension Placket–Method 3

Step 4. Trim seam allowances in extension area to a scant 1/4" (Figure 6.29).

Step 5. Turn extensions *away* from garment, allowing seam allowances to turn *toward* garment. This will create a small fold in the seam allowance at the bottom of the extension. Understitch close to seam to hold extension in place. See Figure 6.29. Finish seam as in Method 1, Steps 6 and 7.

Continuous Lap Placket

A placket with a continuous lap can be made either in a slash or in a seam. When making a placket in a slash, never cut the slash until after it has been stitched for reinforcement.

In a Slash

Step 1. Set machine for 20 stitches to the inch. Make a line of stitching each side of the slash mark. Stitch 1/4" from slash mark at edge of fabric, tapering to a point at the bottom of the slash.

Step 2. Cut on slash mark. See Figure 6.30. Cut all the way to the point, being careful not to cut the stitches. Spread slash open.

Step 3. Cut a strip of garment fabric 1-1/2" wide and twice the length of the slash. Press under 1/4" from edge of strip.

Step 4. Place *wrong* side of opened slash on *right* side of unpressed edge of strip, placing line of stitching 1/4" from edge of strip. Raw edges will not be even. Stitch 1/4" seam on top of previous stitching (Figure 6.30).

Step 5. Press strip and seam away from garment (Figure 6.30).

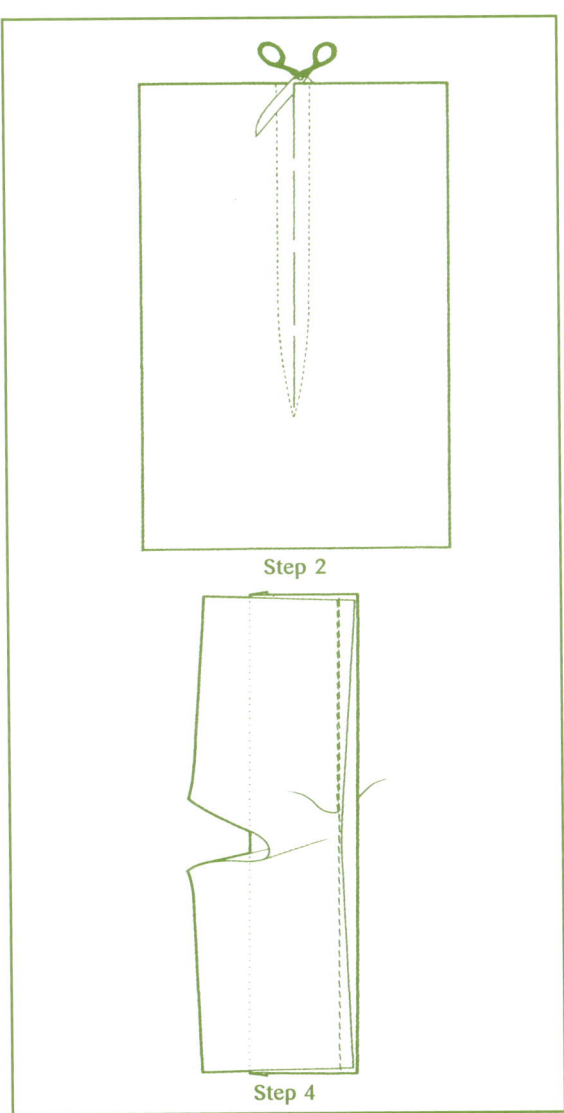

Step 2

Step 4

Figure 6.30–Making a Placket in a Slash

Step 6. Fold strip lengthwise and place pressed edge over seam, covering stitching. Topstitch in place as in Figure 6.30.

Step 7. Close placket. On inside of garment, stitch diagonally back and forth across folded end of lap to hold it in place (Figure 6.30).

Step 8. Press lap to one side, making sure garment laps in the right direction. Machine baste overlap to garment edge at top of placket to hold it in place (Figure 6.30).

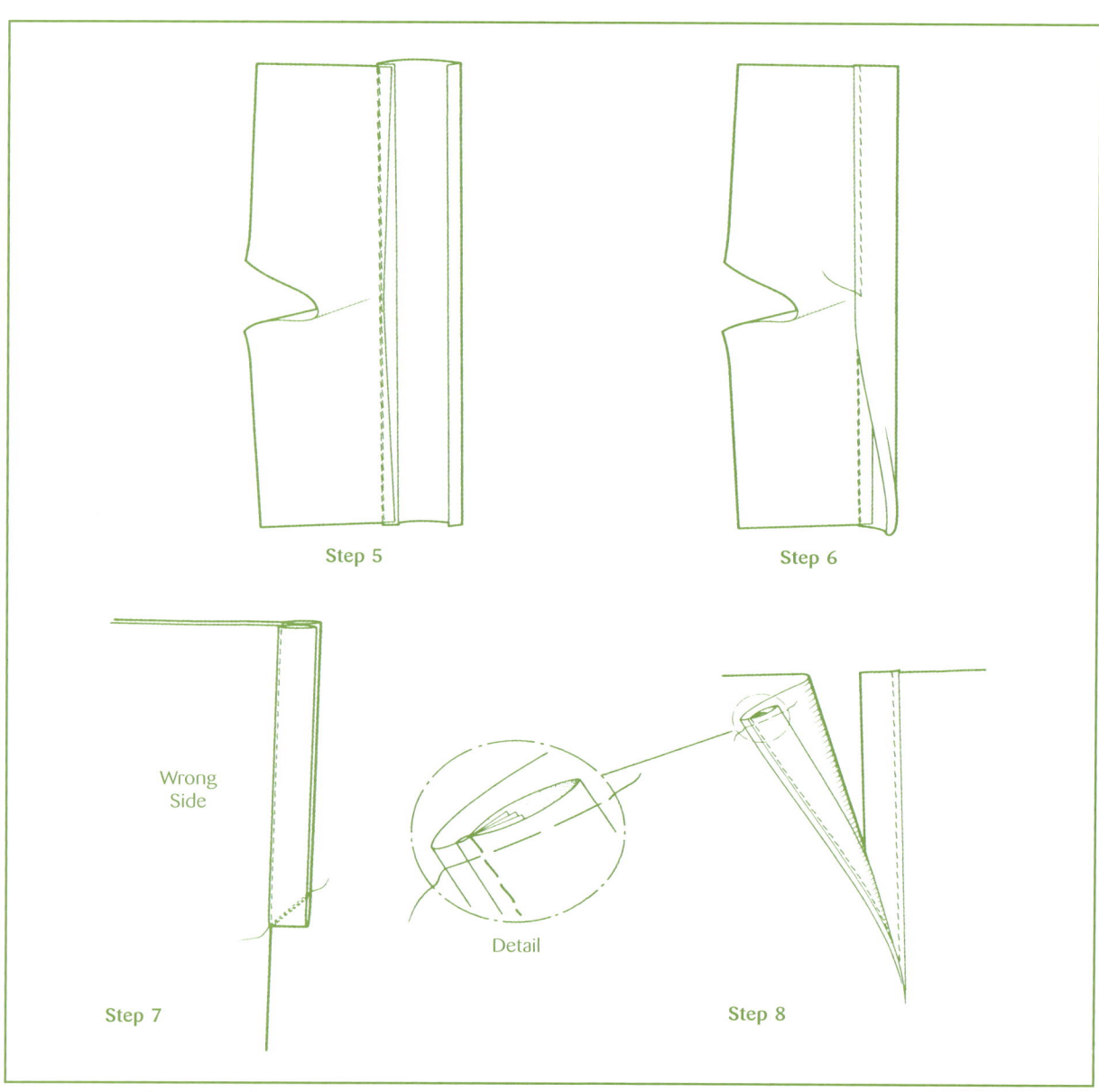

Step 5

Step 6

Wrong Side

Detail

Step 7

Step 8

Figure 6.30–(continued) Making a Placket in a Slash

In a Seam

Step 1. Stitch seam to bottom of placket opening, backstitching at end of stitching. Clip seam allowance to stitching at bottom of placket. Press seam open (Figure 6.31).

Step 2. Cut a strip of fabric 1-3/4" wide and twice the length of the opening. Press under 1/4" on one long edge of strip.

Step 3. Spread placket opening, extending seam allowances. Pin *wrong* side of garment to *right* side of strip. Match edge of seam allowances and edge of strip.

Step 4. Set machine for 20 stitches to the inch. Stitch a 5/8" seam. Reinforce center of seam with a second row of stitching close to the first (Figure 6.31). Trim seam to 1/4". Finish as for a placket in a slash, steps 6 through 8. If you wish to have a hand-finished placket on a fine garment, sew the strips to the *right* side of the slash or seam instead of the wrong side. Follow above directions, finishing by hand on wrong side of garment instead of topstitching on right side, as in Figure 6.32.

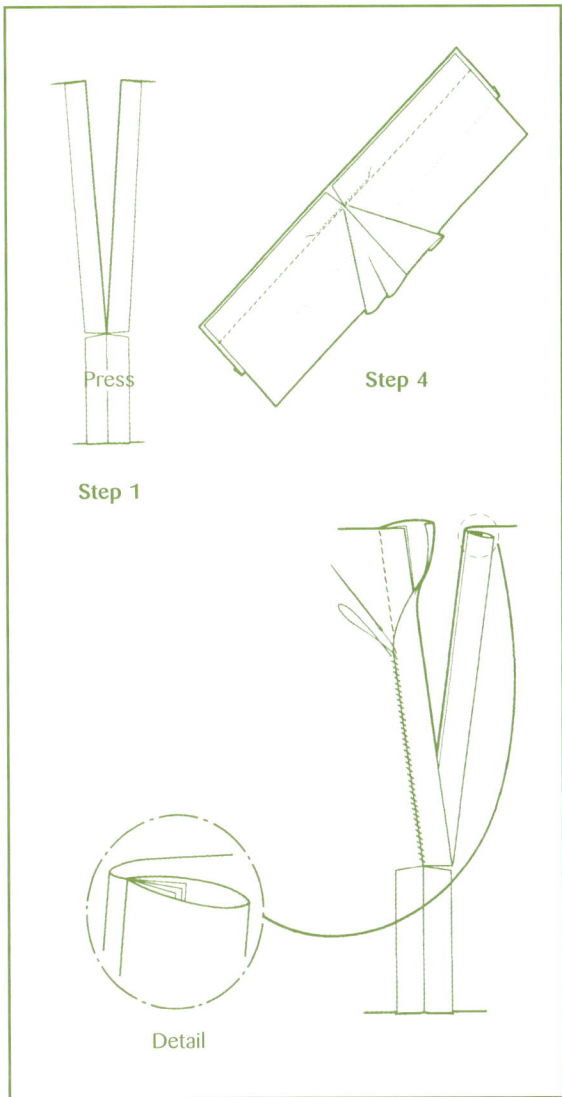

Figure 6.31 – (Top Left and Right) Making Placket in a Seam
Figure 6.32 – (Bottom Left and Right) Hand-Finished Placket

Faced Placket

This placket can be used at the bottom of a cuffed sleeve or at a neckline. It is made with a shaped facing.

Step 1. Clean-finish outer edges of facing, or use any method appropriate to your fabric.

Step 2. Place facing on garment, right sides together, matching raw edges.

Step 3. Set machine for 20 stitches to the inch. Starting 1/4" from slash mark, stitch down one side of slash mark to point. Pivot, take two stitches across point, and pivot again. Stitch up other side of slash mark to edge of fabric, 1/4" from slash mark (Figure 6.33).

Step 4. Slash all the way to the point, being careful not to cut the stitches.

Step 5. Turn facing to inside, carefully straightening fabric at point. Press in place.

Step 6. If garment does not have a collar, neckline facing will be part of placket facing. To attach facing, stitch along neckline seam, then pivot and stitch slash. Pivot again at top of slash and continue with neckline seam. Cut slash (Figure 6.33). Trim, grade, and clip neckline seam. Turn facing to inside and press.

Step 7. Reinforce neckline plackets with a small bar tack on facing only at bottom of opening. See Figure 6.33.

Step 8. To hold facings in place on the sleeves, tack corners to fabric by hand with invisible stitches or use small pieces of fusible webbing.

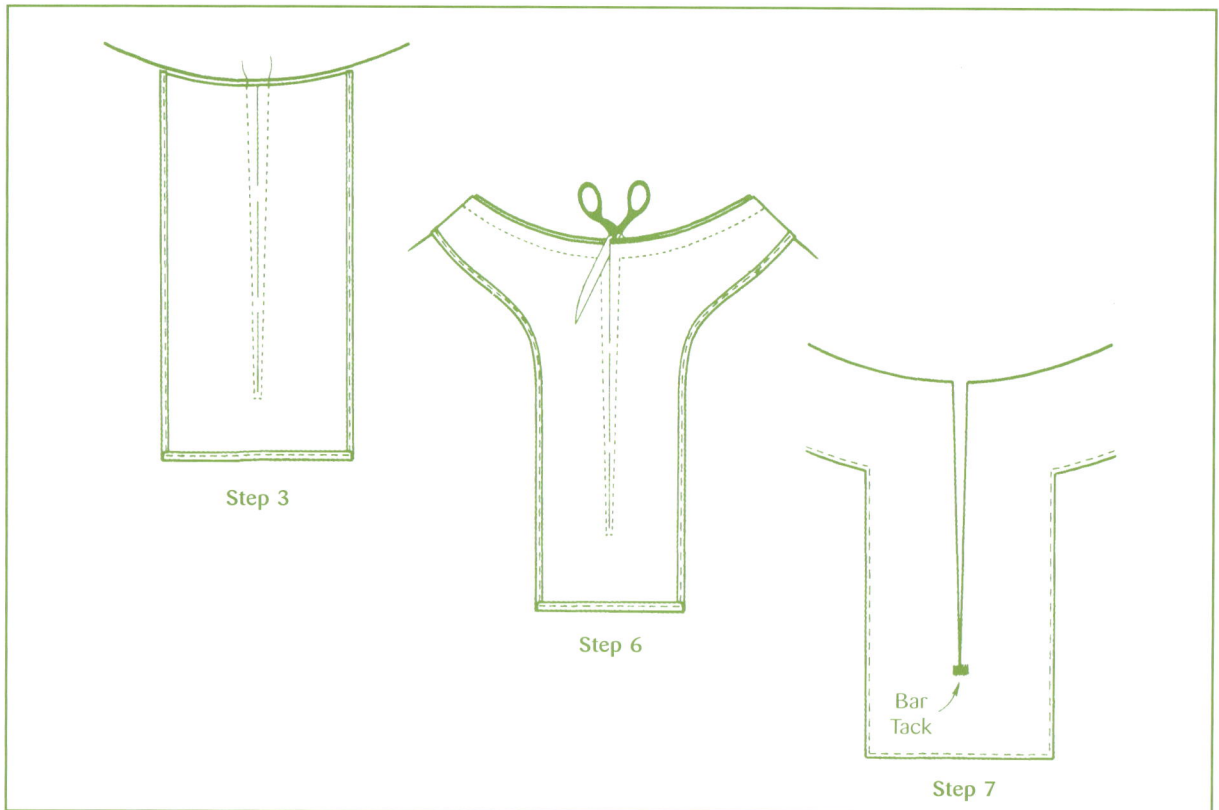

Step 3

Step 6

Bar Tack

Step 7

Figure 6.33—A Placket with a Shaped Facing

A placket facing is sometimes placed on the *outside* of the garment for decoration. The facing is first stitched to the wrong side of the garment. It is turned and topstitched on the right side around the outer edge. It is usually shaped to suit the style of the garment and to give an attractive finish. It is often made from a contrasting fabric. Figure 6.34.

Figure 6.34 – A Placket Facing on the Outside of the Garment

Tab Placket

Tab plackets can be made with either two extension strips or two shaped facings. For plackets that will be worn closed, the extension strip method is very satisfactory and is easy to do. The placket with the shaped facing takes a little more time but is well worth the effort. It is usually used where a tailored collar will be added. The result is a convertible neckline that can be worn open or closed. It is an excellent neckline finish for knit shirts that do not have a front seam.

The tab area of the placket should be interfaced with woven interfacing to provide a backing for the buttonholes. Machine-worked buttonholes are usually used in a tab placket. If you wish to make bound buttonholes, they must be done before the tabs are sewn to the garment.

The length and width of a tab placket can be varied. The most commonly used finished width for men's and women's clothing is 1-1/2". Plackets on men's shirts can be up to 2" wide. On children's clothing, the placket should be 1" wide. The placket opening should allow enough room for the garment to be pulled over the head. A placket 9"-10" long will give sufficient room for a man; a placket 8"-9" long will be adequate for a woman. For a child, make the tab proportionately shorter—7" to 8" is about average.

Instructions below are for a placket 1-1/2" wide and 9" long. You may want to try your hand at making a sample. We think you'll be pleased with the results!

Tab Placket with Extension Strips

The following steps are shown in Figure 6.35 (except Step 7).

Figure 6.35–Tab Placket with Extension Strips

Step 1. On wrong side of garment, draw a line 3/4" each side of center front line. Make each line 9" long. Draw a straight line across the bottom connecting these two lines. This is the outline of your placket. Make sure these lines are very straight and are on the straight grain of the fabric. They should be exactly 1-1/2" apart for their entire length. Stitch on this outline with machine set at 20 stitches to the inch.

Step 2. Slash down center front line to within 1" of bottom of placket. Slash diagonally all the way to the corners. Be careful not to cut stitching.

Step 3. Trim cut edges on each side of center front opening to 1/4".

Step 4. Cut two strips of fabric 3-1/2" wide and 10" long. Cut two strips of interfacing 1-3/4" wide and 10" long. Apply interfacing to one half of each extension strip.

Step 5. Pin right side of strip (the half without the interfacing) to wrong side of garment, matching top and side edges.

Step 6. With garment right side up, stitch 1/4" seam, following previous stitching line. Stitch all the way to the corner, backstitching at end of stitching line. Sew second strip to garment in the same way.

Step 7. Press strips away from garment. Press under 1/4" on long, unfinished edge of strip.

Step 8. Fold each strip in half lengthwise, *right* sides together. Line up outside folded edge of strip with seam. Using 5/8" seam allowance, stitch across top of strip for 3/4" from folded edge to center front line. Backstitch to reinforce.

Step 9. Clip seam allowance at end of stitching. Trim seam allowance from fold to end of stitching.

Step 10. Turn strip right side out. Pin folded edge of strip in place on top of seam, covering previous stitching. Topstitch in place. Topstitch along folded edge of strip if desired. Repeat for other strip.

Step 11. Lap one strip over the other, lining up edges and matching center fronts. Pin or tape in place. Tuck lower ends of strips inside opening. Tuck triangular wedge at bottom of opening to wrong side of garment.

Step 12. Raise lower edge of garment front and position wedge on top of strips, pulling gently to square corners of placket. Pin in place. Check on right side to make sure bottom of placket is straight and corners are square.

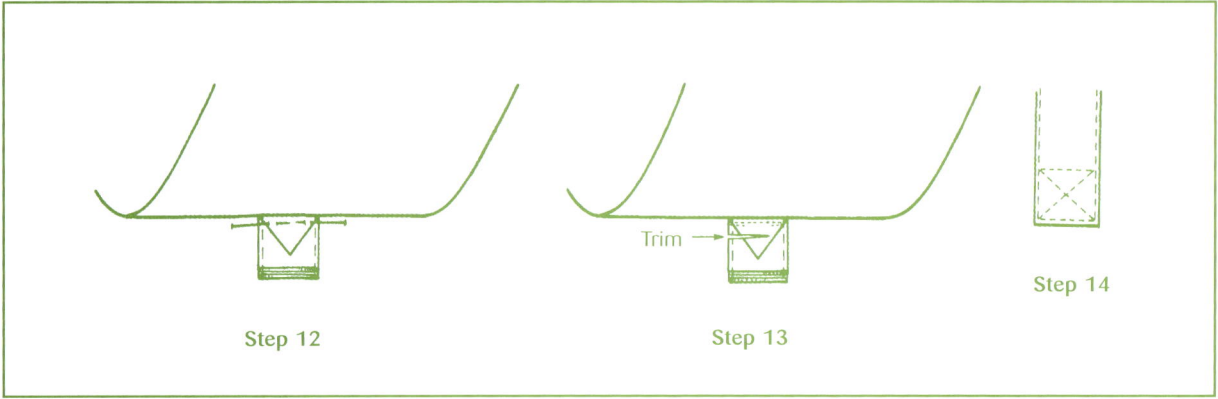

Figure 6.35 – (continued) Tab Placket with Extension Strips

Step 13. Using small stitch (15-20 per inch), stitch across wedge and strips from wrong side of garment, following previous stitching. Backstitch at each end of stitching for reinforcement. Trim seam to 1/4". This is the same technique used on the ends of buttonholes.

Step 14. On outside of garment, make a double triangle of stitching through both strips.

Tab Placket with Shaped Facing

Most patterns with this style of tab front placket and collar will contain a shaped-facing pattern piece. Instructions will, of course, be included in the pattern, but we have given you a preview here so that you can see how they are made. We've even included instructions for making your own pattern for this type of placket. You can convert any plain round neck pattern to this type of opening.

To make your facing pattern, follow these instructions:

Step 1. Cut a 15" square of tissue paper. Draw a line 2-1/2" from one edge.

Step 2. Lay the tissue over your garment front pattern piece with the line on the tissue over the center front line of the pattern piece. Bottom of tissue should be 10" below neckline edge. Trace the neckline and shoulder edge (Figure 6.36).

Step 3. Make a mark on shoulder 2-1/2" from neck edge. Make a mark on bottom edge of tissue 2" from center front line. Connect these two marks with a curved line as illustrated in Figure 6.36.

Step 4. Draw a line 3/4" to the right of the center front line. This will be your foldline.

Step 5. Remove tissue and fold on foldline. Continue neckline marking to edge of fold.

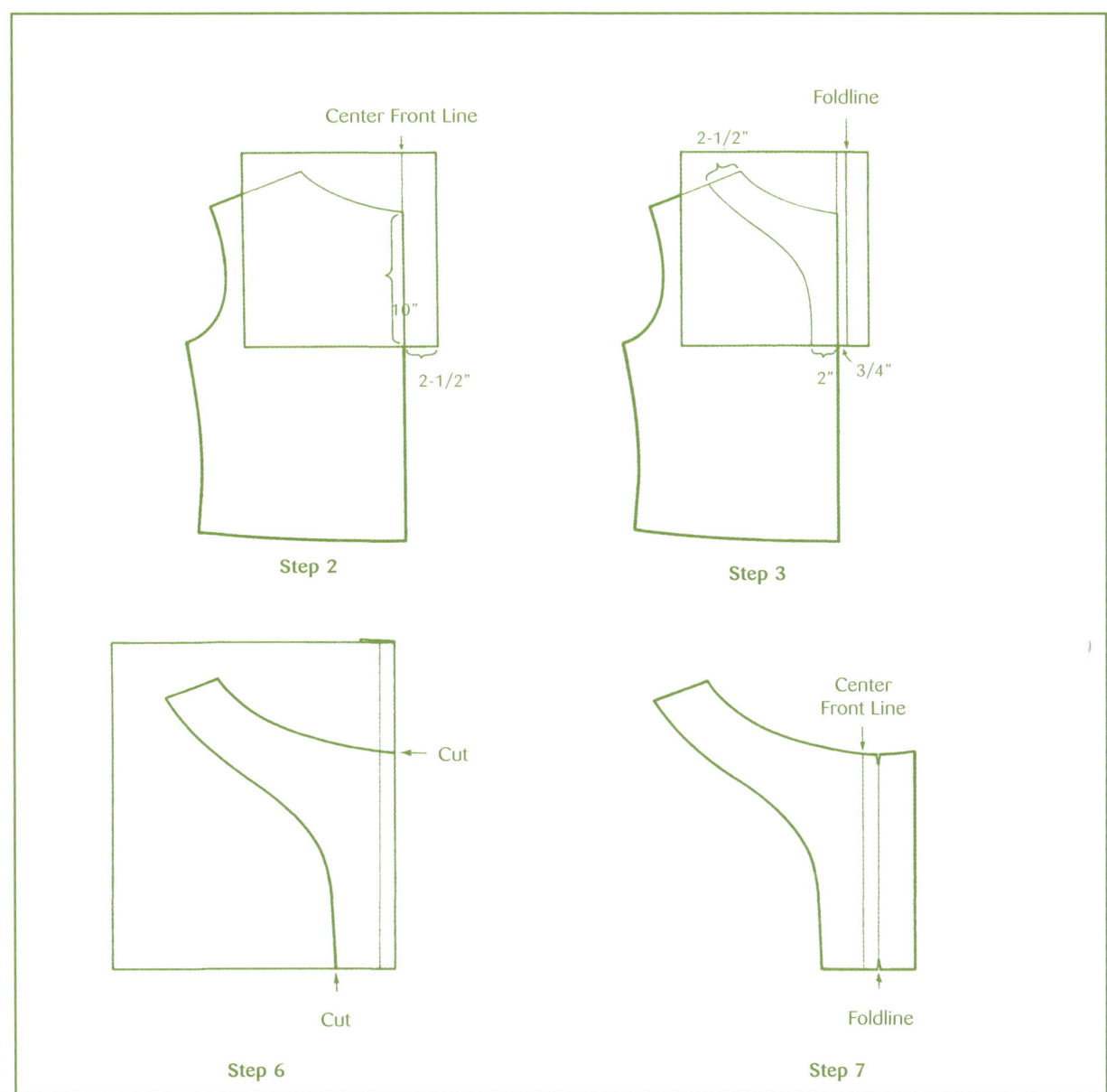

Figure 6.36—Tab Placket with Shaped Facing

Step 6. Cut out your facing pattern, following the lines you have drawn on the tissue (do *not* cut on center front line). See Figure 6.36. Unfold tissue.

Step 7. You now have a pattern for your facing pieces. Make clip marks at top and bottom of foldline. See Figure 6.36.

Now that your pattern is finished, you are ready to make your placket. Cut two facing pieces with this pattern piece.

Study the following instructions for making your placket, as shown in Figure 6.37 (except Step 7).

Step 1. Using tailor's chalk or pencil, draw two straight lines on the outside of your garment front. Make these lines 9" long and draw them 1/2" each side of the center front. These lines must be exactly 1" apart all the way down. They will be your guidelines when stitching. Connect these lines with a chalk line across the bottom.

Step 2. On the wrong side of each facing piece, sew or fuse a strip of interfacing 1-3/4" wide and 10" long.

Step 3. Fold and press each facing piece on the foldline (at the edge of the interfacing), wrong sides together.

Step 4. Reinforce bottom of placket by stitching with a small stitch across the bottom and 1/4" outside each line for about 1" up each side.

Step 5. Unfold facings and place on garment front, right sides together. Edges of facings should be placed on chalk lines. Top edge of facings should be at edge of garment. Stitch facings to garment in 1/4" seams. Seams should be exactly 1-1/2" apart all the way down. Stop exactly at bottom of chalk line. Backstitch to reinforce stitching.

Step 6. Cut garment front on chalk lines to within 1" of bottom. Turn garment to wrong side. Cut diagonally to corners, making a large wedge at bottom of placket. Cut all the way to the corners for a nice, square placket, but be careful not to cut the stitching or the facing fabric.

Step 7. Press seam allowances toward garment (if you plan to topstitch your collar and facing, press seam allowances toward facings).

Step 8. Lay garment right side up and fold facings under on foldlines.

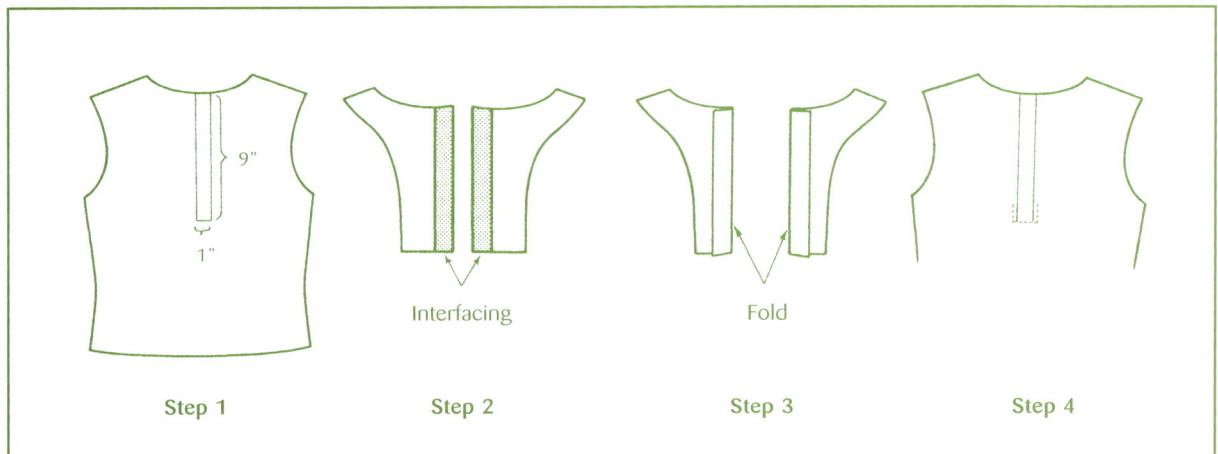

Figure 6.37—Tab Placket with Shaped Facing; Making the Placket

Tuck wedge and lower ends of facings inside garment, lapping tabs in the direction you want them to go. Line up side edge of top tab with seam of bottom tab. Pin or tape in place. Neckline edges of facings will line up with neckline edges of garment. Pin edges in place.

Step 9. Lift bottom of garment and position wedge on top of facings. Pin in place. Check on right side to make sure bottom is straight and corners are square. Stitch across wedge and facings with small stitch to secure wedge. Your placket is finished and ready for a collar.

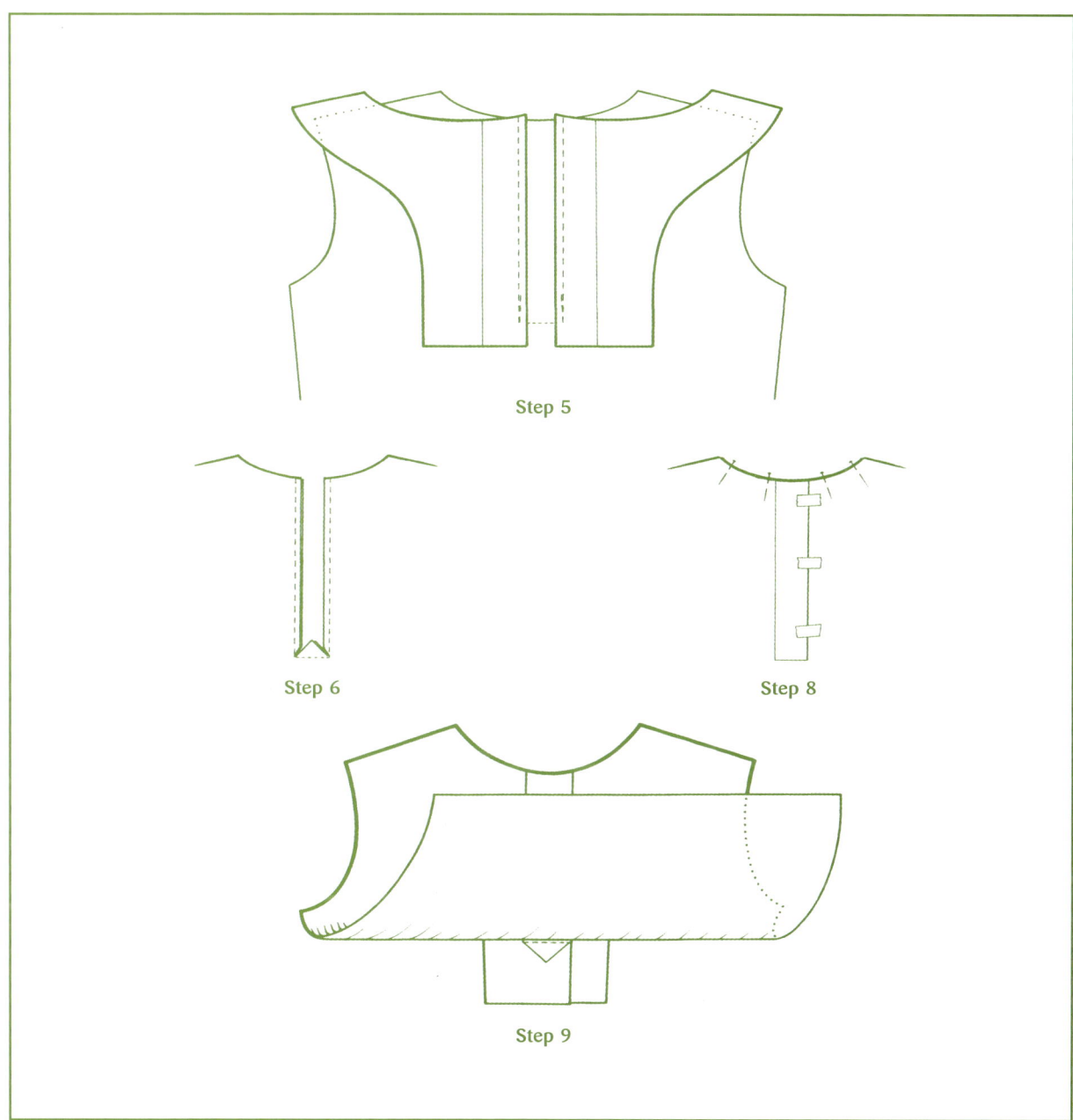

Figure 6.37—(continued)

Before continuing with your reading, answer the following multiple-choice questions to check what you have already learned.

1. Pleats with folds all turned to the side in one direction are _____ pleats.

    a. accordion
    b. knife
    c. inverted

2. Pleats with two folds that meet in the center on the underside are _____ pleats.

    a. box
    b. inverted
    c. accordion

3. _____ pleats work best in soft fabrics.

    a. Unpressed
    b. Sunburst
    c. Pressed

4. _____ should always be finished before the pleats are pressed or edge-stitched.

    a. Hems
    b. Plackets
    c. Gathers

5. A/an _____ placket is used most often on sleeves with cuffs.

    a. extension
    b. tab
    c. continuous lap

6. The _____ placket is commonly seen on sportswear.

a. faced

b. tab

c. extension

Check your answers with those provided on page 199.

PART FOUR

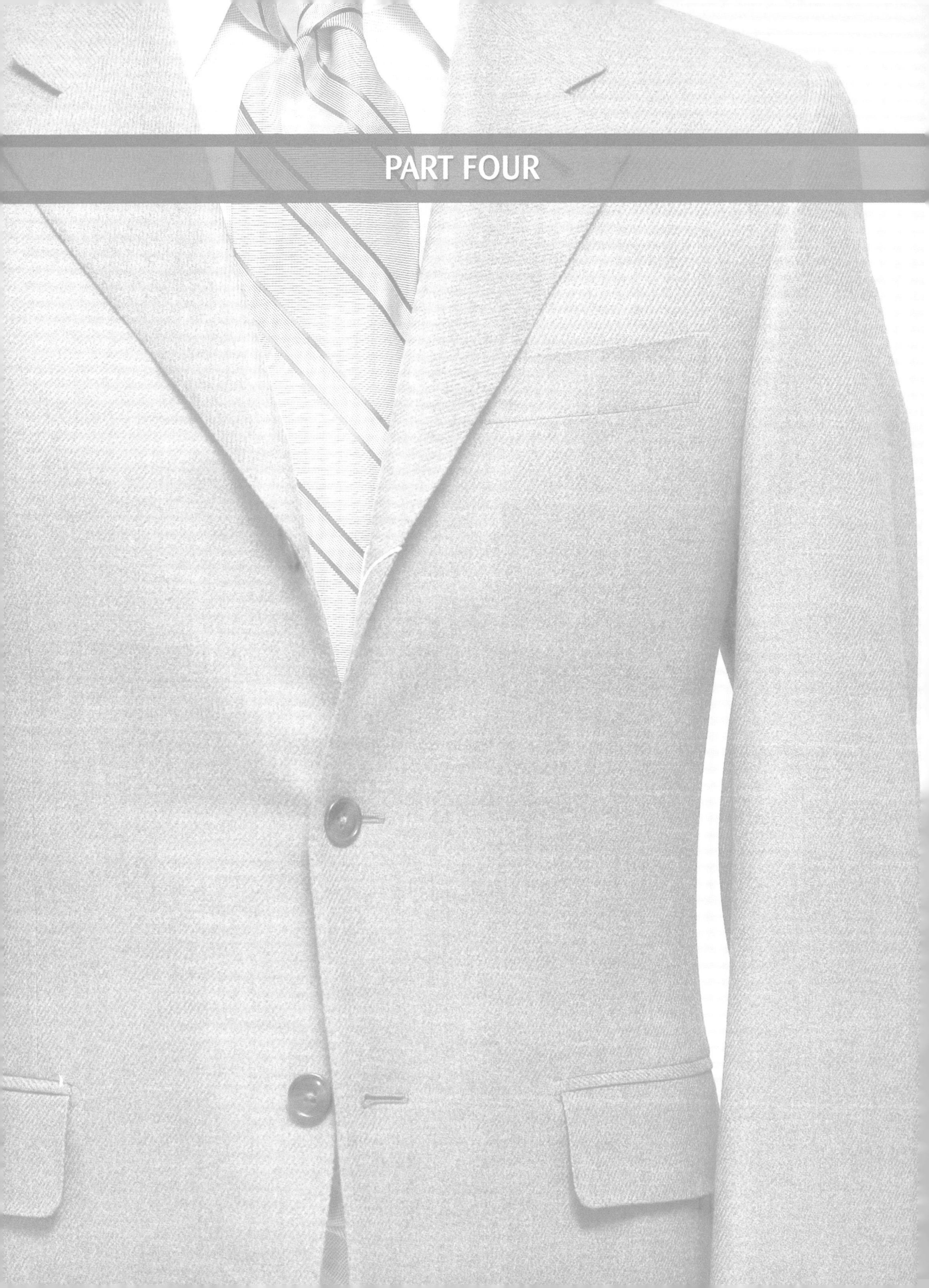

RUFFLES, FACINGS, COLLARS, AND SLEEVES

Overview

In this fourth part, we will continue the explanation of detail techniques. Facings, ruffles, collars, and sleeves, covered in this part, all add to the shape and style of a garment. Perfecting these construction techniques can add to the professional look of a garment you sew. At the completion of this part, you will be able to

- Name different types of facings and explain construction methods
- List and define the different ruffles
- Explain the construction techniques used with collars
- Match names and definitions connected with sleeves and sleeve styles

FACINGS

Introduction

A facing is a piece of fabric that finishes the raw edge of a garment. It is used most frequently at necklines and sleeveless armholes. A facing is usually made of the garment material, but when the fabric is bulky a lining material can be used. Facings do not show on the right side, except on garments with lapels that turn back. There are basically three types of facings:

1. *Shaped*—cut to the same shape as the garment edge to be faced (Figure 7.1).

2. *Extended*—attached to the garment and cut in one piece with the garment piece (Figure 7.2).

3. *Bias*—a bias strip used singly, or folded and used double (Figure 7.3).

Shaped Facings

Shaped facings are cut the same shape as the garment edge to be finished. They are sewn flat to the garment and turned to the underside after stitching. The raw edge of the facing is finished in any manner suitable to the garment. On firm knits and fabrics that don't ravel, no finish is needed. On bulky fabrics, the raw edge can be stitched and pinked. On lightweight and medium-weight fabrics, the raw edge can be clean-finished (turned under 1/4" and stitched). To make it easier to turn under a curved edge, make a line of stitching 1/4" from the edge and fold on this line.

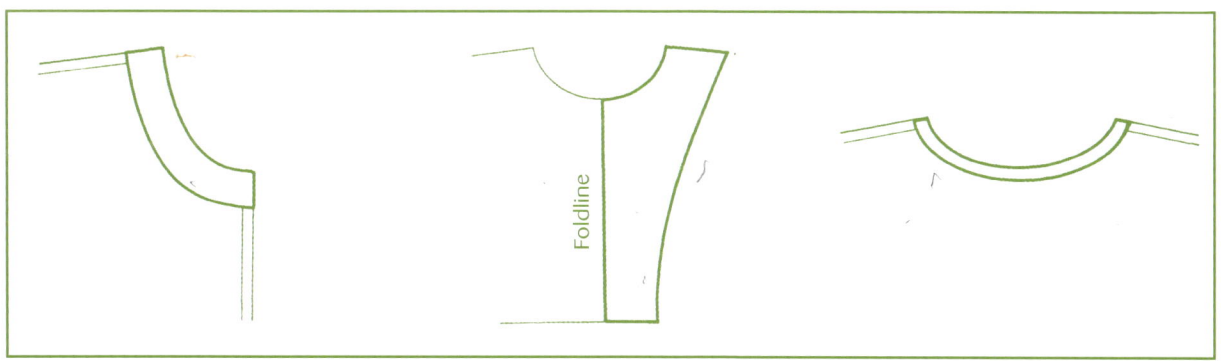

Figure 7.1–Shaped Facing   Figure 7.2–Extended Facing   Figure 7.3–Bias Facing

Most faced edges need an interfacing to help them hold their shape. If *regular interfacing* is used, it is sewn to the *garment* fabric before the facing is applied. Trim the outer edge of the interfacing if it is cut from the facing pattern. This will keep it from showing beyond the edge of the facing. If *fusible interfacing* is used, it is applied to the *facing* rather than the garment, to prevent a ridge from showing on the outside of the garment. Be sure to trim seam allowances from interfacing before fusing.

To apply a shaped neckline facing, follow these directions:

Step 1. Sew facing pieces together at shoulder seams. Trim seam allowances to 1/4". Press seams open (Figure 7.4).

Step 2. Finish outer edge of facing in any manner appropriate to your fabric.

Step 3. Place facing on garment right sides together, matching notches and shoulder seams. Stitch around neck on seamline (Figure 7.5).

Step 4. Trim and grade seam allowance. Turn seam allowance toward facing. Understitch facing close to seam; this helps the facing to roll to the wrong side of the garment and stay in place (Figure 7.6).

Step 5. Turn facing to underside of garment and press in place. Tack loosely at seams by hand, or hold in place with a piece of fusible web; or stitch in the ditch on the right side of the fabric (Figure 7.7).

If your neckline is V-shaped or square, be sure to reinforce the corners with small stitches when applying the facing. Clip all the way to the corners before turning, but be careful not to cut

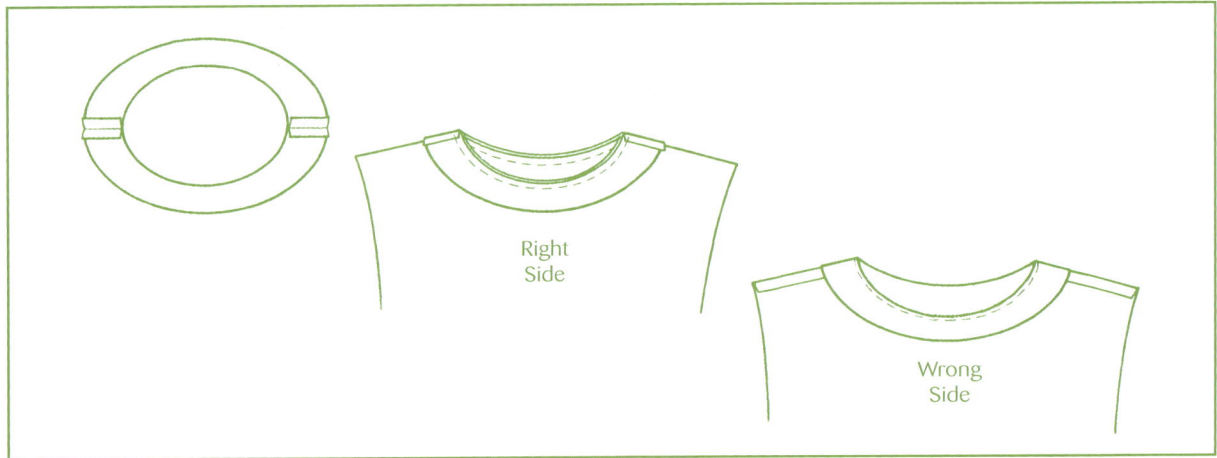

Right Side

Wrong Side

Figure 7.4 – Sew neckline facing pieces together.
Figure 7.5 – Sew facing to neck.
Figure 7.6 – Turn facing to wrong side.

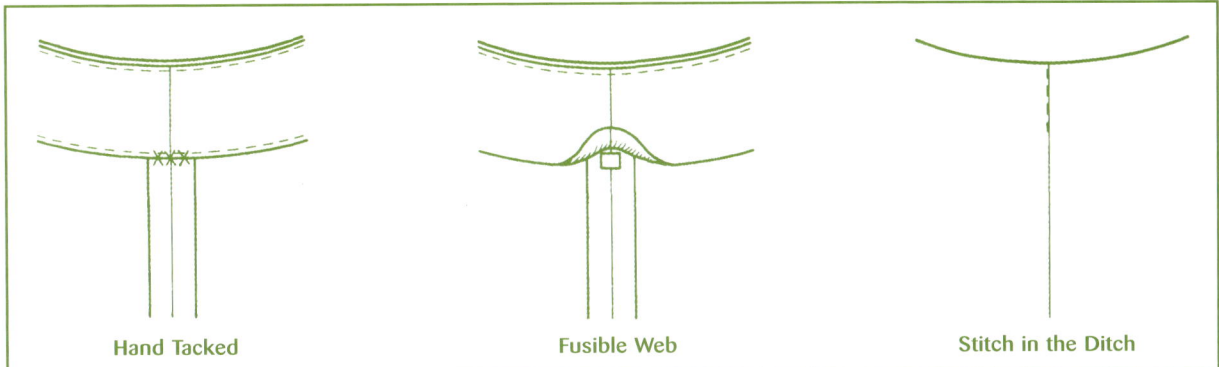

| Hand Tacked | Fusible Web | Stitch in the Ditch |

Figure 7.7–Attach facing to inside.

stitching. *If corners are not clipped far enough, the facing will not lie flat when turned* (Figure 7.8).

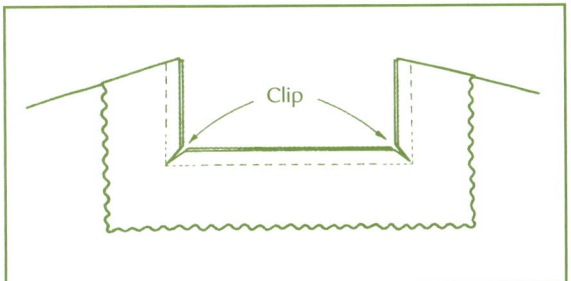

Figure 7.8–Clipping the Corners on a Square Neckline

If your garment has a back opening, you may insert the zipper either before or after you apply the facing. If you insert the zipper first, open the zipper before applying the facing. Wrap the ends of the facing around the zipper at the openings before stitching. Stitch through all thicknesses. Make sure the seamlines meet at the back opening edges (Figure 7.9). Turn the facing to the inside of the garment and slipstitch the facing to the zipper tape (Figure 7.10). Finish the top of the garment with a hook and eye.

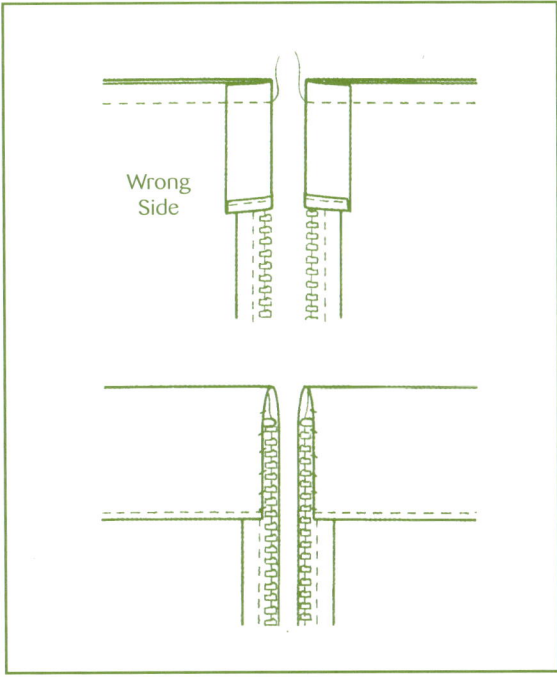

Figure 7.9–(Top) Inserting the Zipper Before the Facing
Figure 7.10–(Bottom) Turning the Facing to the Inside and Slipstiching It to the Zipper Tape

If facing is applied first, insert zipper in usual manner for centered application. Trim zipper tape at neck seamline before stitching to reduce bulk (Figure 7.11). Turn facing down after stitching and slipstitch facing to zipper tape.

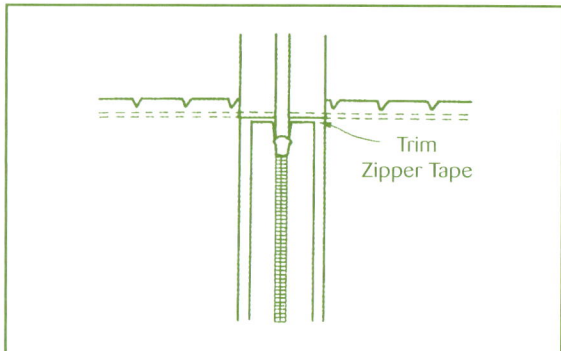

Figure 7.11–Inserting the Zipper After the Facing is Applied

Shaped Facing with a Slash

Round necklines will sometimes have a slashed opening that is cut after the facing is stitched to the garment. Prepare the facing in the usual way. Pin it to the garment right sides together. Pin or baste the facing to the garment down the center of the slash mark. Stitch around the neckline, pivoting at the corners of the slash. Reinforce the point of the slash by using small stitches for 2" each side of point (Figure 7.12).

Slash the opening to the point, being careful not to cut stitches. Trim and grade the seam allowance and trim the corners at the top of the slash. Understitch the facing as far as possible around the neck edge. Turn the facing to the inside of the garment and tack at the shoulders (Figure 7.13).

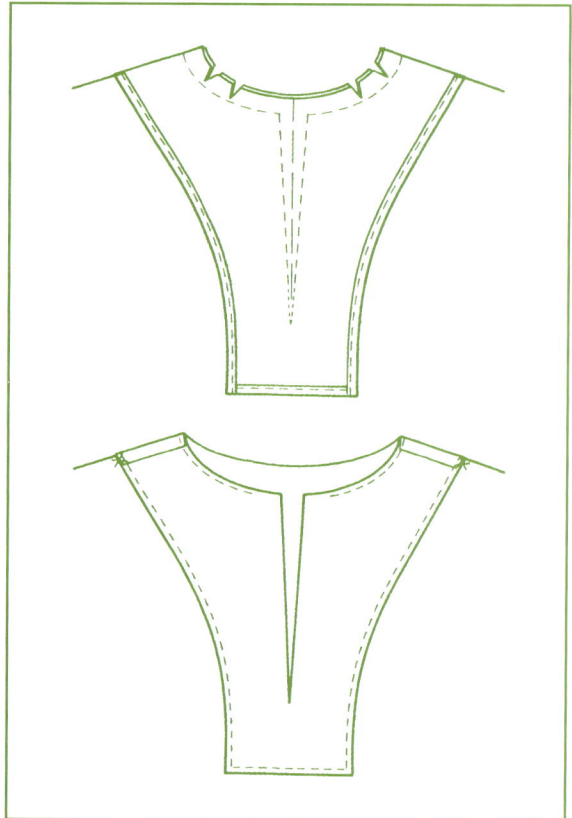

Figure 7.12–(Top) Stitching a Neckline with a Slash
Figure 7.13–(Bottom) Turning the Facing of a Neckline with a Slash

Combined Facings

On sleeveless garments you will sometimes come across a combined neckline and armhole facing. The two facings are cut in one piece. This is especially common on scoop-necked dresses that have narrow shoulder seams. Here is a way of sewing them completely by machine, with no hand finishing. This method is used in factory sewing. It may sound confusing at first, but it really isn't, once you've done it. Don't sew the shoulder seams of the garment or facing before you start this, or it won't work. It will work with the side seams stitched, but we prefer to leave them open.

Step 1. Finish bottom edges of front and back facing pieces separately, (Figure 7.14).

Step 2. With a pin, make a narrow tuck in front and back shoulders of *garment only* (Figure 7.15). These tucks will make the garment shoulder slightly larger than the facing shoulder when sewn. Facing seams will then stay hidden and will not peek out at the shoulders when worn.

Step 3. Right sides together, sew facing front to garment front at neck and armhole edges. Repeat for garment back. Because of the pin, edges will not match exactly, so follow the *facing* seamline when stitching, not the garment seamline. Be *sure* the distance between stitching lines is the same on all shoulder pieces (Figure 7.16).

Step 4. Trim and grade seam allowances and clip curves. Remove pins. Turn facings to inside. Understitch as far as possible. If shoulders are narrow, you will not be able to understitch all the way to the shoulder. Press both pieces.

Step 5. Right sides together, pin garment together at shoulders through *garment fabric only*. Do not pin facings (Figure 7.17).

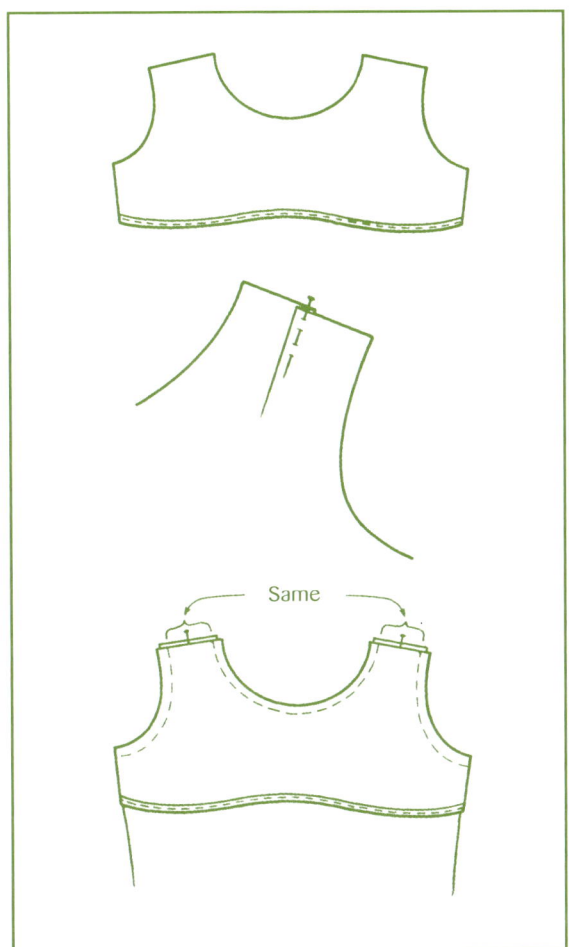

Figure 7.14 – (Top) Finishing Bottom Edge of Combined Neckline and Armhole Facing
Figure 7.15 – (Center) Pin tuck in garment ensures hidden facing seams.
Figure 7.16 – (Bottom) Sewing Facing to Garment

Step 6. Turn back facing inside out over garment front. Garment front is now sandwiched between back and back facing.

Step 7. Open and match seams and continue pinning shoulder in a circle. Stitch all the way around (Figure 7.18). Trim seam and pull garment to right side. Your shoulder seam is finished—a nice, neat seam.

Step 8. If your shoulder is narrower than 1-1/2" - 2", you won't be able to sew in a circle. Instead, sew flat across all four layers (Figure 7.19). Remember that the garment is slightly wider than the facing. Side seams will roll slightly toward the facing. Trim and grade seam. Pull garment right side out and press.

Step 9. To sew garment underarm seams, turn facings away from garment. Match facing seams and stitch from edge of facing to bottom of

garment in one continuous seam (Figure 7.20). Trim seam in facing area. Press seam open.

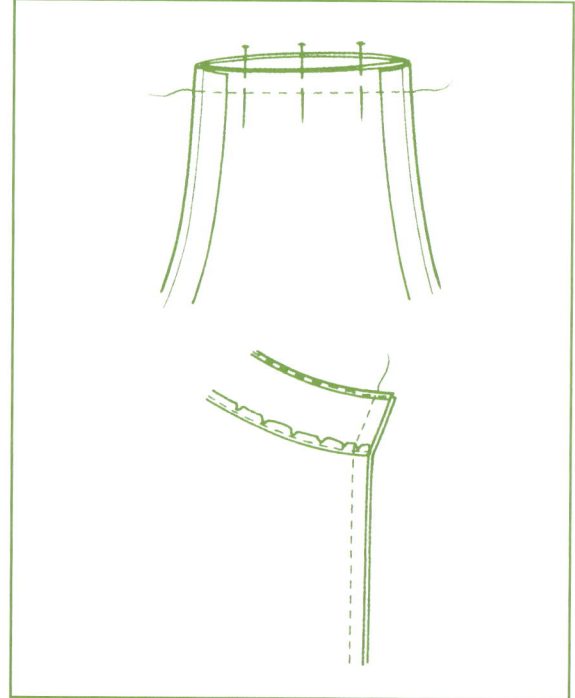

Figure 7.19 – (Top) For a narrow shoulder, sew the seam flat.
Figure 7.20 – (Bottom) Sewing Underarm Seams

Step 10. Turn facing to inside of garment. Tack in place or stitch in the ditch.

Extended Facings

An extended facing is one that is cut in one piece with the garment. It is used most often on the front of blouses and jackets. When turned back, it creates a folded edge.

Step 1. Always interface an extended facing to give firmness to the foldline. Apply interfacing only to the foldline of the facing (Figure 7.21).

Step 2. If a shaped facing is used at the back edge of the neckline, seam it to the extended facing at the shoulders. Seam shoulders of garment (Figure 7.22).

Step 3. Finish outer edge of facing in any manner suitable to the garment.

Step 4. Turn facing to right side of garment on foldline. Stitch around neck edge (Figure 7.23).

Step 5. Trim and clip neckline seam. Turn facing to wrong side of garment.

Interfacing is usually applied to the *garment* fabric to prevent seam allowances from showing through. When bound buttonholes are used on a garment edge, the interfacing must be applied to the garment fabric to reinforce the buttonholes. When machine-worked or handworked buttonholes are used, the interfacing can be applied to the *facing*.

Since fusible interfacing sometimes leaves a ridge where it ends, it should be applied to the *facing* fabric. If you wish to use fusible interfacing on a garment front, interface the entire garment front, first cutting out the interfacing in the dart area and trimming off all seam allowances.

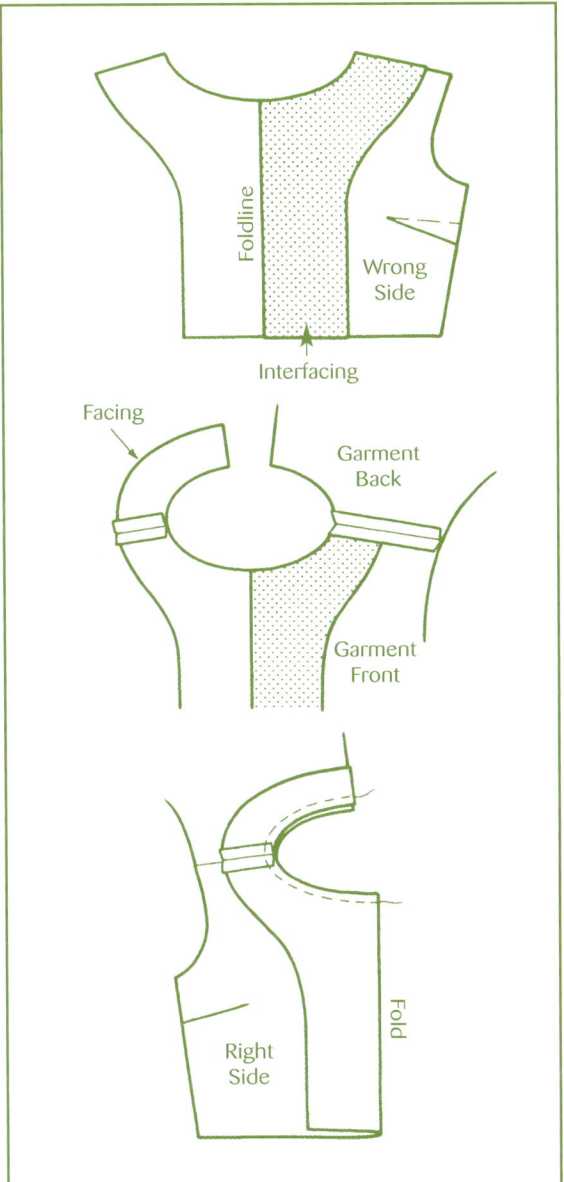

Figure 7.21–(Top) Applying Interfacing to an Extended Facing
Figure 7.22–(Center) Seaming a Shaped Facing to an Extended Facing
Figure 7.23–(Bottom) Trimming and Stitching an Extended Facing

When a garment has lapels that will be turned back, the interfacing should be applied to the *facing* fabric (unless bound buttonholes will be used). Sometimes a lighter weight interfacing can be used on both garment and facing. Remember that interfacing adds body to a fabric, so choose accordingly. On sheer fabrics, a piece of the garment fabric can be used as interfacing.

Here is a technique for applying interfacing that will give a smooth finished edge to the garment facing. It is used quite often in factory sewing. It looks nice on unlined jackets or on sheer fabrics. It cannot be used, however, with bound buttonholes or fusible interfacing.

Step 1. Sew facing seams together. Sew interfacing seams together. Trim seams and press open.

Step 2. Pin interfacing to facing, right sides together, matching seamlines and raw edges. Stitch around *outer* edge (Figure 7.24). Trim and clip seam allowance.

Step 3. Turn right side out and press. Edgestitch close to seamed edge, if desired.

Step 4. Pin raw edges together. Sew to garment with facing fabric against right side of garment fabric (Figure 7.25). Finish facing in the usual way. This method can be used on necklines and armholes.

Bias Facing

A bias facing is a substitute for a shaped facing. It is especially suitable

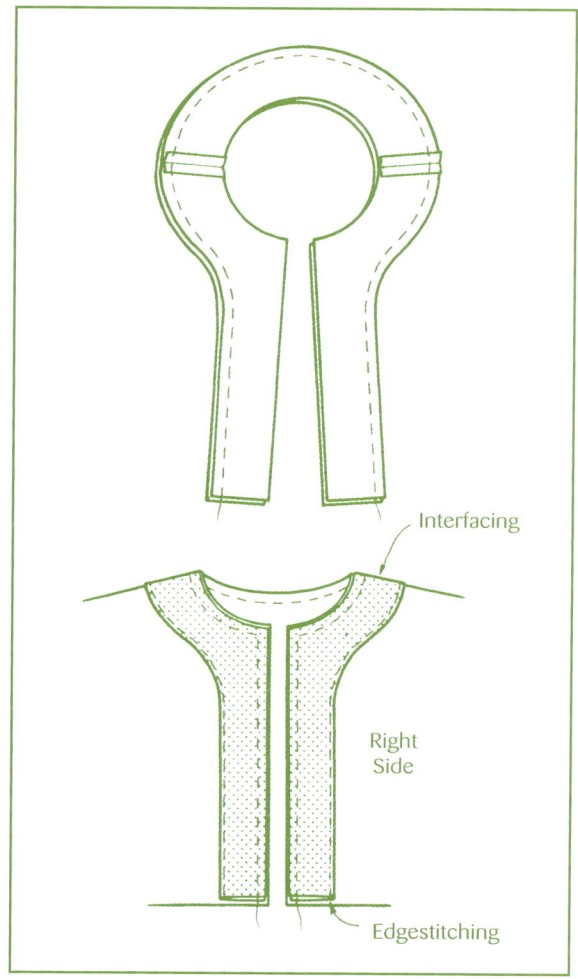

Figure 7.24 – (Top) Sewing Interfacing to Facing for Unlined Jacket
Figure 7.25 – (Bottom) Sewing Facing and Interfacing to Garment of Unlined Jacket

for sheer fabrics where a shaped facing would show through. It can be used on armhole edges, hemlines, and slightly curved necklines. It is an easy facing to make.

To make a bias facing for a neckline, follow these directions:

Step 1. Trim neckline seam allowance to 1/4".

Step 2. Cut a strip of bias fabric 1-1/2" wide and 1" longer than neckline. On knit fabrics, cut the strip on the crosswise grain of the fabric for greater stretch.

Step 3. Fold bias strip in half lengthwise, wrong sides together, and press. After first pressing, steam press bias strip into neckline shape, stretching folded edge to fit curve of neckline (Figure 7.26).

Step 4. Stitch strip to right side of garment in 1/4" seam, matching raw edges of strip and neckline (Figure 7.27).

Step 5. Clip seam and turn bias away from garment. Turn ends of bias to wrong side of facing. Turn bias facing to inside of garment, rolling seam to inside so it won't show.

Step 6. From outside, topstitch close to garment edge. If desired, make another row of topstitching 1/4" from the first (Figure 7.28). If an invisible finish is desired, eliminate topstitching and slipstitch facing to garment with invisible stitches (Figure 7.29).

When a bias facing is used on a sleeveless armhole, cut facing strip 1/2" longer than armhole seamline. Seam ends of facing together in a 1/4" seam. Press seam open before folding bias in half.

A bias facing is also a good substitute for a shaped facing on bulky or scratchy fabrics. Use a piece of lining fabric or other soft material in a color to match the garment fabric. Purchased bias binding may also be used. Press out the folds in purchased binding before folding it in half to make the facing.

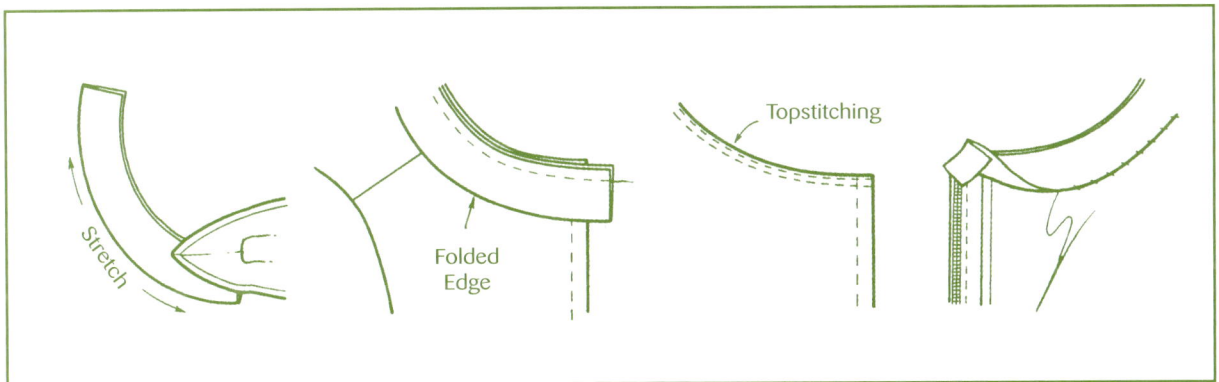

Figure 7.26—(Left) Pressing Bias Facing to Fit Neckline Curve
Figure 7.27—(Center Left) Stitching Bias Facing to Neck Edge
Figure 7.28—(Center Right) Topstitching Bias Facing
Figure 7.29—(Right) Alternate Method of Slipstitching Bias Facing

Before continuing with your reading, answer the following questions. True or False?

1. A facing is a piece of lining material that shows on the right side of all garments.

2. No finish is needed on facings made from firm knit fabrics that don't ravel.

3. In garments with a back opening, you can insert the zipper before or after you apply the facing.

4. An extended facing is one that is cut one piece with the garment.

5. A bias facing is not a substitute for a shaped facing.

Check your answers with those provided on page 199.

RUFFLES AND COLLARS

Ruffles

A soft, graceful touch is often added to a garment with the use of ruffles. A *straight ruffle* is usually cut on the crosswise grain and receives its fullness from two rows of gathering. It is often used as a flounce around a skirt (Figure 8.1). It is also used frequently on lightweight curtains. A *circular* ruffle receives its drape from the way it is cut (on a curve). It is sewn to the garment without gathers. It is used mostly at necklines and on sleeves (Figure 8.2).

Straight Ruffles

The fullness of a straight ruffle is determined by the amount of gathers in it. For a very full ruffle, use a strip of fabric three times the length of the finished ruffle. For a moderately full ruffle, use twice the length. For slight fullness, use one and a half times the length. Sheer, lightweight fabrics look best in ruffles. The width of the ruffle is determined by its usage and the type of fabric being used. Usually, the sheerer the fabric, the wider and fuller the ruffle.

Figure 8.1—(Top) Straight Ruffle
Figure 8.2—(Bottom) Circular Ruffle

A straight ruffle is usually cut on the crosswise grain, occasionally on the bias. A straight ruffle cut on the lengthwise grain does not gather as well or fall as gracefully as one cut on the crosswise or bias.

A ruffle is usually made of a single layer of fabric. A double layer can be used on sheer or lightweight fabrics to give the ruffle more body and eliminate the need for a hem finish. The ruffle is cut twice the width and folded wrong sides together. The raw edges are gathered as one (Figure 8.3). On a single layer of fabric, the edge of the ruffle is usually finished with a tiny hem, which can be sewn either by hand or by machine (Figure 8.4).

Ruffles will sometimes need to be pieced in order to make them long enough. Be sure to piece the fabric on the straight grain, even if the ruffle is cut on the bias (Figure 8.5).

Gathering Ruffles

Raw ends of ruffles can be left unfinished if the edge is to be included in a seam (Figure 8.6). If the edge is to be left free, hem the ruffle ends the same as the ruffle bottom (Figure 8.7). On a folded ruffle, finish the ends by hand (Figure 8.8), or stitch the right

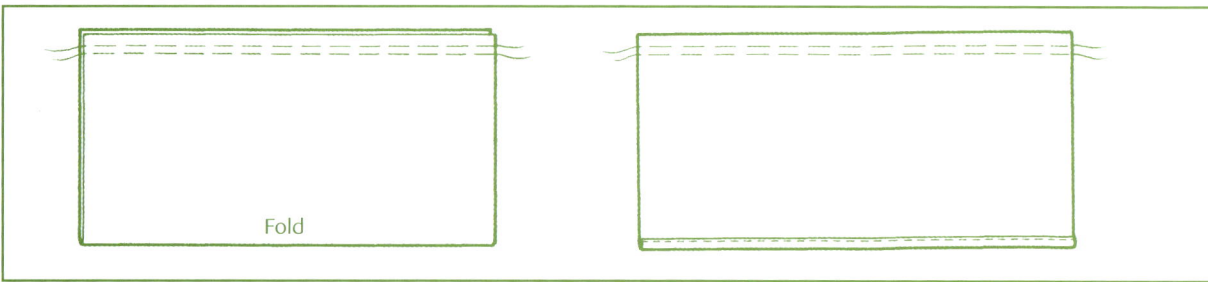

Figure 8.3–(Left) Gathering the Edges of a Double-Layer Ruffle
Figure 8.4–(Right) Hemming and Gathering a Single-Layer Ruffle

Figure 8.5–Always piece ruffles on the straight grain.

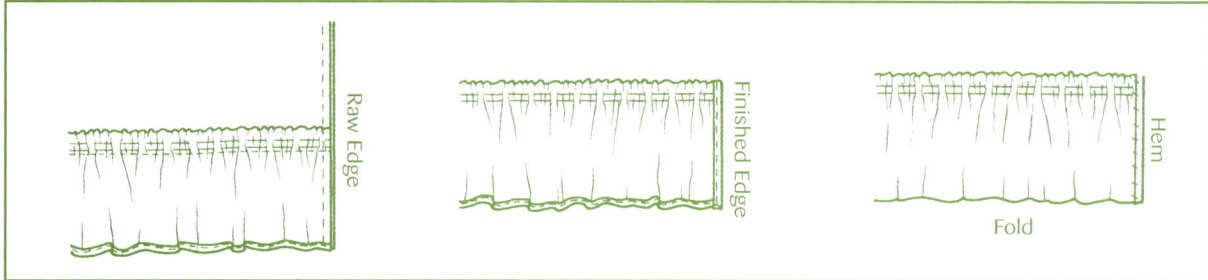

Figure 8.6–(Left) Leave the ends of a ruffle raw when they will be sewn into a seam.
Figure 8.7–(Center) Hem free end of ruffle.
Figure 8.8–(Right) Hem the free end of a folded ruffle by hand.

sides together and turn before gathering.

To gather a straight ruffle, sew two rows of machine basting along the top edge of the ruffle. Place one row on the seamline and the other row on the seam allowance, 1/4" from the first. Use a strong bobbin thread to prevent breakage when gathering. If ruffle is very long, divide in half or in quarters and gather each section separately (Figure 8.9). If the ruffle has seams, stop machine basting at each seamline; then continue (Figure 8.10).

Stitching Ruffle to Garment

When attaching a ruffle to a garment, pin the ends in place, right sides together, and pull up the gathers to fit. If the area is large, gather in sections (Figure 8.11). Secure ends by wrapping gathering threads around pins (Figure 8.12). Stitch in place along the seamline

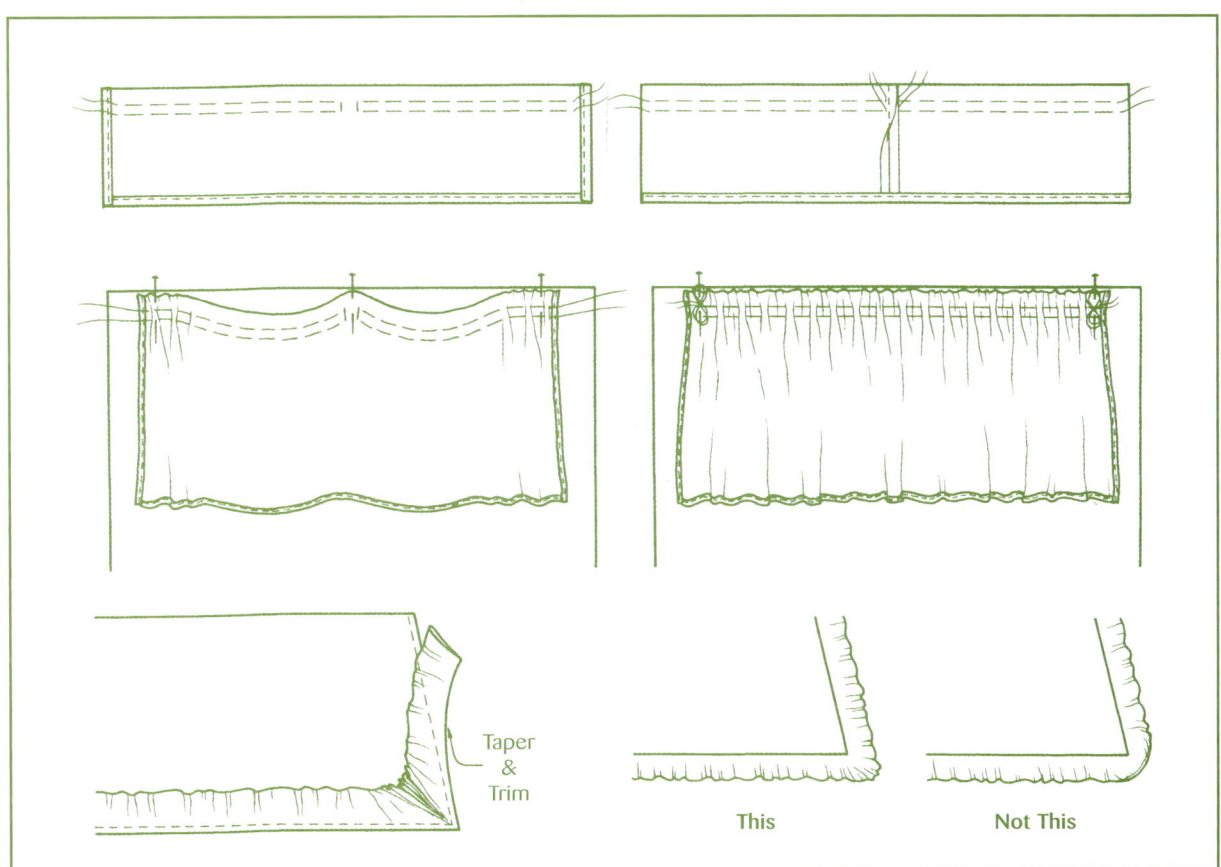

Figure 8.9–(Top Left) Two rows of machine basting prepare a straight ruffle for gathering.
Figure 8.10–(Top Right) Stop the basting at any seamline on a ruffle; then continue.
Figure 8.11–(Center Left) Pin the ruffle ends to the garment.
Figure 8.12–(Center Right) Pull the basting threads to fit and secure the ends.
Figure 8.13–(Bottom Left) Taper the ruffle ends in a collar that is to be faced.
Figure 8.14–(Bottom Right) Allow ruffle fullness at a corner.

with the gathering layer on top. If the garment piece is to be faced (as in a collar), machine baste the ruffle in place, tapering the ends into the seam allowance at the end of the stitching (Figure 8.13). Trim off excess ruffle in seam allowance. Be sure to allow plenty of fullness at the corners so the ruffle will not pull when turned out (Figure 8.14). Place facing right side down over ruffle and pin or baste in place. Turn all garment sections over. Stitch in place through all thicknesses, following machine basting line. Turn right side out.

When a ruffle is attached to a hem or a sleeve edge of a garment, the raw edge of the seam can be finished with overcasting or machine zigzag. If desired, the seam edge can be enclosed in a bias strip of binding or self-fabric. Sew the bias along the seamline on top of the ruffle (Figure 8.15). Trim seam allowance. Press seam toward garment. Turn bias and hem by hand to garment (Figure 8.16). Take tiny stitches so they will not show on right side of garment.

When a ruffle is attached to a neckline, it is usually finished with a facing. The application of facings will be discussed in a later section.

Double Ruffles

A double ruffle and a ruffle with a heading have finished edges on both top and bottom edges. A double ruffle has two rows of machine gathering down the center (Figure 8.17); a ruffle with a heading has two rows of gathering near the top (Figure 8.18). They are both

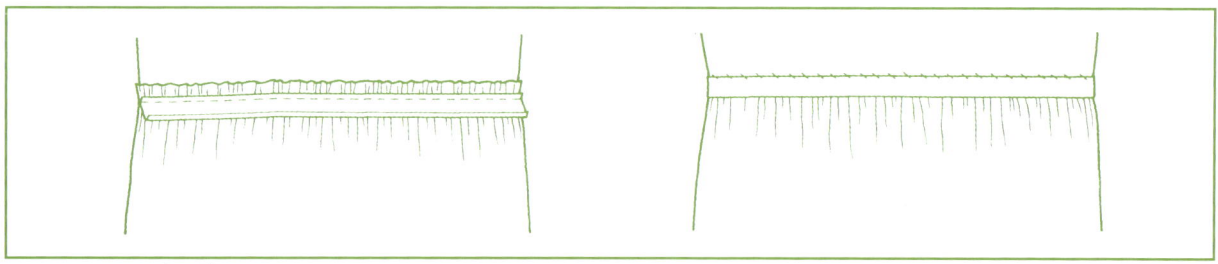

Figure 8.15–(Left) Attaching a Bias Strip to a Ruffle Seam
Figure 8.16–(Right) Finishing a Bias Strip Attached to a Ruffle Seam

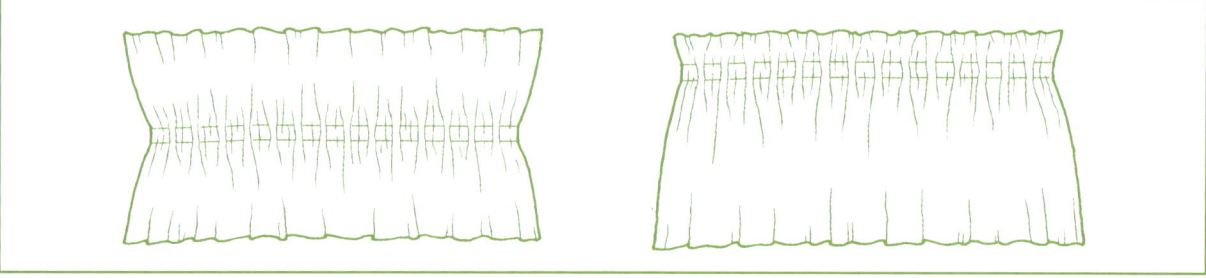

Figure 8.17–(Left) For a double ruffle, the machine basting is done at the center.
Figure 8.18–(Right) For a ruffle with a heading, the machine basting is done near the top.

applied by topstitching over the gathering lines.

A ruffle with a heading may be attached to the raw edge of a garment in the following manner:

Step 1. With the ruffle right side up, place *wrong* side of ruffle against *wrong* side of garment edge. Match bottom row of machine gathering to seamline of garment. Pin in place.

Step 2. Stitch ruffle to garment along bottom row of machine gathering (Figure 8.19).

Step 3. Trim seam allowance of garment to scant 1/4". Turn ruffle to right side of garment.

Step 4. Pin to garment along top row of machine gathering. Raw seam edge will be covered.

Step 5. Stitch ruffle to garment along top row of machine gathering (Figure 8.20).

Circular Ruffles

A circular ruffle is cut in a circle, then clipped and straightened to make a soft flounce with a gentle drape. The size of the circle will depend on the size of the ruffle desired. The length of the top edge of the ruffle will equal the circumference (distance around) of the inner circle of the ruffle. If a long ruffle

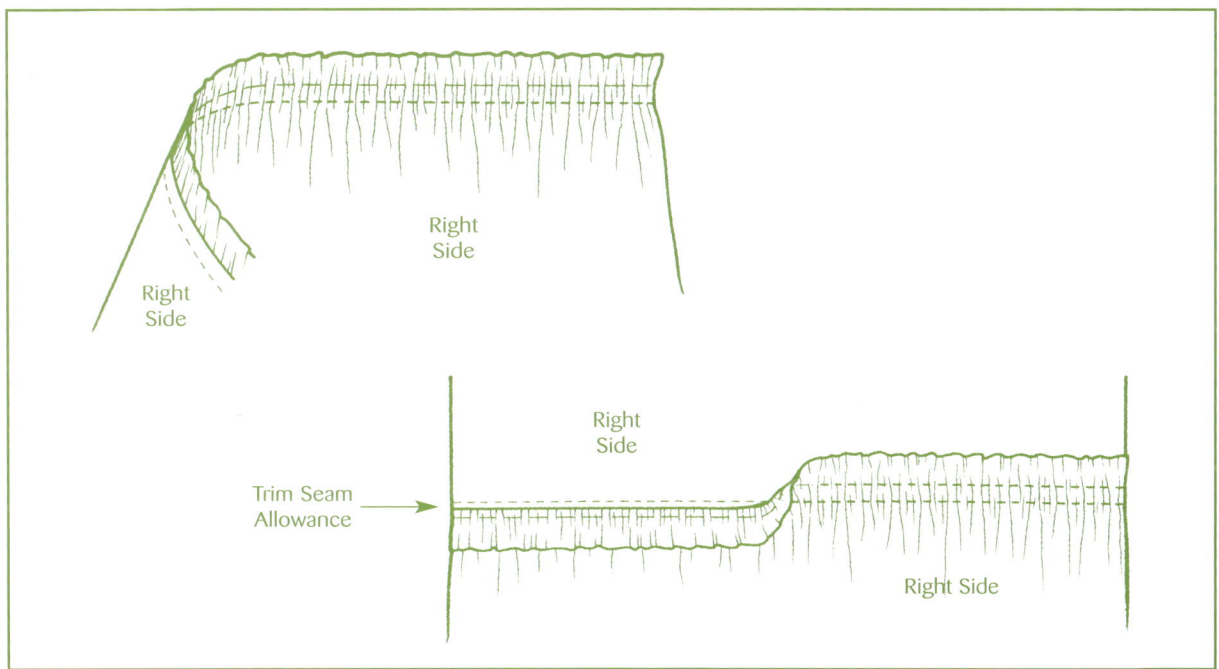

Figure 8.19–(Left) For a ruffle with a heading, stitch the wrong side of the ruffle to wrong side of the garment at the bottom row of machine gathering.
Figure 8.20–(Right) Stitch a ruffle with a heading on the right side at the top row of machine gathering.

is needed, several circles are cut, then pieced together. The width of the ruffle will be the distance between the inner and outer circles (leave seam allowance on both edges).

To cut a circular ruffle, cut around outer edge of circle of desired size, then cut *along grainline* to inner circle. Cut inner circle according to desired dimensions. Staystitch on seamline of inner circle (Figure 8.21). Clip all around edge of inner circle until ruffle will straighten out and lie flat along the edge. If more length is needed, cut another circular ruffle and seam to first ruffle at straight grain edge.

Finish the outer edge of the circular ruffle with a narrow hem (Figure 8.22). It is easier to do this by hand than by machine because of the curve of the fabric. Attach ruffle to garment along staystitched edge.

If a double layer of ruffle is desired, cut two ruffles and sew them right sides together along the outer edge and on each end (Figure 8.23). Trim and clip seam. Turn ruffle to right side and press. Staystitch inner edges together; then clip (Figure 8.24). Straighten ruffle and attach to garment.

Figure 8.21 – (Top Left) Staystitching and Clipping Circular Ruffle
Figure 8.22 – (Top Right) Circular Ruffle with Edges Hemmed
Figure 8.23 – (Bottom Left) Double Layer of Ruffle with Right Sides Sewn Together
Figure 8.24 – (Bottom Right) Turned Double Ruffle with Inner Circle Staystitched and Clipped

Collars

The perfect collar can be the making of a beautiful garment. The fine points of construction that we give you here will assure you a perfect collar every time. These are the characteristics that are essential to a professional-looking collar:

- The collar must be symmetrical. It should be centered on the neckline. Points or curves should be identical on both sides of the collar.

- The collar should lie smooth and flat. It should encircle the neck without ripples or bulges. A rolled collar should fall gracefully.

- All neckline seams should be hidden by the collar when the garment is worn.

- The undercollar should never show. It should not peek out from under the upper collar at any spot.

- The edges and points of the collar should lie smooth and flat without curling up.

- The shape of the collar should be preserved. The correct choice of interfacing and careful stitching will ensure you of a perfectly shaped collar.

Types of Collars

The shape of the inner (neck) edge of a collar determines what type of collar it is and how it fits the neck. Although there are many, many shapes and varieties of collars, there are three basic collar shapes:

Flat—This is the easiest collar to make. It is applied flat to the garment and finished with a neckline facing. The shape of the collar is basically the same as the shape of the neckline. The Peter Pan collar is a flat collar (Figure 8.25). The flat collar is used mostly on untailored garments such as women's dresses. It is also used on children's clothing.

Standing—This collar stands up straight from the neck. The neck edge of the collar is straight or very, very slightly curved. The Mandarin collar is a standing collar (Figure 8.26). The turtleneck is a standing collar that folds back on itself. A man's shirt collar on a separate stand (band around the neck between collar and shirt) is a variation of a standing collar.

Rolled—This is a collar that stands up from the neck and folds over on itself in a soft roll (Figure 8.27). The *roll line* is the line along which the collar is turned. The depth of the roll is determined by the shape of the inner edge of the collar. The neck seam of a

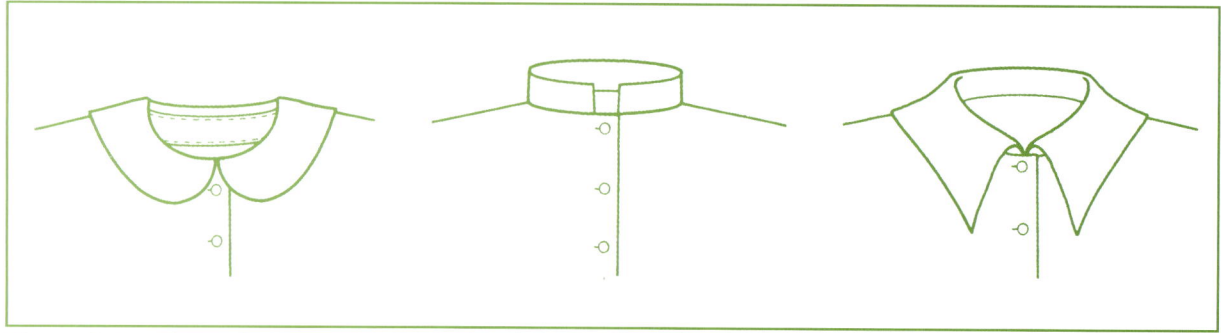

Figure 8.25—Flat Collar   Figure 8.26—Standing Collar   Figure 8.27—Rolled Collar

rolled collar should be completely covered. Notched collars found on jackets and coats are examples of rolled collars.

Cutting a Collar

The *upper collar* is the part of the collar that shows when the garment is worn. The *undercollar* (facing) is the underneath part of the collar that lies against the garment. A collar is usually cut in two pieces. A collar with a straight edge can be cut in one piece and folded in half along the straight edge. One half of the collar then forms the facing (Figure 8.28). When the collar is cut in two pieces, it can be cut from *one* pattern piece—the two pieces will then be the same size. If the collar is cut from *two* pattern pieces (an upper collar and an undercollar), the undercollar is slightly smaller than the upper collar (Figure 8.29). This gives a better shape and roll to the collar. This method is usually used on better jackets and coats. It is always used in tailoring.

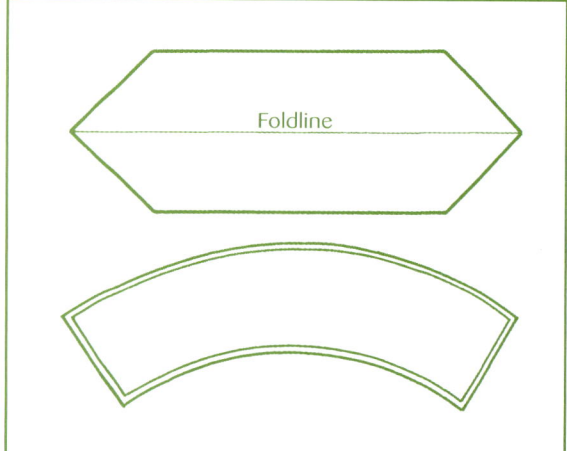

Foldline

Figure 8.28–(Top) A One-Piece Collar
Figure 8.29–(Bottom) A Two-Piece Collar with the Undercollar Slightly Smaller Than the Upper Collar for a Better Fit

Interfacing

Most collars should be interfaced. The exception would be very soft fabrics or relaxed styles such as very softly draped garments (usually blouses). The weight of the interfacing you use depends on the weight of your fabric and the type of collar on your garment.

A collar interfacing is usually cut on the straight grain, the same as the collar. An interfacing can be cut on the bias grain to give a better, softer roll to a rolled collar. Fusible interfacings are good for collars, because they are trimmed to the seamline before fusing. This reduces bulk in the collar seam. Fuse an extra triangle of interfacing at the points to help them lie flat. Be sure to trim 1/8" off the points of any interfacing in a collar to reduce bulk. An extra piece of interfacing can be fused to the stand area for extra strength, if desired (Figure 8.30).

Interfacing should be applied to the wrong side of the *upper* collar to prevent seam allowance from showing through. On tailored coats and jackets the interfacing is applied to the *undercollar* for greater support. When using fusible interfacings, check on a scrap of fabric first to see if the interfacing shows through or leaves a line where it ends. If so, fuse the interfacing to the *undercollar.*

Construction

When two collar pieces are cut from the same pattern, they will be the same size. When pinning them together, it will be necessary to stretch one piece and ease the other so that one will be larger than the other along the *outside* edges (not the neck edges). The smaller piece will be the *upper* collar. Stitch with this one on top, holding both pieces taut as you sew. When the collar is

turned the upper collar will become the larger piece (Figure 8.31).

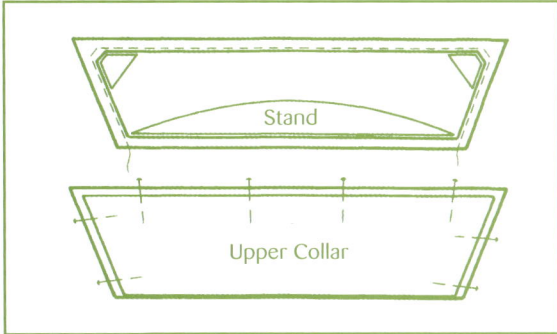

Figure 8.30–(Top) When using fusible interfacing, apply extra pieces to the corners and the stand area.
Figure 8.31–(Bottom) Pinning Two Collar Pieces of the Same Size by Stretching One Piece

When two collar pieces are cut from different patterns, the upper collar will be *larger* than the undercollar. Pin the collar sections right sides together with the *undercollar* on top. It will be necessary to ease the upper collar into the *undercollar,* stretching the undercollar if necessary. Hold both pieces taut as you sew (Figure 8.32).

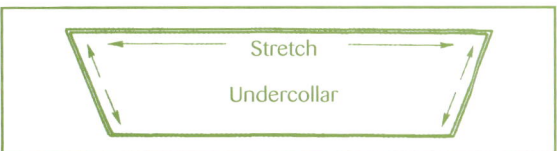

Figure 8.32–Pinning Two Collar Pieces when the Upper Collar is Larger

Professional Tips for Perfect Collars

Always stitch directionally from center to ends, overlapping stitching 1/2" at center of collar. Stitching from the center to the ends will aid you in easing and stretching the two pieces to fit.

For identical collar points, stitch off the material at the corners. The point of the collar will land where the stitching crosses. Reinforce the corner 1" each side of the point with small stitches (15-20 per inch). Take one or two stitches on the diagonal across the point for turning ease (Figure 8.33).

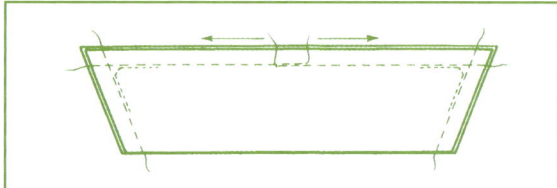

Figure 8.33–Extra Stitches at Collar Points and Diagonals

Trimming is the most important element in creating an attractive collar. It is especially important at the points. Trim as closely as possible to the stitching; then trim diagonally. Remove as much material as possible in the point area, except on fabrics that ravel easily. Fabrics that ravel a lot should be trimmed only to within 1/4" from the stitching; otherwise they will pull out when turned. Curves must be notched and clipped, or trimmed with pinking shears. The bulkier the fabric, the more notching you will have to do. Collar seams must be graded to avoid bulk at the collar edge. The seam on the upper collar should be left the widest. Trim interfacing close to the stitching line.

Turning a Collar

Press the collar flat before turning; then press the seam open over a point presser, or use the following method:

With the undercollar on top, press the seam allowance open (Figure 8.34). Then press both seam allowances toward the undercollar (Figure 8.35). If desired, the collar seam may be understitched as far into the corner as possible, as shown in Figure 8.36.

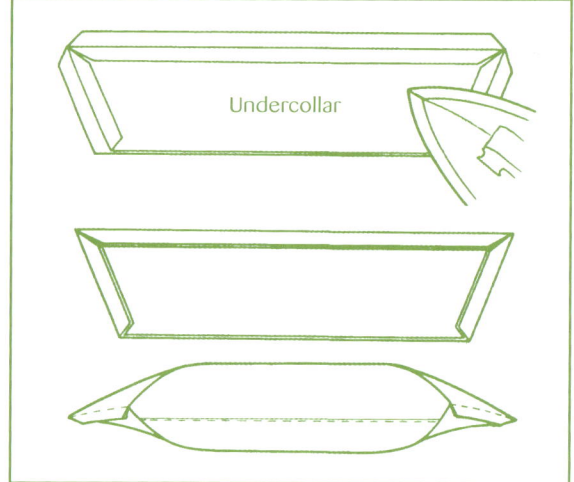

Figure 8.34–(Top) First press the seam allowances open.
Figure 8.35–(Center) Then press the seam allowances toward the undercollar.
Figure 8.36–(Bottom) If desired, understitch the collar seam as far as possible.

To turn the collar, slip your hand inside the collar, palm up. Holding the seam allowances in one corner with your thumb, pull the upper collar forward over your hand (Figure 8.37). Repeat for other corner. Use a strong needle or pin to pull out the corners.

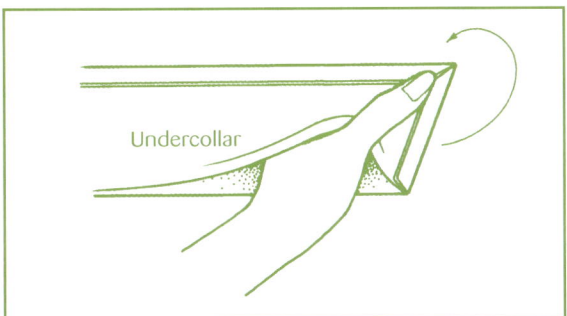

Figure 8.37–Turning the Collar with Your Thumb

Never push the corners out with your scissors—you may poke a hole in the fabric. Pull the corners out gently, being careful not to tear the fabric. Roll the collar seam slightly toward the undercollar. Press collar lightly, using a press cloth.

You will notice that the neck edge seams of the collar no longer match. The upper collar is now slightly narrower than the undercollar. Before sewing these edges together, fold the collar over your hand to establish the roll of the collar (Figure 8.38). For a flat collar you will need only a slight roll.

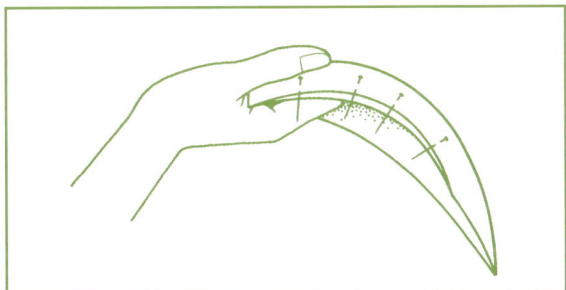

Figure 8.38–Fold the collar over your hand to establish the roll of the collar.

For a rolled collar, or if your fabric is very bulky, use this method to establish the roll:

Step 1. Lay the collar on the sewing machine with the *undercollar* on top. Starting at the outer edge, roll up the collar. The upper collar will be on the outside.

Step 2. The two cut edges will assume the correct position for the roll of the collar. Pin these edges together (Figure 8.39). Unroll the collar.

Step 3. Once the roll has been established, make a row of machine basting through both layers 1/2" from the edge of the undercollar. The top collar will have a slight bubble when lying flat (Figure 8.40).

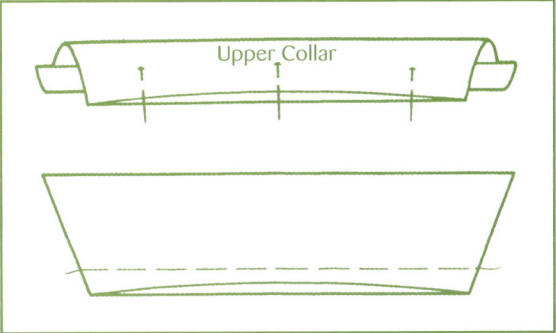

Figure 8.39–(Top) Pinning Together the Cut Edges of a Rolled Collar
Figure 8.40–(Bottom) Machine baste along the cut edges of the rolled collar.

Collar Application

To prepare your garment for the collar application, stitch the shoulder seams and any other seams that affect the neckline of the garment. Finish seams and press open. Staystitch around neck edge if you haven't already done so. You will need to clip to the staystitching before applying the collar if your collar is straight or if the curve of the collar does not match the curve of the neckline. It is easier to apply the collar if the side seams of the garment are left open. The garment will then lie flat on the sewing machine.

Flat Collar

Step 1. Lay garment flat, right side up.

Step 2. Lay collar on garment, undercollar against garment fabric. Collars made of two separate units should be joined before being attached to garment. Match front edges at seamline, allowing seam allowances to overlap. Baste together by hand or machine at seamline (Figure 8.41). Match all notches and other markings on collar and neckline. Baste or pin in place.

Step 3. If garment front has an extended facing, fold back on foldline. Be sure the same amount of fabric extends beyond each end of the collar (Figure 8.42).

Step 4. Lay facing over collar, right side down. Stitch around neckline through all layers (Figure 8.43). Grade and clip seam. Clip as close to stitching as possible without cutting stitching;

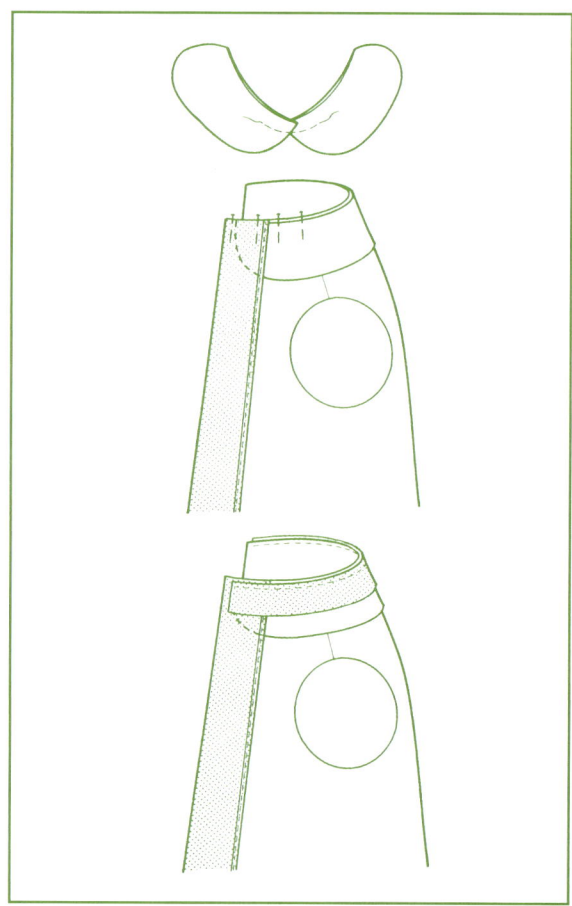

Figure 8.41 – (Top) Basting Together Two Collar Units
Figure 8.42 – (Center) Folding Extended Facing over Collar
Figure 8.43 – (Bottom) Stitching Collar through All Layers, Including Facings

your collar will lie flatter that way. Turn seam allowances toward facing. Understitch facing as far as possible around neck edge. Turn facing to inside and press. Tack in place at shoulder seams and front facing edges.

Standing Collar

Step 1. If standing collar is made from two pieces, sew interfacing to outer collar piece. If collar is made from one piece, sew interfacing only as far as the foldline. If you wish to have a very firm collar, you may interface the entire collar; use your interfacing on the bias to ensure a smooth foldline.

Step 2. Prepare garment by sewing all seams that affect the neckline. Finish garment opening, including zipper, if used. Staystitch neck edge and clip to stitching. Straighten neckline to match collar edge (Figure 8.44).

Step 3. For a one-piece collar, fold in half, right sides together. Turn back neck seam allowance on facing side of collar and press in place. Trim to 3/8". Stitch across ends of collar with small stitches. Clip corners diagonally at folded edge. Trim and grade seam allowances (Figure 8.45). Turn right side out and press, using press cloth (Figure 8.46).

Step 4. For a two-piece collar, pin right sides together. Turn back neck seam allowance on facing piece of collar and press in place. Trim to 3/8". Stitch top and side edges of collar. Reinforce corners. Cut corners diagonally. Trim and grade seam allowances (Figure 8.47). Turn right side out and press, using press cloth.

Step 5. Pin outer collar to neckline of garment, right sides together. Place each end of collar a hairline *inside*

Figure 8.44 – (Top) Neck edge is stitched, clipped, and straightened to receive a standing collar.
Figure 8.45 – (Center) One-Piece Standing Collar Stitched with Corners Clipped
Figure 8.46 – (Bottom) One-Piece Standing Collar Turned and Pressed

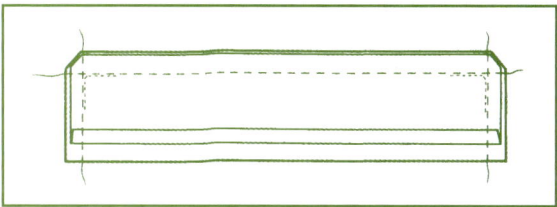

Figure 8.47 – Two-Piece Standing Collar Stitched with Corners Clipped

garment edge (Figure 8.48). This will prevent the collar from protruding beyond the garment edge when the collar is finished. Sew a 5/8" seam, tapering to a 1/2" seam for about 1" at each end of the seam. Trim and grade seam allowance, leaving collar seam allowance the widest. Press seam allowance up into the collar.

Step 6. Pin facing side of collar over seam allowance, covering stitching line.

Push outer edges of garment 1/8" up into collar at seamline. Line up outer edges of garment and collar so that there is no jog on the outer edge of the garment (Figure 8.49). Overcast facing to collar seam allowance by hand (Figure 8.50).

If you wish, you can apply this collar to the inner edge of the garment instead of the outer edge. You can then topstitch the collar from the outside instead of hand finishing the inside. Be sure to topstitch from outer edges to center on each side of garment. This will preserve your straight line at the edge of the garment (Figure 8.51).

For Knits Only

A standing collar on a knit garment can be applied in the following way:

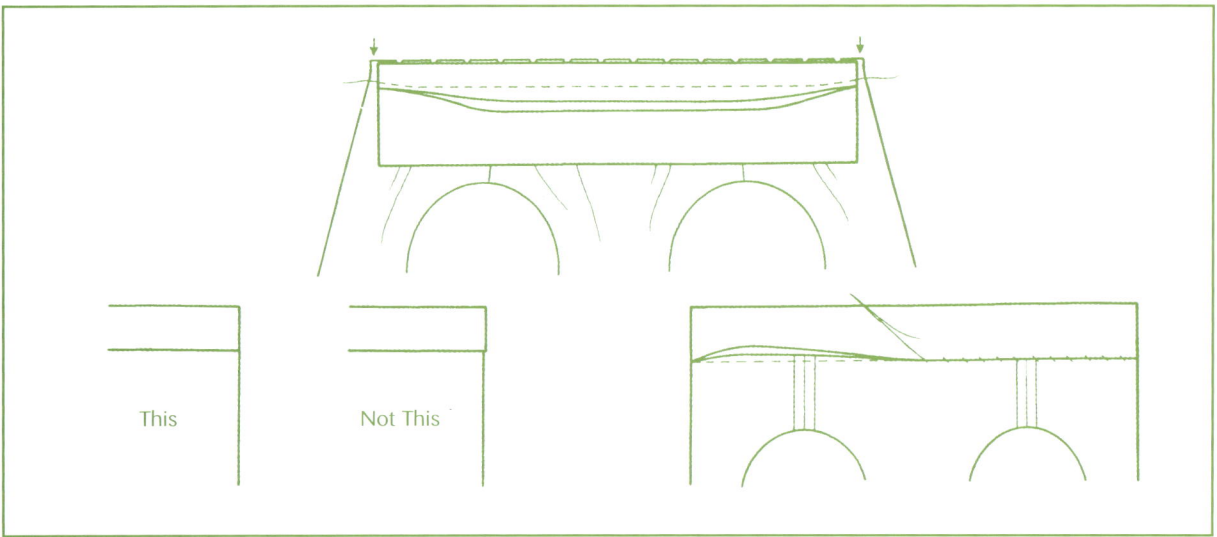

Figure 8.48 – (Top) Attaching Standing Collar to Neckline Along Outer Collar
Figure 8.49 – (Bottom Left) Be sure the edge of the garment and the edge of the standing collar form a straight line (no jog).
Figure 8.50 – (Bottom Right) Stitching the Facing of a Standing Collar to the Inside of a Garment

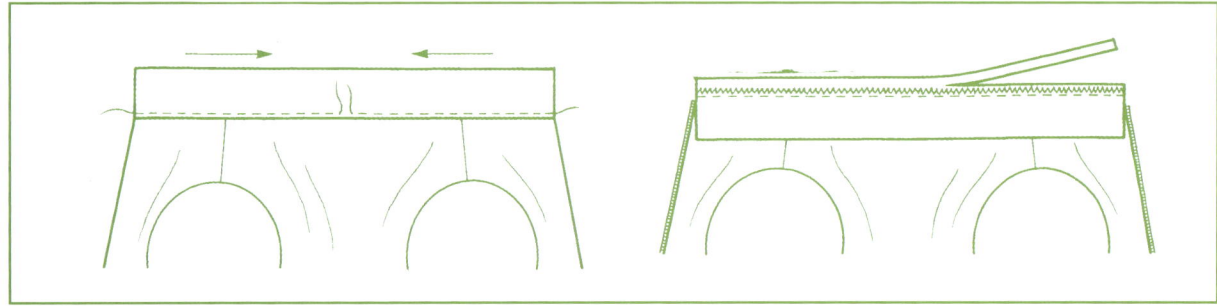

Figure 8.51 – (Left) Topstitching a Standing Collar Attached to the Inner Edge
Figure 8.52 – (Right) Attaching and Finishing a Standing Collar on a Knit Garment

Place finished collar on garment, right sides together. Stitch on seamline through all layers. Make a row of zigzag stitching close to first stitching. Trim seam allowance close to stitching (Figure 8.52). Press seam allowance toward garment.

This seam can also be done with an overedge stitch. This type of collar must be worn closed. If worn open, the seam allowance will show.

Collar with a Stand

This is a variation of the standing collar. The stand may be part of the collar or it may be cut as a separate piece (Figure 8.53). If cut as a separate piece, the collar is completed first, then sewn to the stand. Both collar and stand should be interfaced.

For a collar with an attached stand, make and apply the collar to the garment as for a standing collar. If the garment has a front facing, finish the edge of the facing and turn the facing to the inside of the garment before applying the collar. Machine baste the

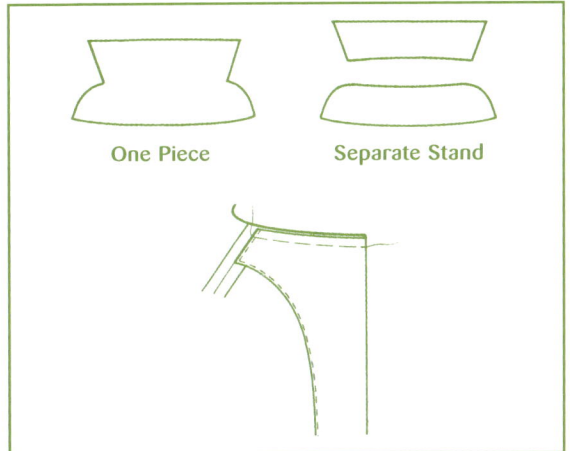

Figure 8.53–(Top) Two Types of a Collar with a Stand
Figure 8.54–(Bottom) Basting the Facing to the Garment to Receive a Collar with an Attached Stand

facing to the garment along the neck edge to hold it in place while attaching the collar (Figure 8.54).

For a collar with a separate stand, sandwich the completed collar between the right sides of the stand. The *undercollar* should be against the *outer* layer of the stand. Turn under the seam allowance on the neck edge of the *inner* stand. Match all notches, *making sure the collar is centered on the stand.* Stitch through all layers around the outer edge of the stand, shortening stitches on the curves (Figure 8.55).

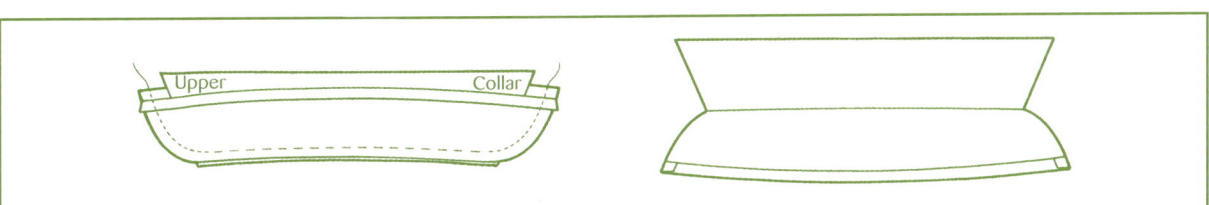

Figure 8.55–(Left) Stitching through All Layers of a Collar with a Separate Stand
Figure 8.56–(Right) Turned Collar with a Separate Stand

Trim, grade, and clip seam allowance. Turn the stand right side out (Figure 8.56). Press, using a press cloth. Apply the collar to the garment, following the directions for a standing collar.

Rolled Collar

A rolled collar is probably the most commonly used type of collar. It can be applied with or without a neck facing. On lined jackets and coats there is usually a neck facing. On blouses and unlined jackets a facing is usually omitted. When a back neck facing is used, the collar is applied in the same way as a flat collar with a facing. The outer edges of the facing are not finished, since they are sewn to the garment lining. When a back neck facing is not used, the collar is applied in the following manner:

Step 1. Prepare neck edge of garment by staystitching and clipping seam allowance.

Step 2. Make collar but do not baste raw edges together. Hand baste collar and facing together through roll line instead. To establish roll line, shape collar around a tailor's ham, a dress form, or your own neck (Figure 8.57). Mark with pins; then baste together while still rolled. Some patterns have the roll line marked on them.

Step 3. Pin *undercollar* to garment across back neck edge for about 1" past shoulder seam. Stitch in place (Figure 8.58).

Step 4. Turn garment front facing to outside of garment, covering front part of collar on each side of garment opening. Be sure the same amount of fabric extends beyond the collar on both front garment edges. Turn back the shoulder seam allowance on the facing. Stitch through all layers from garment front edge to shoulder seams, overlapping previous stitching. Clip

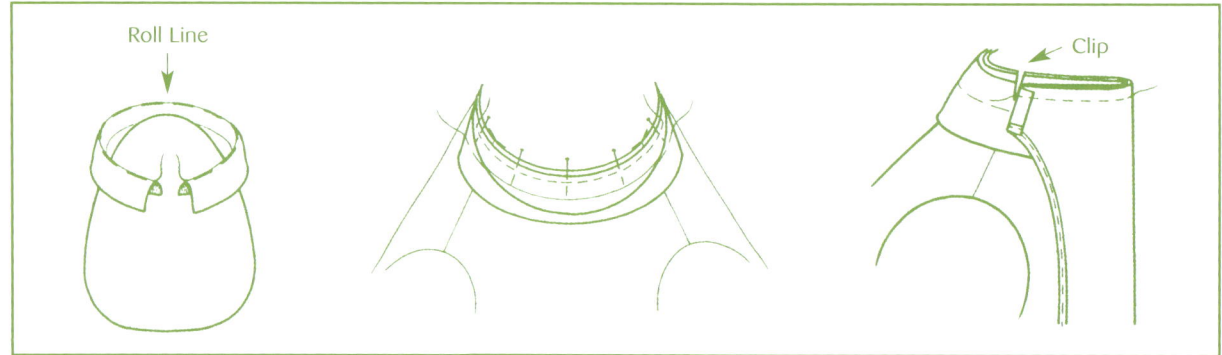

Figure 8.57 – (Top) Establishing the Roll Line on a Rolled Collar
Figure 8.58 – (Center) Pinning and Stitching the Undercollar of a Rolled Collar to the Garment
Figure 8.59 – (Right) Stitching and Clipping Rolled Collar

seam allowance and upper collar to neck seamline at shoulder seams (Figure 8.59).

Step 5. Trim, grade, and clip neckline seam allowance. Turn front facing to inside of garment. Press seam allowance into collar at back of neck. Turn under remaining seam allowance of upper collar and pin to collar seam allowance, covering stitching. Slipstitch by hand or topstitch close to seamline. Slipstitch folded edge of front facing to shoulder seam allowance, as shown in Figure 8.60. Remove roll line basting threads.

On knit garments, all back neck seam allowances can be turned down toward garment. Clip at shoulder seam will not be necessary. Topstitch close to neckline seam and trim seam allowances close to stitching (Figure 8.61).

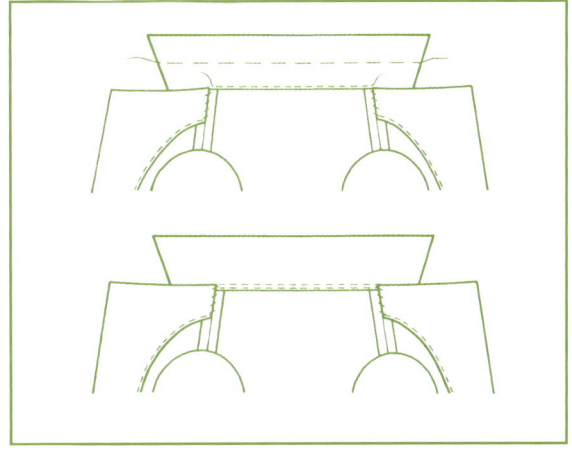

Figure 8.60–(Top) Finishing the Inside of a Garment with a Rolled Collar
Figure 8.61–(Bottom) Finishing the Inside of a Knit Garment with a Rolled Collar

Before continuing, answer the following multiple-choice questions.

1. A _____ ruffle receives its drape from the way it is cut.

   a. straight
   b. circular
   c. double

2. A _____ ruffle is usually cut on the crosswise grain.

   a. circular
   b. double
   c. straight

3. The Peter Pan collar is an example of a _____ collar.

   a. standing
   b. flat
   c. rolled

4. Notched collars are examples of a _____ collar.

   a. rolled
   b. standing
   c. flat

5. For a professional-looking collar, always stitch directionally _____.

   a. from end to end
   b. from center to ends
   c. diagonally

Check your answers with those provided on page 199.

SLEEVES

Introduction

A well-set sleeve can be the mark of a professionally sewn garment. Don't be afraid of sleeves. They aren't as hard as they look. Once you've understood how to manipulate them, setting sleeves will be a breeze.

To be attractive, a sleeve must fit well. It must hang straight and have enough room for movement. It should be comfortable and should not bind or

pull when the arm is raised. The length of a sleeve can vary but should always be in proportion to the rest of the garment. Keep in mind your own body structure when determining the length of your sleeves. Wear the length that is the most becoming to you.

Sleeve Styles

Although there are many variations of styles, sleeves fall into three basic categories:

1. *Set-in sleeve*—This is by far the most widely used type of sleeve. It is set into the armhole of the garment. The fullness at the top of the sleeve (sleeve cap) is eased into the garment to give shape to the sleeve and allow room for arm movement. The puffed sleeve is a type of set-in sleeve. The set-in sleeve is usually cut in one piece. In tailored garments, such as suits and coats, the sleeve is often cut in two pieces.

2. *Raglan sleeve*—This is an easy type of sleeve to fit. It is constructed of diagonal seams extending to the shoulder. The shape of the shoulder is determined by a curved shoulder dart

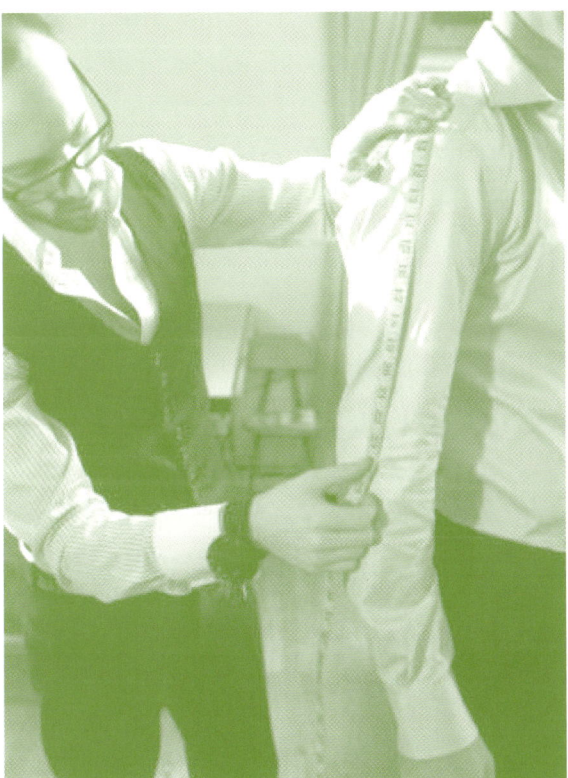

or a seam down the center of the sleeve. It is a comfortable sleeve to wear.

3. *Kimono sleeve*—This is the easiest sleeve to make, since it is cut in one with the garment. If the sleeve is loose-fitting or short, the underarm seam is reinforced at the curve to prevent strain on the seam. If the sleeve is long or close-fitting, a gusset may be needed in the underarm area to allow room for movement. The dolman sleeve, with its deep armhole, can be a variation of the kimono sleeve, or the set-in sleeve, depending on whether or not there is an armhole seam.

Set-in Sleeves

The sleeve cap of a set-in sleeve is always larger than the armhole of the garment. The fullness of the sleeve cap must be eased into the armhole carefully and smoothly for the proper fit and hang of the sleeve. Most sleeves allow 1-1/2" of ease in the sleeve cap. Patterns made only for knits allow less—usually 1"—because knit fabrics already have built-in stretch. Knits are also quite closely woven and are more difficult to ease than loosely woven fabrics. Heavy or tightly woven fabrics, such as denim and velveteen, can also be difficult to ease. Permanent-press fabrics cannot be eased without difficulty because of the firmness of the finish on the fabric. Vinyl and imitation leather will not ease at all, so some of the fullness in the sleeve cap must be removed.

To find out how much fullness must be removed, proceed as follows.

Step 1. Fit the pattern for the sleeve into the armhole, easing any excess fullness toward the shoulder seam of the garment. Excess ease will form a tuck at the shoulder (Figure 9.1).

Step 2. Remove sleeve from armhole and open out this tuck. Measure the amount of fullness in it. This is the amount of ease you will need to remove (Figure 9.2).

Step 3. Divide this amount by four and make a crosswise tuck this size in the cap of the sleeve pattern. If excess fabric is 1", tuck in pattern will be 1/4" (Figure 9.3). If excess fabric is 1/2", tuck will be 1/8". Recut sleeve according to the adjusted pattern.

An alternate method for removing fullness is to slit the pattern lengthwise in several places (Figure 9.4). Overlap the slits the desired amount (Figure 9.5).

Step 1. To check the ease in the sleeve cap before cutting out the sleeve, stand your tape measure on edge and measure around the cap of the sleeve along the seamline, from one underarm seam allowance to the other (Figure 9.6).

Step 2. To measure the armhole, overlap front and back pattern pieces, matching shoulder seams. Stand tape on edge and measure around armhole from one underarm seam to the other (Figure 9.7). The difference between the two measurements is the amount of ease in the sleeve cap.

When setting sleeves, be sure to match the sleeve notches to the garment notches. Sleeves must be set in the proper armhole, that is, the *right* sleeve must be placed in the *right*

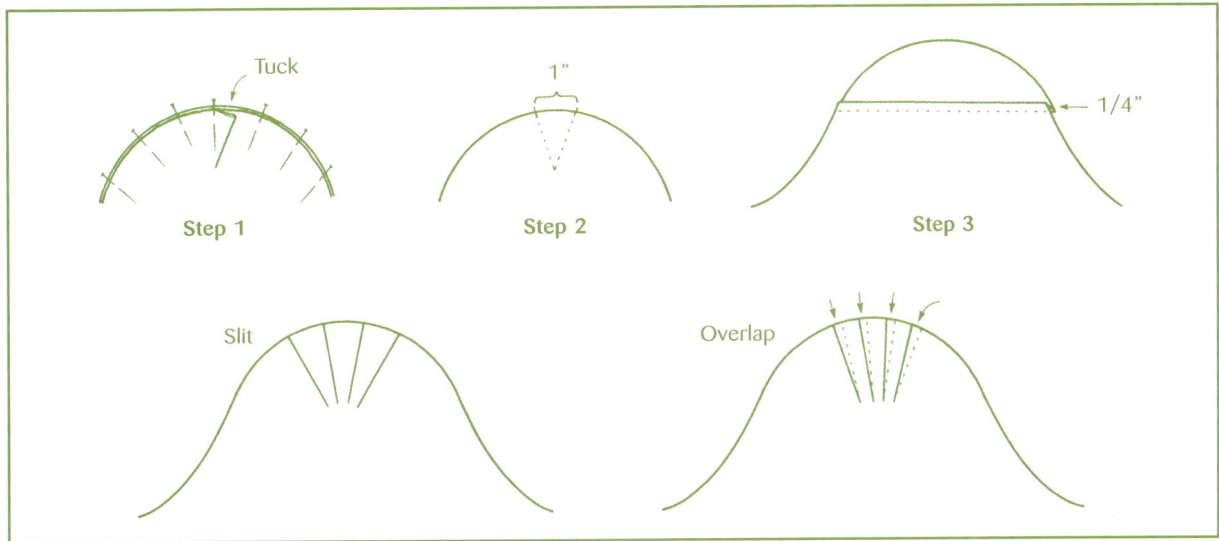

Figure 9.1 – (Top Left) Step 1: Removing Fullness from Set-in Sleeve Pattern
Figure 9.2 – (Top Center) Step 2
Figure 9.3 – (Top Right) Step 3
Figure 9.4 – (Bottom Left) Step 4: Alternate Method for Removing Sleeve Fullness: Slitting the Pattern
Figure 9.5 – (Bottom Right) Step 5: Alternate Method for Removing Sleeve Fullness: Overlapping the Slits Cut in Figure 9.4

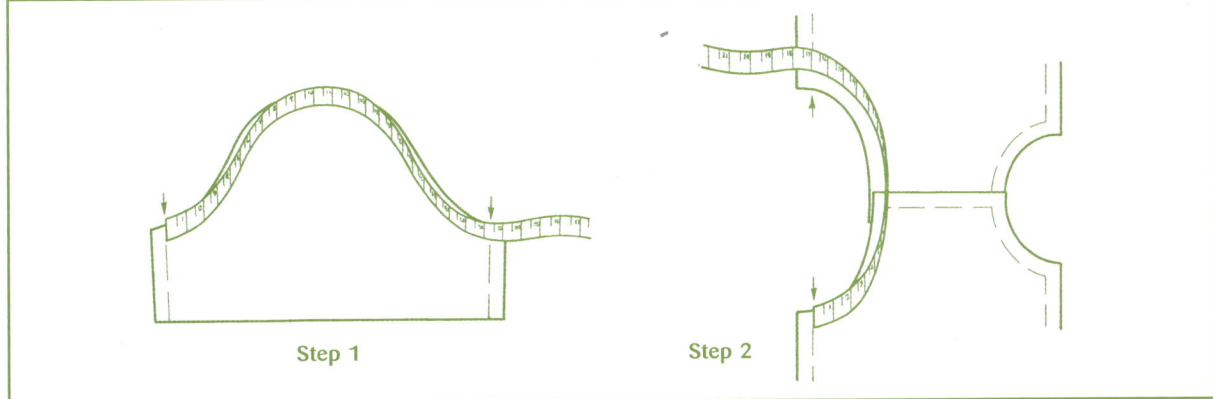

Figure 9.6 – (Left) Step 1: Determining the Ease in a Sleeve Cap by Measuring the Cap
Figure 9.7 – (Right) Step 2: Determining the Ease in a Sleeve Cap by Measuring the Armhole

armhole and the *left* sleeve in the *left* armhole. The back of the sleeve cap usually has more curve than the front to allow for arm movement. If sleeves are set in the wrong armhole, they will pull across the back. Long sleeves often have darts or ease in the elbow to allow for movement. The darts or ease will be on the back edge of the sleeve seam.

The fit of the garment at the shoulder will determine the hang of the sleeve. The shoulder seam must be halfway between the back and front of the body (Figure 9.8). The armhole seam must be exactly at the point of the shoulder (Figure 9.9). The sleeve will not hang properly if the shoulder does not fit properly.

Wherever possible, follow the unit method of construction and finish the sleeve before setting it into the armhole. It's easier to work on the sleeve before it is attached to the garment. However, if you're not sure of the finished length, wait until the garment is finished to sew on the cuff or finish the sleeve hem. On some garments, you may wish to insert the sleeve in the armhole before stitching the underarm seam.

Armhole seams can be finished in any way appropriate to your garment fabric. Armhole seams of set-in sleeves are not pressed open. They are turned

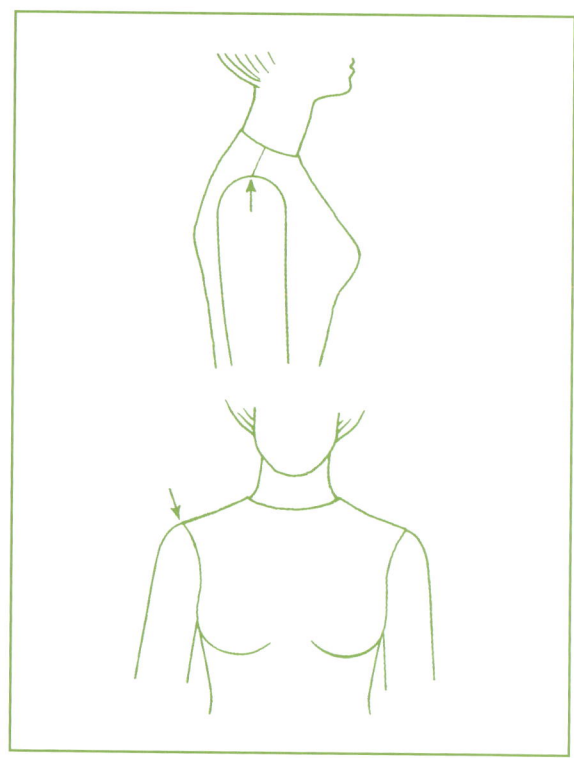

Figure 9.8–(Top) Shoulder seam should be right at shoulder line.
Figure 9.9–(Bottom) Armhole seam should come at the point of the shoulder.

toward the sleeve. On knits, a second row of stitching can be made 1/8" - 1/4" from the first, and the seam allowance can be trimmed close to the stitching.

Here is the most commonly used method of inserting a set-in sleeve:

Step 1. Match a notch or clip at shoulder marking on sleeve.

Step 2. Make a row of easestitching in sleeve cap between notches. Use 8-10 stitches per inch and sew just a hairline outside the seamline. If desired, make a second row of stitching in the seam allowance 1/8" from the first, as shown in Figure 9.10. We find that one row works best on a sleeve with a small amount of ease.

Step 3. Stitch sleeve seam and press open. If long sleeves have elbow darts or ease, stitch these before stitching sleeve seams.

Step 4. Finish bottom of sleeve if length has been determined. If not, leave this until garment is finished.

Step 5. With garment wrong side out and sleeve right side out, insert sleeve into armhole, right sides together. Be sure shoulder and underarm seams of garment are pressed open. Put pins in from sleeve side at right angles to the edge. Pin sleeve to shoulder seam at shoulder marking, right sides together. Pin 1/2" each side of shoulder seam. This 1" at the top of the sleeve cap is cut on the straight grain of the fabric and will not be eased. Pin at underarm seam and at notches. See Figure 9.11.

Step 6. Pull up gathering threads between notches and shoulder pins until sleeve fits armhole. Spread gathers with fingers until sleeve fits loosely and no puckers remain. Do not pull sleeve too tight. Adjust ease carefully until sleeve fits smoothly. Don't give up until all the ease has been smoothed out. A poorly set sleeve is the sign of unprofessional sewing. Pin every 1/2" around the armhole when ease has

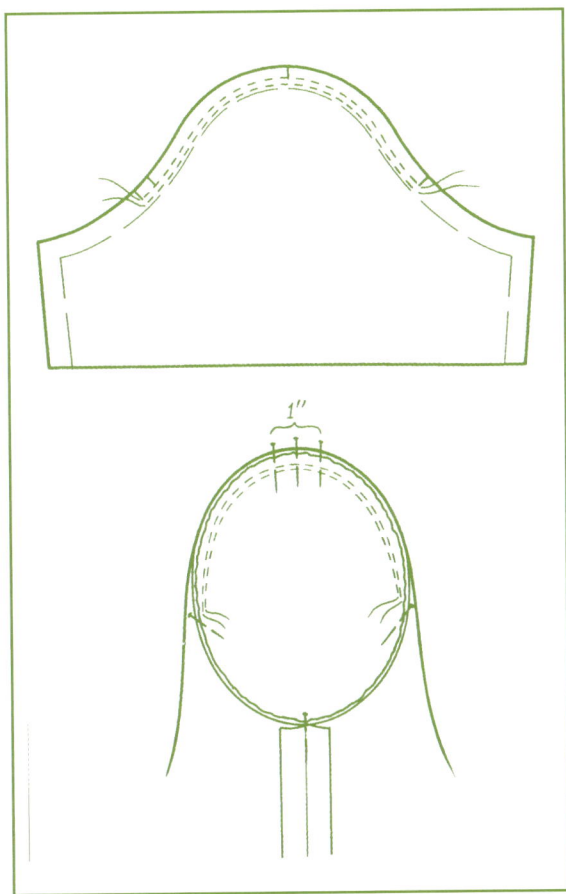

Figure 9.10–(Top) Easestitching on the Sleeve Cap
Figure 9.11–(Bottom) Sleeve Pinned into Armhole at Notches, Shoulder Seam, and Underarm Seam

been worked into place. Check around armhole on wrong side of garment to make sure fabric is flat and smooth.

Step 7. If you have trouble easing the sleeve cap, wrap ends of gathering threads around a pin in figure eight fashion. Remove sleeve from armhole and place sleeve over the end of an ironing board or a tailor's ham. Steam out excess fullness (Figure 9.12). Some fabrics steam more easily than others.

Wools are the easiest to steam. If fullness cannot be eased or steamed out, sleeve cap will have to be made smaller.

Step 8. Pin sleeve back into armhole. Starting at underarm seam, stitch around armhole with sleeve on top. Remove pins as you come to them (Figure 9.13). To aid in easing sleeve into armhole, spread fabric with both hands as you sew. Overlap ends of stitching at underarm seam.

Step 9. Check the garment from the outside to see if the sleeve is inserted smoothly in armhole. If there are any tucks or puckers in the sleeve, remove stitching, adjust with fingers, and restitch.

Step 10. To reinforce armhole, make a second row of stitching 1/8" from the first. Trim seam allowance in underarm seam to 1/4". Trim remaining seam allowance to 3/8". Overcast edges if needed.

Step 11. Press armhole seam allowance flat from sleeve side, using tip of iron. Press from edge of fabric to seamline. Turn seam allowance toward sleeve but *do not press*. Only tailored garments have armhole seams that are pressed.

Step 12. When making a puffed sleeve, fullness is not eased out. Spread gathers evenly across shoulder area between notches. Hold hands on either side of stitching line and smooth gathers as you sew (Figure 9.14). Do not allow gathers to overlap while stitching. Press as above.

Flat Construction

An easy way to stitch a set-in sleeve is to use the flat construction method. The sleeve is sewn to the armhole *before* the underarm sleeve and garment side seams are sewn. This is a good method to use on children's clothes, because the

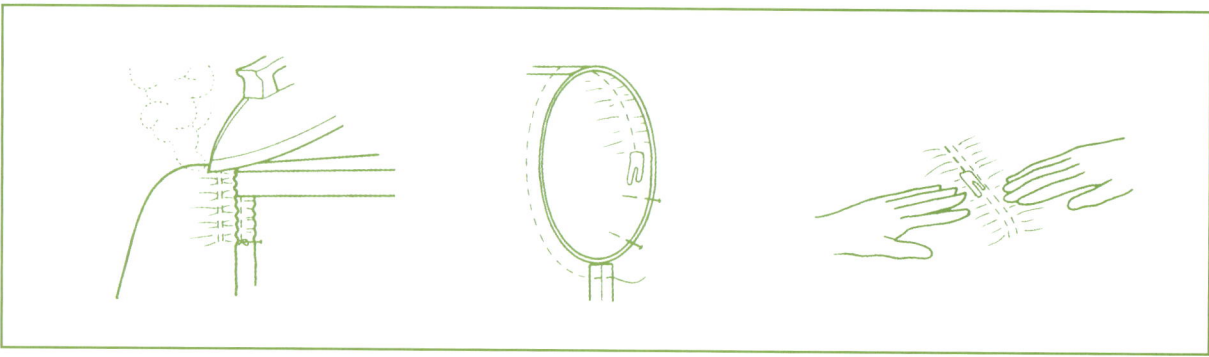

Figure 9.12 – (Left) Steaming out the Excess Fullness of a Sleeve
Figure 9.13 – (Center) Stitching Sleeve into Armhole
Figure 9.14 – (Right) Stitching a Puffed Sleeve

armholes are small. This method works well on stretchy knits and lightweight fabrics. It is also used on sleeves that have a small amount of ease, such as T-shirt sleeves and men's shirt sleeves.

If needed, make a row of easestitching along the seamline of the sleeve cap. Stitch the sleeve to the armhole, easing the sleeve and matching notches and shoulder markings (Figure 9.15). Trim the seam

to 1/4" in the underarm area, between notches. Stitch the entire underarm seam of the sleeve and the garment in one operation, turning armhole seam toward the sleeve (Figure 9.16).

On bulky fabrics, stitch the sleeve to the armhole above the notches only, in the sleeve cap area. Sew the sleeve underarm seam and garment underarm seam separately; then finish sewing the armhole seam below the notches. Trim underarm seam to 1/4" as usual.

Raglan Sleeve

A raglan sleeve is usually set into a garment by the flat construction method.

Step 1. Stitch shoulder dart or seam. Slash dart and press dart or seam open.

Step 2. Stitch sleeve to bodice front and back, right sides together, matching notches. Clip curves and press seams open.

Step 3. Right sides together, join entire underarm seam. Use a small stitch on underarm curve for reinforcement. Clip curves and press seam open (Figure 9.17).

A raglan sleeve can also be inserted like a set-in sleeve. This gives a smoother finish under the arm.

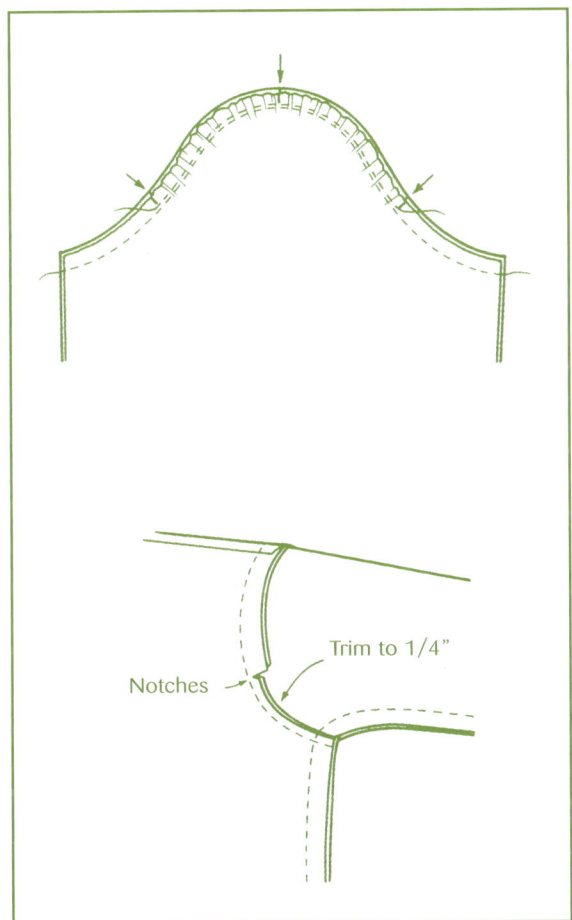

Figure 9.15 – (Top) Stitching a Sleeve to the Armhole Before Other Seams Are Sewn
Figure 9.16 – (Bottom) Stitching Sleeve and Garment Seams After the Sleeve Is Attached to the Armhole

Notches

Trim to 1/4"

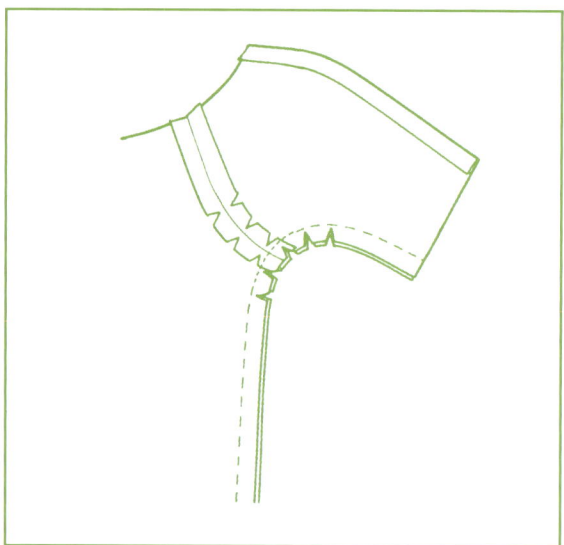

Figure 9.17—Stitching the Underarm Seam After a Raglan Sleeve Is Attached

Step 1. Stitch shoulder dart or seam. Slash dart and press dart or seam open.

Step 2. Stitch sleeve seam.

Step 3. Stitch underarm seam of garment.

Step 4. Stitch sleeve to garment around entire U-shaped armhole.

Step5. At front and back notches, clip seam allowance to stitching. Press seam allowance open above clips.

Step 6. Below clips, trim underarm seam to 1/4" and overcast raw edges.

Dolman Sleeve

A dolman sleeve has a very deep armhole. If the sleeve is separate from the garment, it is sewn to the garment by the flat construction method. There is very little ease in the sleeve cap of a dolman sleeve. Clip seam and press open. With right sides together, sew entire underarm seam. Clip underarm curve and press open. If the dolman sleeve is cut in one with the garment, it is treated as a kimono sleeve.

Kimono Sleeve

This is a simple sleeve to make, but it requires reinforcement. The sleeve is cut in one piece with the garment. All that is required to form the sleeve is to stitch the shoulder seam and the entire underarm seam. To reinforce the underarm area, use one of the following methods:

Method 1. Stretch a piece of bias tape with the iron and sew it in with the seam, using small stitches (Figure 9.18). Clip seam and press open. Do not clip the bias tape.

Method 2. Use a piece of regular woven seam binding. Sew it into the underarm seam, using small stitches. Fold the tape on an angle as it goes around the curve (Figure 9.19). Clip seam and press open.

Method 3. Stitch entire underarm seam, using small stitches in the curve area. Clip seam and press open. On right side, stitch close to seam in the curve area through both the garment and the seam allowance. Stitch on both sides of seam, taking one stitch across seam at each end of stitching. Make sure that seam allowance underneath lies flat while stitching (Figure 9.20).

Gussets

A gusset is a piece of fabric inserted in the underarm seam of a kimono sleeve to allow more flexibility of movement. If you find that your kimono sleeve it too close-fitting to allow for enough movement, your best bet is to insert a gusset in the underarm area. A gusset should always be cut on the bias to allow for maximum movement of the arm. It can be one diamond-shaped piece of fabric or two triangular pieces (Figure 9.21). The two-piece gusset is easier to insert because the underarm seam is not stitched until after the gusset pieces have been stitched in place.

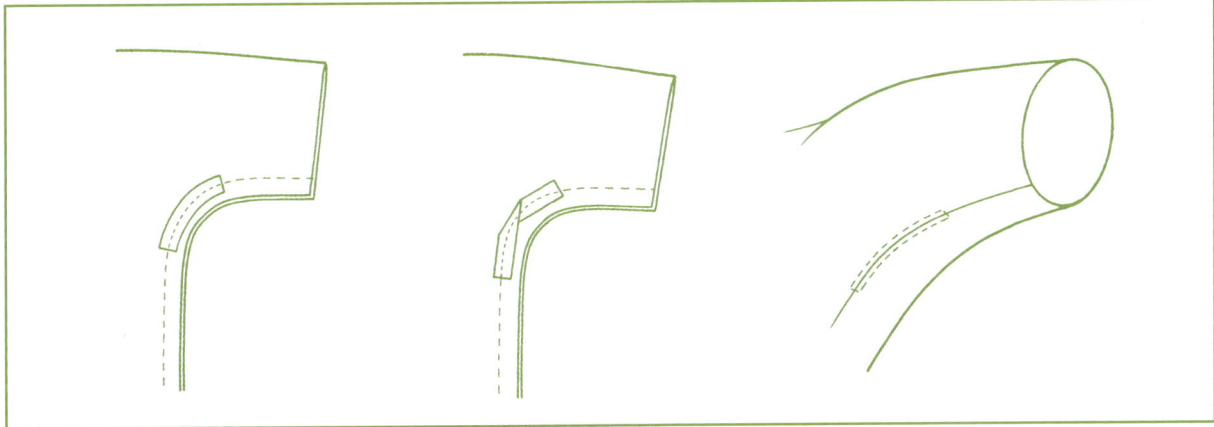

Figure 9.18—(Left) Method 1: Reinforcing a Kimono Sleeve with Bias Tape
Figure 9.19—(Center) Method 2: Reinforcing a Kimono Sleeve with Seam Binding
Figure 9.20—(Right) Method 3: Reinforcing a Kimono Sleeve with Small Stitches

Figure 9.21—Inserting Gussets for Ease in a Kimono Sleeve

Because underarm gussets are subject to a great deal of strain, it is necessary to reinforce the slash in the garment where the gusset will be inserted. The slash can be reinforced at the point with a small bias square of fabric, a piece of seam binding, or fusible interfacing. On firmly woven fabrics, a small stitch 1" each side of the point is sufficient reinforcement. For fabrics that ravel a lot or for a top-stitched insertion, the entire slash can be faced with a piece of lining fabric or other lightweight material.

Don't panic when you think about inserting a gusset. If your pattern includes a gusset, follow the pattern directions. Accuracy is the key in inserting a gusset. There are several different methods that can be used. We've given you an easy topstitched method to start with. We recommend trying it out on a sample piece of fabric. Once you've cut into your garment, there's no turning back. After you've mastered the mechanics of the topstitched gusset, you'll be ready to try the set-in gusset.

Two-Piece Topstitched Gusset

To make an easy *two-piece* topstitched gusset, follow these directions, illustrated in Figures 9.22 through 9.28:

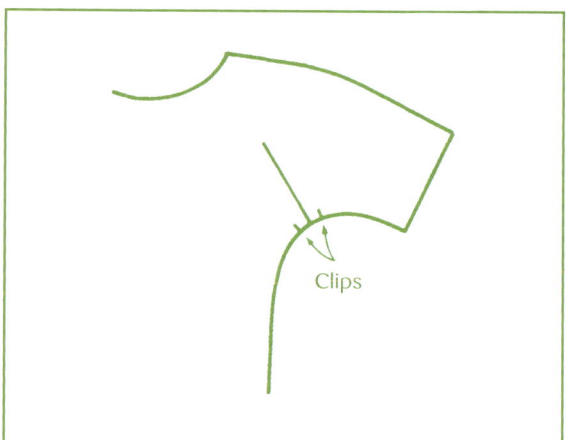

Figure 9.22–Step 1: Two-Piece Gusset

Step 1. At the deepest point of the underarm curve, mark a diagonal slash line 4-1/4" long on bodice front and back. Slash should point toward neck. Make clips in seam allowance 1/2" each side of slash mark (Figure 9.22).

Step 2. From garment fabric, cut two gusset pieces (for each underarm), using enclosed pattern as shown in Figure 9.23 (trace gusset pattern onto tissue paper). Place long edge of pattern on the true bias of the fabric. Mark stitching lines on wrong side of fabric. Thread-trace to right side, if desired. Note that the two short sides have 1/2" seam allowances and the long side has a 5/8" seam allowance.

Step 3. From a piece of lining fabric, cut two facing strips, each 2" wide and 5" long. Fold facing strips in half lengthwise, wrong sides together. Press a crease down the middle. Lay folded strip on right side of garment, lining up folded edge with slash mark. Unfold strip and pin to garment. Mark end of slash mark on facing strip. Make clip marks in edge of strip to correspond to clip marks in garment (Figure 9.24).

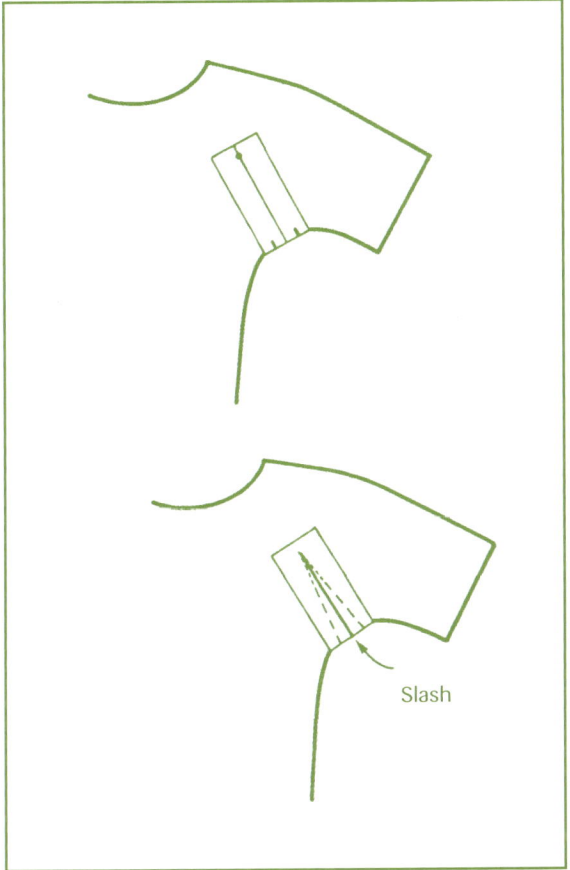

Slash

Figure 9.23–(Top) Step 2: Two-Piece Gusset
Figure 9.24–(Bottom) Step 3: Two-Piece Gusset

Step 4. Starting at edge of garment, stitch around slash, tapering from clip marks to point. Take one or two stitches across point. Use small stitches (20 per inch) for 1" each side of point. Press flat. Slash to stitching at point (Figure 9.25).

Step 5. Turn facing inside and press, rolling seam slightly toward facing (Figure 9.26).

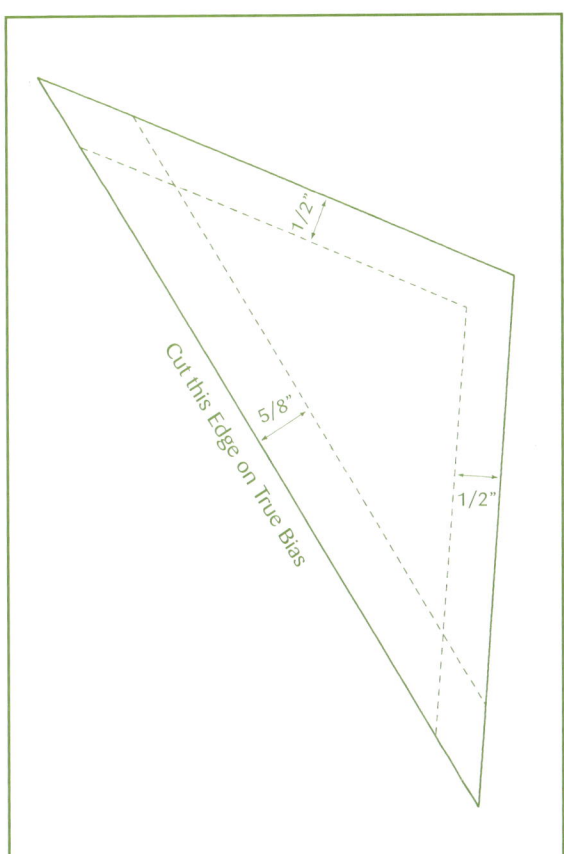

Cut this Edge on True Bias
1/2"
5/8"
1/2"

Figure 9.25–Step 4: Pattern for Two-Piece Gusset

Step 6. With right sides up, spread slash and position garment over gusset, lining up faced edges of slash with 1/2" seamline on gusset. Topstitch close to faced edge of slash, pivoting at point (Figure 9.27). On wrong side, carefully trim any edges of facing fabric that stick out past gusset.

Install other gusset piece in remaining bodice piece in the same way.

Step 7. Right sides together, stitch entire underarm, gusset, and sleeve seams in one operation (Figure 9.28). Press seam open, clipping if needed.

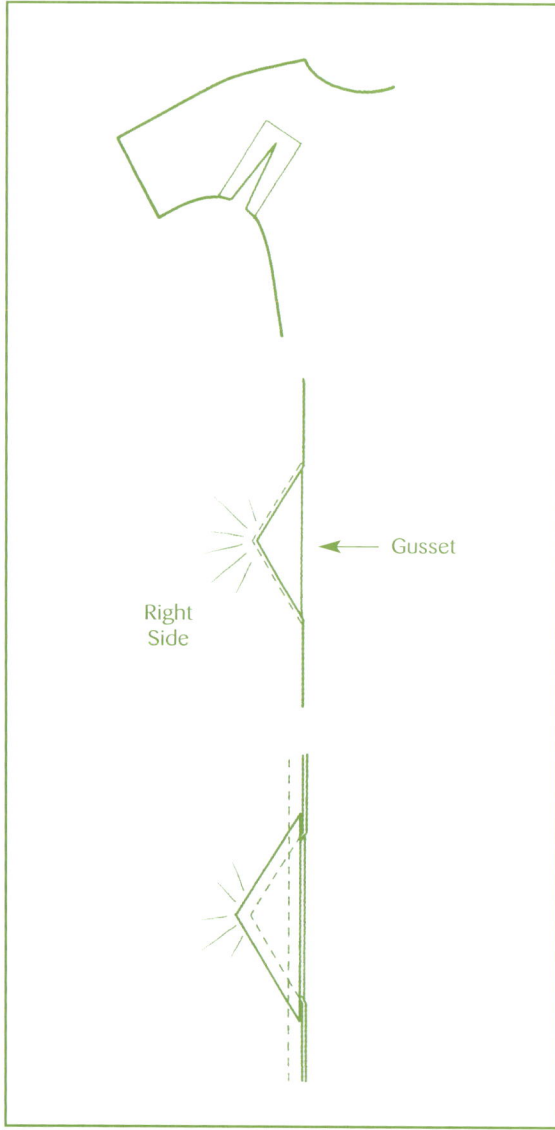

Gusset

Right Side

Figure 9.26–(Top) Step 5: Two-Piece Gusset
Figure 9.27–(Center) Step 6: Two-Piece Gusset
Figure 9.28–(Bottom) Step 7: Two-Piece Gusset

If you prefer a *one-piece* top-stitched gusset, follow these directions:

Step 1. Face garment slash in both bodice pieces as described in two-piece gusset.

Step 2. Stitch underarm seam and side seam separately, being sure to match faced edges exactly. Backstitch to secure stitching at facing edges. Press seams open, clipping curves where needed (Figure 9.29).

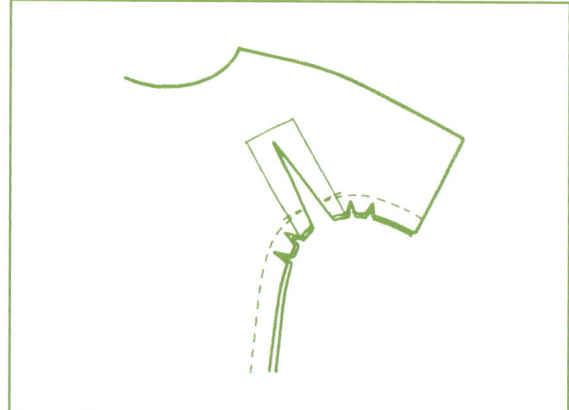

Figure 9.29–Reinforcing the Slash and Stitching the Underarm Seam for a One-Piece Gusset

Step 3. Place gusset pattern in Figure 9.25 on a bias fold of fabric, lining up 5/8" stitching line with bias fold (Figure 9.30). Cut out and unfold gusset. Mark 1/2" seam allowance on all four sides of wrong side of gusset. Thread-trace to right side of fabric, if desired.

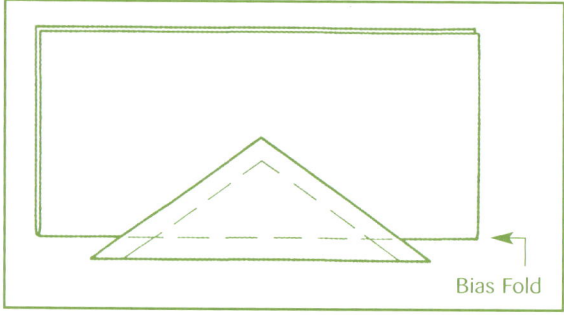

Bias Fold

Figure 9.30–Cutting a One-Piece Gusset

Step 4. Turn garment right side out. With right sides up, position garment opening over gusset, lining up faced edges with 1/2" seamline on gusset. Topstitch around garment opening edge close to faced edge, pivoting at corners (Figure 9.31). On wrong side of garment, carefully trim away any edges of facing that stick out past edge of gusset.

Set-in Gusset

A set-in gusset is sewn to the garment so that no stitching shows on the outside (Figure 9.32). The slash is not usually faced but the point of the slash must be reinforced. A set-in gusset can be one piece or two. We have given directions first for a *two-piece* set-in gusset:

Figure 9.31 – (Top) Topstitching One-Piece Gusset
Figure 9.32 – (Bottom) A Set-In Gusset

Two-Piece Gusset

Step 1. Cut out a two-piece gusset as previously described.

Step 2. Make slash mark on garment and stitch around slash opening, reinforcing point of slash (Figure 9.33).

Step 3. Cut on slash mark to point of stitching, cutting through reinforcement fabric. Turn reinforcement fabric to wrong side and press to make it lie flat (Figure 9.34).

Step 4. Right sides together, pin top half of slash to top half of gusset. Line up stitching on slash with 1/2" on

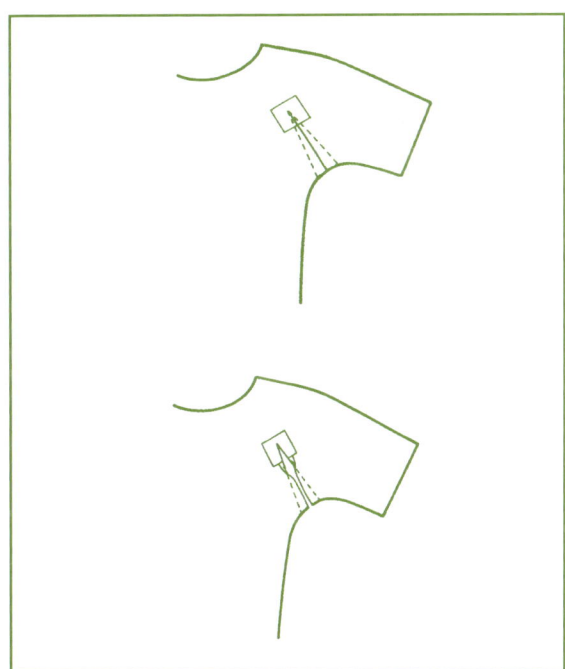

Figure 9.33 – (Top) Reinforcing the Slash for a Two-Piece Set-In Gusset
Figure 9.34 – (Bottom) Turning the Reinforcement to the Wrong Side

gusset. Fabric edges will not match. Point of slash should be at corner of seamline on gusset. Stitch to corner, following slash stitching line. Stitch just a hairline inside slash stitching line (Figure 9.35). Use small stitches 1" each side of corner. Pivot at corner and line up second side of slash with seamline on second side of gusset. Stitch to edge of fabric (Figure 9.36).

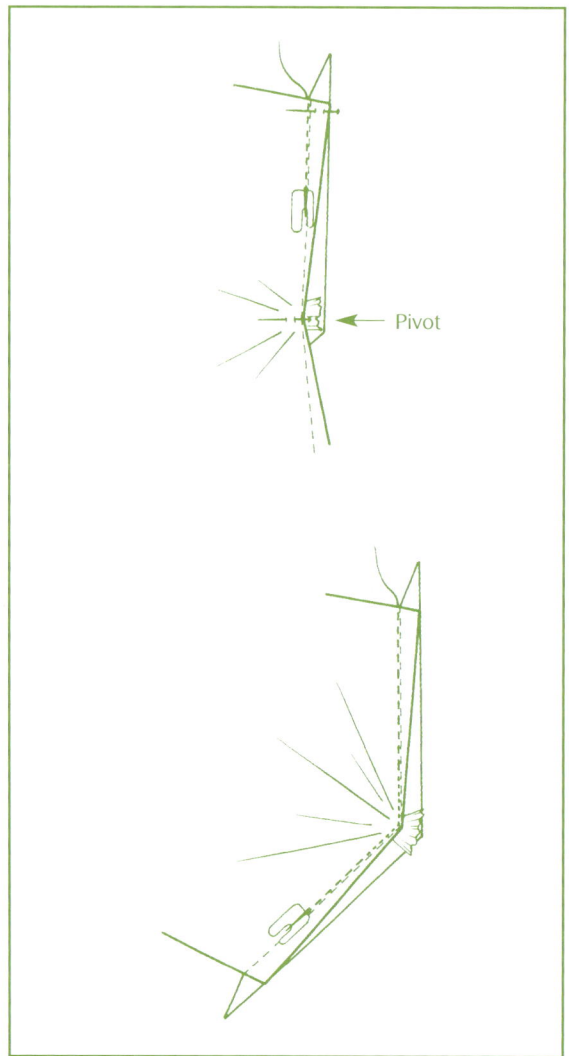

Figure 9.35–(Top) Stitching the First Side of the Gusset to the First Side of the Slash
Figure 9.36–(Bottom) Stitching the Second Side of the Gusset to the Second Side of the Slash

Step 5. Insert other half of gusset in other bodice piece in the same way.

Step 6. Press seams toward garment. Right sides together, stitch entire underarm, gusset, and sleeve seam. Be sure to match gusset edges. Press seam open, clipping if needed. Carefully trim away edges of reinforcement fabric.

One-Piece Gusset

To make a *one-piece* set-in gusset, follow these directions:

Step 1. Prepare slash openings as described for two-piece gusset.

Step 2. Cut a one-piece gusset as previously described.

Step 3. Right sides together, stitch underarm seam and sleeve seam separately. Stitch *only* to slash stitching line. Backstitch for reinforcement (Figure 9.37). Press seams open, clipping if needed.

Step 4. Right sides together, pin one bodice piece to one side of gusset, matching slash stitching to 1/2" seam allowance on gusset. Fabric edges will not match. Stitch a hairline inside slash stitching, pivoting at corner of slash. Begin and end stitching where sleeve and underarm seams end. Reinforce ends of stitching or pull thread ends through and tie (Figure 9.38).

Figure 9.37–(Top) Stitching Underarm and Sleeve Seams Separately for One-Piece Set-In Gusset
Figure 9.38–(Bottom) Stitching Gusset to Bodice for One-Piece Set-In Gusset

Step 5. Repeat for other half of gusset on other bodice piece. Press all seams toward garment. Carefully trim excess reinforcement fabric beyond edge of gusset.

Before continuing with your reading, answer the questions. True or False?

1. The puffed sleeve is a type of raglan sleeve.

2. The kimono sleeve is cut in one with the garment.

3. Vinyl and imitation leather ease without difficulty.

4. Sleeves must be set in the proper (right or left) armhole.

5. The raglan sleeve is usually set into a garment by the flat construction method.

6. A dolman sleeve has a very narrow armhole.

7. A gusset is a piece of fabric inserted in the underarm seam of a dolman sleeve.

8. A set-in gusset is sewn to the garment so that decorative stitching shows on the outside.

Check your answers with those provided on page 199.

ANSWERS TO SELF-TEST QUESTIONS

Self-Test 1
1. F
2. T
3. F
4. T
5. T
6. F
7. F
8. F
9. T
10. T

Self-Test 2
1. A
2. C
3. B
4. A
5. A
6. B
7. B
8. C
9. B
10. A

Self-Test 3
1. B
2. C
3. A
4. A
5. B

Self-Test 4
1. F
2. T
3. F
4. T
5. T
6. T
7. T
8. F
9. T
10. T

Self-Test 5
1. T
2. T
3. F Easing is used when a small amount of fullness must be put into a seam.
4. T
5. T

Self-Test 6
1. B
2. A
3. A
4. A
5. C
6. B

Self-Test 7
1. F
2. T
3. T
4. T
5. F

Self-Test 8
1. B
2. C
3. B
4. A
5. B

Self-Test 9
1. F
2. T
3. F
4. T
5. T
6. F
7. F
8. F